PJ-PK

ORIENTAL PHILOLOGY AND LITERATURE, INDO-IRANIAN PHILOLOGY AND LITERATURE

Library of Congress Classification

2000 EDITION

Prepared by the
Cataloging Policy
and Support Office,
Library Services

Library of Congress, Cataloging Distribution Service, Washington, D.C.

The additions and changes in Class PJ-PK adopted while this work was in press will be cumulated and printed in List 277 of *LC Classification — Additions and Changes*

Library of Congress Cataloging-in-Publication Data

Library of Congress.
Library of Congress classification. PJ-PK. Oriental philology and literature, Indo-Iranian philology and lieterature / prepared by the Cataloging Policy and Support Office, Library Services. — 2000 ed.
p. cm.
Includes index.
1. Classification—Books—Indo-Iranian philology. 2. Classification, Library of Congress. I. Title: Oriental philology and literature, Indo-Iranian philology and literature. II. Library of Congress. Cataloging policy and Support Office. III. Title.

Z696.U5P7 2000
025.4'64911—dc21 00-020688
CIP

ISBN 0-8444-1010-1

For sale by the Library of Congress,
Cataloging Distribution Service,
Washington, DC 20541-5017

PREFACE

The first edition of Class P: Subclasses PJ-PK (Oriental Philology and Literature, Indo-Iranian Philology and Literature) was published in 1933 and was reprinted in 1965 with supplementary pages of additions and changes. A second edition was published in 1988. This 2000 edition includes for the first time a full index, prepared by Lawrence Buzard, editor of classification schedules. It has been produced using a new automated system developed at the Library of Congress for this purpose. The system will allow for the production of new editions on a regular and frequent basis.

In 1992, Rebecca Guenther, Network Development and MARC Standards Office, began overseeing the conversion of Library of Congress Classification data to machine-readable form using the provisionally approved USMARC format for classification data. In 1993-1994, the Cataloging Distribution Service developed programs for producing printed classification schedules from the MARC records in cooperation with Lawrence Buzard, Paul Weiss, senior cataloging policy specialist, and Rebecca Guenther. The Cataloging Distribution Service also coordinated the layout and design of the new schedules.

New or revised numbers and captions are added to the L.C. Classification schedules as a result of development proposals made by the cataloging staff of the Library of Congress and cooperating institutions. Upon approval of these proposals by the weekly editorial meeting of the Cataloging Policy and Support Office, new classification records are created or existing records are revised in the master classification database. The Classification Editorial Team, consisting of Lawrence Buzard, editor, and Barry Bellinger, Kent Griffiths, Nancy Jones, and Dorothy Thomas, assistant editors, is responsible for creating new classification records, maintaining the master database, and creating index terms for the captions.

Thompson A. Yee, Acting Chief
Cataloging Policy and Support Office

January 2000

ORIENTAL PHILOLOGY AND LITERATURE

INDO-IRANIAN PHILOLOGY AND LITERATURE

INDEX

OUTLINE

PJ	1-(9500)	Oriental philology and literature
	1-489	General
	1-(195)	Languages
	306-489	Literature
	601-995	Special groups
	601-621	Christian Oriental
	701-(989)	Mohammedan
	991-995	Hamito-Semitic
	1001-1989	Egyptology
	1091-1109	Egyptian writing and its decipherment
	1111-1439	Language
	1481-1989	Literature. Inscriptions
	2001-2199	Coptic
	2340-2399	Lybyco-Berber languages. Berber languages
	2353-2367	Libyan group
	2369-2399	Berber languages
	2401-2594	Cushitic languages
	3001-3097	Semitic philology and literature
	3101-(4091)	East Semitic languages
	3101-(3971)	Assyriology. Akkadian
	3231-3595	Language
	3601-(3971)	Literature. Inscriptions
	4001-(4091)	Sumerian
	4101-4197	West and North Semitic languages
	4171-4197	Phenician-Punic
	4501-5192	Hebrew
	4543-4937	Language (Biblical and modern)
	4951-5000	Medieval Hebrew
	5001-5060	Literature
	5050-5060	Individual authors and works
	5061-5192	Other languages used by Jews
	5111-5192	Yiddish
	5201-5329	Aramaic
	5211-5289	West Aramaic
	5211-5219	Biblical (Chaldaic)
	5229	Palmyrene inscriptions
	5239	Nabataean inscriptions
	5241-5249	Christian Palestinian
	5251-5259	Jewish Palestinian
	5271-5279	Samaritan
	5281-5289	Neo-Aramaic
	5301-5329	East Aramaic
	5321-5329	Mandaean
	5401-5909	Syriac
	5414-5493	Language
	5601-5695	Literature
	5701-5709	East Syriac (Nestorian)

OUTLINE

OUTLINE

Oriental philology and literature
Languages
Periodicals and societies
1 International
2 American (United States)
3 British
4 French
5 German
Including Austrian
6 Italian
7 Russian
9 Other
10 Annuals. Yearbooks, etc.
Congresses
20 International congress of orientalists
Arrange as follows:
1st, 1873
20.A73 Acts. Transactions. Proceedings
20.A73b Bulletin
20.A73c Other regular serials
20.A73k Circulars. Announcements. Programs
20.A73l Lists of members
20.A73m Miscellaneous
Later congresses
20.A74-A89 1874-1889
Subarrange as follows:
.x Acts. Transactions. Proceedings
.xb Bulletin
.xc Other regular serials
.xk Circulars. Announcements. Programs
.xl List of members
.xm Miscellaneous
20.A91 9th statutory congress, London, 1891
Subarrange as follows:
.x Acts. Transactions. Proceedings
.xb Bulletin
.xc Other regular serials
.xk Circulars. Announcements. Programs
.xl List of members
.xm Miscellaneous
20.A92 9th regular congress, London, 1892
Apply table at PJ20.A91
20.A93 10th statutory congress, Lisbon, 1892
Apply table at PJ20.A91
20.A94 10th regular congress, Geneva, 1894
Apply table at PJ20.A91
20.A97-A99 1897-1899
Apply table at PJ20.A91
20.B02-B99 1902-1999
Apply table at PJ20.A91
Works about the congresses. By date

	Languages
	Congresses
	International congress of orientalists
	Works about the congresses. By date -- Continued
20.Z99	General works
20.Z999	Miscellaneous uncataloged matter
21.A-Z	Other congresses, A-Z
	e.g.
21.C7	Congrès provincial des orientalistes. By date
21.C79	Miscellaneous uncataloged matter
	Collections
(23)	Texts. Sources, etc.
	see PJ347-PJ489
(24)	Translations
	see PJ408-PJ489
	Monographs. Studies, etc.
25	Various authors. Series
26.A-Z	Studies in honor of a particular person or institution, A-Z
27	Individual authors
31	Encyclopedias. Dictionaries
33	Atlases. Maps. Charts, etc.
37	Philosophy. Theory. Method
	History of philology
51	General
52	General special
	By period
54	Earliest
55	Middle ages
57	Renaissance
58	Modern
59	19th-20th centuries
60.A-Z	By region or country, A-Z
	Cf. PJ68.A+, Study and teaching
	By university, college, etc , see PJ69
(62)	Bibliography. Bio-bibliography
	see Z7046+
	Biography. Memoirs. Correspondence
63	Collective
64.A-Z	Individual, A-Z
	Study and teaching
65	General works
68.A-Z	By region or country, A-Z
69	By university, college, etc.
	General works
	Treatises
70	Early through 1800
71	1801-
73	General special
75	History
91	Compends
95	Popular

Languages -- Continued
(97) Script
see P211+
Grammar
120 Early to 1800
121 1801-
127 Conversation. Phrase books
Phonology. Phonetics. Alphabet
128 General works
(138) Transliteration
see P226+
139 Morphology. Inflection. Accidence
149 Parts of speech (Morphology and syntax)
171 Syntax
181 Prosody. Metrics. Rhythmics
183 Etymology
Lexicography
187 Treatises
(191) Dictionaries
see P361
(193) Vocabularies. Glossaries
see P361
(195) Special lists
see P361
Literature
Periodicals and societies, see PJ1+
Yearbooks, see PJ10
Congresses, see PJ20+
History
Treatises. Compends
306 Early works through 1800
307 1801-
308 Outlines, syllabi, etc.
309 Collected essays
310 Lectures. Essays. Pamphlets
311 Relations to history, civilizations, etc.
Relations to other literatures
Cf. PA3010
312 General works
313 Translations (as subject)
314.A-Z Treatment of special subjects, A-Z
314.N3 National characteristics
314.P4 Peace
Biography of authors
317 Collective
Individual
see the respective literature, PJ-PL
319.A-Z Special classes of authors, A-Z
e.g.
319.I55 Ismaili
327 Poetry
334 Drama
336 Prose. Fiction

PJ

Literature
History -- Continued
341 Other
(345) Folk literature
see subclass GR
Collections
Original texts
347 General
349 Selections. Anthologies
356 Poetry
371 Drama
379 Prose. Prose fiction
383 Other
(393) Folk literature
see subclass GR
Translations of Oriental literature
English
408 General
409 Selections. Anthologies
Poetry
416 General
418 Selections. Anthologies
Drama
431 General
433 Selections. Anthologies
439 Prose (General)
Fiction
440 General
441 Selections. Anthologies
443 Other
(455) Folk literature
see subclass GR
French
460 General
461 Selections. Anthologies
Poetry
462 General works
463 Selections. Anthologies
464 Drama
466 Prose
467 Prose fiction
469 Other. Fables, proverbs, etc.
German
470 General
471 Selections. Anthologies
Poetry
472 General works
473 Selections. Anthologies
474 Drama
476 Prose
477 Prose fiction
479 Other. Fables, proverbs, etc.
481 Dutch

Literature
Collections
Translations of Oriental literature -- Continued
483 Italian
485 Scandinavian
486 Slavic
487 Spanish and Portuguese
489.A-Z Other languages, A-Z
Special groups
Christian Oriental
Comprises: Syriac, Christian Arabic, Coptic, Ethiopic, Armenian, Georgian (Grusinian)
Languages
see PJ, PK. General, PJ; special languages, PJ and PK
Literature
601 Periodicals. Societies. Congresses
Collections
603 Texts. Sources, etc.
605 Series. Monographs (various authors)
607 Collected works, studies, etc. (individual authors)
611 Treatises (General)
621 Special topics
Mohammedan
Comprises prevailingly Arabic, Persian, and Turkish; also other languages used by Muslims, e.g. Urdu, Afghan, etc.
Languages
701 Periodicals. Serials
703 Societies
705 Congresses
Collections
709 Texts. Sources, etc.
711 Anthologies
Monographs. Studies, etc.
713 Serial
714.A-Z Studies in honor of a particular person or institution, A-Z
715 Individual authors
721 Encyclopedias. Dictionaries
725 History of philology
(726) Bibliography. Bio-bibliography
see Z7046+
727 Biography
Prefer PJ63-PJ64
Treatises
731 General
733 General special
Grammar
735 General works
Phonology. Phonetics
(737) General works

Special groups
Mohammedan
Languages
Grammar
Phonology. Phonetics -- Continued
(738) Script
see PJ6123
(739) Transliteration
see P226+
741 Morphology. Inflection. Accidence
745 Syntax
751 Style. Composition. Rhetoric
761 Etymology. Semantics
(771) Dictionaries
see PJ6601-PJ6680, especially, PJ6633
Literature
History and criticism
Treatises. Compends
806 Early works through 1800
807 1801-
808 Outlines, syllabi, etc.
809 Collected essays
810 Lectures. Essays. Pamphlets
811 Relations to history, civilizations, etc.
Relations to other literatures
812 General works
813 Translations (as subject)
814.A-Z Treatment of special subjects, A-Z
814.I84 Islam
Laylī and Majnūn, see PJ814.M35
814.M35 Majnūn Laylā. Laylī and Majnūn
814.M83 Muḥammad, d. 632
Biography of authors
817 Collective
Individual
see the respective literature, PJ-PL
819.A-Z Special classes of authors, A-Z
e.g.
819.I55 Ismaili
819.S5 Shiite
819.S9 Sufi
827 Poetry
834 Drama
836 Prose. Fiction
841 Other
(845) Folk literature
see GR
Collections
Original texts
Cf. PJ709+
847 General
849 Selections. Anthologies
856 Poetry

Special groups
Mohammedan
Literature
Collections
Original texts -- Continued
871 Drama
879 Prose. Prose fiction
883 Other
(893) Folk literature
see subclass GR
Translations
English
908 General
909 Selections. Anthologies
Poetry
916 General
918 Selections. Anthologies
Drama
931 General
933 Selections. Anthologies
939 Prose (General)
Fiction
940 General
941 Selections. Anthologies
943 Other
(955) Folk literature
see subclass GR
French
960 General
961 Selections. Anthologies
Poetry
962 General works
963 Selections. Anthologies
964 Drama
966 Prose
967 Prose fiction
969 Other. Fables, proverbs, etc.
German
970 General
971 Selections. Anthologies
Poetry
972 General works
973 Selections. Anthologies
974 Drama
976 Prose
977 Prose fiction
979 Other. Fables, proverbs, etc.
981 Dutch
983 Italian
985 Scandinavian
986 Slavic
987 Spanish and Portuguese
989.A-Z Other languages, A-Z

Special groups -- Continued
Semitic
General, see PJ3001+, PJ3097
Special
see PJ3101-PJ9278
Indo-Aryan
Special
see PK201-PK6996
Iranian
Special
see PK6097-PK7111
Ural-Altaic
General, see PL1+
Special, see PL1+, PL400+, PL450+
Far East, see PL490+
Indo-Chinese
General, see PL3521+
Special
see PL3601-PL4001
Malayo-Polynesian
General, see PL5021+
Special
see PL5051-PL6579

991-995 Afroasiatic languages. Hamito-Semitic languages.
Hamitic languages (Table P-PZ9)
For Chadic languages, see PL
For Nilo-Hamitic languages, see PL
For Semitic languages, see PJ3001-PJ9293

Egyptology
Egyptology comprises the philological, archaeological, and historical study of the languages, culture, and history of ancient Egypt. Treatises devoted to the investigation of a subject are classified by subject
Cf. DT43+, Egyptian history

Periodicals
1001 International
1002 English and American
1003 French
1004 German
1005 Italian
1009 Other

Societies
1011 International
1012 English and American
1013 French
1014 German
1015 Italian
1019 Other

1021 Congresses

Collections
Texts. Sources, etc , see PJ1501+
Monographs. Studies, etc.
1025 Serial

Egyptology
Collections
Monographs. Studies, etc. -- Continued
1026.A-Z Studies in honor of a particular person or institution, A-Z
1027 Individual authors
1031 Encyclopedias. Dictionaries
Philosophy. Theory. Methods
1035 General works
1037 Relations
History (of Egyptology)
Cf. PJ1090.2+, Egyptian writing and its development
1051 General
1052 General special
1053 Early period to ca. 1800/30
1055 19th and 20th centuries
1060.A-Z By region or country, A-Z
(1062) Bibliography
see Z7064
Cf. Z3561+
Biography. Memoirs. Correspondence
1063 Collective
1064.A-Z Individual, A-Z
e.g.
1064.C6 Champollion, J.F.
Study and teaching (Curricula, etc.)
1065 General
1066 General special
1068.A-Z By region or country, A-Z
1069.A-Z By university, college, etc., A-Z
1071 General works
Includes H. Brugsch, Aegyptologie, 1891
1081 Compends
1085 Popular
1089 Special philological-archaeological studies
Cf. PJ1805, Demotic literature
Egyptian writing and its decipherment
Cf. PJ1531.R3+, Rosetta stone
History, see PJ1051+
Hieroglyphic
Horapollo
Cf. PA4211.H67, Greek literature
1091.A3 Greek texts. By date
1091.A5-Z Translations. By language
1093 Other early works, to 1800
1095 1800-1870
1097 1871-
(1103) Symbolism
see PJ1090.2-PJ1097
1105 Hieratic
Cf. PJ1650+, Literature

Egyptology
Egyptian writing and its decipherment -- Continued
1107 Demotic
Cf. PJ1801+, Literature
1109 Specimens, types, etc.
Cf. Z250+
Language
Class here works on the "Classical" or "Middle" Egyptian as well as works on other periods
1111 Treatises (General: History, relations, etc.)
Grammar
1121 Comparative
1125 Historical
Descriptive
1131 Early through 1800
1135 1801-
1139 Outlines. Syllabi. Tables, etc.
1141 Readers. Chrestomathies
1151 Phonology
1155 Orthography
Morphology. Inflection. Accidence
1161 General works
1171 Noun
1181 Verb
1191 Other. Miscellaneous
1201 Syntax
1251 Style. Composition. Rhetoric
1301 Rhythmics. Versification
Etymology
1350 Treatises
1351 Dictionaries (exclusively etymological)
1355.A-Z Special elements. By language, A-Z
1355.A3 Foreign elements in general
1357 Other special
1361 Semantics
1371 Synonyms. Antonyms
Lexicography
1401 Collections
1411 Treatises (History, etc.)
1417 Criticism, etc., of particular dictionaries
Dictionaries
1423 Polyglot
Cf. P361+, Comparative lexicography
Bilingual
1425.A-Z English. By author, A-Z
1430.A-Z Other. By author, A-Z
Special
Etymological, see PJ1351
Particular periods
1433 Demotic
1435 Names
1439 Other (Technical, etc.)
Literature

Egyptology
Literature -- Continued
History
1481 Treatises
1482 Compends
1483 Lecture, essays, etc.
By period
(1484) Ancient
see PJ1481-PJ1780
(1485) New (Late)
see PJ1481-PJ1780
(1486) Demotic
see PJ1801-PJ1921
1487 By form
1488 Special topics (not A-Z)
Texts (Inscriptions, papyri, etc.)
Collections
1501 General
1511 Museums. Institutions
1515 Minor (Private, etc.)
Inscriptions. Stelae
1521 General. Miscellaneous
1526.A-Z By place where found, A-Z
(1529) By place where preserved
see PJ1511-PJ1515
1531 Particular inscriptions
e.g.
1531.C6 Cleopatra's needle, New York
Rosetta stone
1531.R3 Texts. By date
1531.R4A-Z Translations. By language, A-Z
1531.R5 History and criticism
1531.S4 Stela of Sebek-khu
Religious literature
Collections. Selections
1551 General works
Pyramid texts
1553.A1 Collections. By date
1553.A11-A19 Selections. By editor
1553.A2-A29 Translations
Prefer PJ1961, for translations without texts
1553.A3 Special pyramids
1553.A5-Z Criticism, etc.
1554 Coffin texts (Spells. Incantations)
Book of caverns
1554.5.A1 Complete texts
1554.5.A2A-Z Translations. By language, A-Z
Abridged version. Summary
1554.5.A3 General works
1554.5.A4 Translations
Selections. Selected hours
1554.5.A5 General works

PJ

	Egyptology
	Literature
	Texts (Inscriptions, papyri, etc.)
	Religious literature
	Book of caverns
	Selections -- Continued
1554.5.A6	Translations
1554.5.A7-Z	Works about the Book of caverns
	Book of the Dead (Per-m-hru)
1555.A3	Texts (Hieroglyphic or Hieratic). By date
1555.A5	Demotic. By date
1555.A7-Z	Translations. By language and translator
1556	Particular incantations ("Chapters" or "books")
1557	Commentaries, criticism, etc.
1557.Z8	Glossaries, indices, etc. By date
1558	Book of that which is in the nether world. Am duat, Am tuat, Shat am tuat, etc.
1558.A1	Complete texts
1558.A2A-Z	Translations. By language, A-Z
	Abridged version. Summary
1558.A3	General works
	Includes Jacquier. Le livre de ce qu'il y a dans l'Hadès
1558.A4	Translations
	Selections. Selected hours
1558.A5	General works
1558.A6	Translations
1558.A7-Z	Works about the Am duat
1559	Other works
	Amen-em-apt
1559.A6	Texts
1559.A7	Criticism
	Book of breathings
1559.B42	Texts
1559.B43	Criticism
	Book of gates
1559.B6	Texts
1559.B7	Criticism
	Book of openings of the mouth
1559.B72	Texts
1559.B73	Criticism
	Book of the Fayum
1559.B736	Texts
1559.B7362	Criticism
	Book of the night
1559.B738	Texts
1559.B7382	Criticism
	Book of the two roads of the blessed dead
1559.B75	Texts
1559.B76	Criticism
	Book of the two ways
1559.B78	Texts

Egyptology
Literature
Texts (Inscriptions, papyri, etc.)
Religious literature
Other works
Book of the two ways -- Continued
1559.B79 Criticism
Buch von Durchwandeln der Ewigkeit
1559.B83 Texts
1559.B832 Criticism
Liturgy of funeral offerings
1559.L6 Texts
1559.L7 Criticism
1565 Hymns
1569 Poems
Includes Epic of Penta-our
1571 Dramatic texts
Hieratic literature
1650 General. Miscellaneous
1661 Museums. Institutions
1665 Minor collections (Private, etc.)
1670 Inscriptions (Hieratic only)
(1671) Particular inscriptions
see PJ1531
1675 Ostraka
Papyri
(1678) General. Miscellaneous
see PJ1650
(1679) By place where preserved
see PJ1650+
1680 By place where found
1681.A-Z Particular papyri, A-Z
Including facsimiles (and originals if not placed in the Manuscript department), also typographical reproductions of the text entire in hieroglyphic type, or transliterated in Roman characters; for editions of papyri containing parts of the "Book of the dead," see PJ1555.A3-PJ1557.Z8
Cf. PJ1849, Demotic literature
For editions of parts of papyrus which are classified according to contents, see PJ1701+
For translations (without text) for popular use, see PJ1941+
For treatises (Linguistic, critical, archaeological, etc.), see PJ1089, or see the subject, if written from that point of view
By form, subject, etc.
(1701) Religion
see PJ1551-PJ1571

Egyptology
Literature
Hieratic literature
Papyri
By form, subject, etc. -- Continued
1725 Poetry
Cf. PJ1569, Poems
(1729) Drama
see PJ1571
Prose
1731 General. Miscellaneous
1735 Narrative. Tales
1741 Didactic. Moral
1745 Letters
1761 History. Geography
1771 Science (Mathematics. Medicine. Magic)
1775 Other
(1780) Individual works
classified according to contents in PJ1735-PJ1775
Cf. PJ1681
Demotic literature
History
1801 Treatises. Compends
1803 Lectures. Essays
1805 Special philological and archaeological studies
Texts
1809 General. Miscellaneous
1811 Museums. Institutions
1819 Minor collections (Private, etc.)
Inscriptions
(1820) General. Miscellaneous
see PJ1809
1821 By place where found
(1823) By place where preserved
see PJ1811-PJ1819
(1825) Particular inscriptions
see PJ1531
1829 Ostraka
Papyri
(1840) General. Miscellaneous
see PJ1809
By place where preserved, see PJ1811
1845 By place where found

Egyptology
Literature
Demotic literature
Texts
Papyri -- Continued
1849 Particular papyri
Including facsimiles (and originals if not placed in the Manuscript department), also typographical reproductions of the text entire in hieroglyphic type, or transliterated in Roman characters; for editions of papyri containing parts of the "Book of the dead," see PJ1555.A3-PJ1557.Z8
For editions of parts of a papyrus which are classified according to contents, see PJ1701+
For translations (without text) for popular use, see PJ1941+
For treatises (Linguistic, critical, archaeological, etc.), see PJ1089, or see the subject, if written from that point of view
Literary texts
1860 General. Miscellaneous
1871 Narrative. Tales, etc.
By subject
Prefer PJ1849, for special papyri
1881 Religion. Mythology
Cf. PJ1551+, Religious literature
1891 Magic
1895 History. Politics. Administration
1901 Documents (Law. Contracts, etc.)
For legal documents, e.g. contracts, wills, etc., see Subclass KL
1911 Medicine
1921.A-Z Other special, A-Z
Translations of Egyptian literature
Class here mainly translations of Egyptian literature (without the addition of text) intended for popular use
1941 Collections
1943 Selections. Anthologies, etc.
1945 Poetry
Prose (General. Miscellaneous)
1947 General works
1949 Narrative. Tales, etc.
1959 Didactic. Moral
By subject
1961 Mythology
Religion, see BL2430
1963 History
1967 Science (Magic, etc.)

Translations of Egyptian literature -- Continued
Individual works
1981 Inscriptions
1985 Papyri
1989 Other
Prefer PJ1949-PJ1967
2001-2199 Coptic (Table P-PZ3)
2001 Periodicals. Societies. Collections
2015 History of philology
2019 Study and teaching
2023 Treatises
2028 Script
Grammar
2029 Comparative. Historical
2033 Descriptive
2037 Readers. Chrestomathies
2040 Phonology
2059 Morphology. Inflection. Accidence
2070 Parts of speech (Morphology and syntax)
2113 Syntax
2135 Style. Composition. Rhetoric
2153 Prosody. Metrics. Rhythmics
2161 Etymology
2181 Lexicography. Dictionaries
Linguistic geography. Dialects
2187 General
(2188) Special
Including Sahidic (Theban), Akhmimic, Fayumik (Bashmeric), Bahairic
see PJ2029-PJ2081
Literature
2190 History
Texts
2193 Inscriptions
Collections
2195 General. Miscellaneous
2196 Institutions
2197 Minor (Private, etc.)
2198 Translations
2199 Single works or authors
Libyco-Berber languages. Berber languages
General
Collections
2340 General works
2341 Texts. Sources, etc.
2343 General works
2344 Alphabet. Writing. Tifinag
2345 Grammar
2347 Etymology
2349 Dictionaries, glossaries, etc.
Libyan group
General, see PJ2340+
Egyptian, see PJ1001+

Libyco-Berber languages. Berber languages
Libyan group -- Continued
Coptic, see PJ2001+
2353 Libyan (Ancient)
Including Numidian, Mauretanian, etc.
Modern dialects
Class here dialects spoken in the various oases of the region comprised within ancient Libya
2357 Audil (Aujila)
2359 Ghadames
2361 Siwa (Siwi) (Table P-PZ15a)
2365 Socna
2367 Temissa
Berber languages
General, see PJ2340+
2369.A-Z Special. By region or country, A-Z
Special languages
2371 Guanche (Extinct) (Table P-PZ15a)
2373 Kabyle (Kabail) (Table P-PZ15a)
2375 Zouave (Table P-PZ15a)
2377 Rif (Table P-PZ15a)
2379 Shilha (Shlu, Chleuh) (Arabic name, Sölha) (Table P-PZ15a)
Tuareg (Tawarek, Tamashek)
2381 General works (Table P-PZ15a)
Dialects
2382.G4 Ghat
2382.T3 Tahaggart
2391 Zenaga (Table P-PZ15a)
2395.A-Z Other special, A-Z
2395.B2 Baamarani
2395.C4 Chenoua
2395.J43 Jebel Nefusa
2395.M97 Mzab
2395.O87 Ouargla
2395.T3 Tamazight (Table P-PZ16)
2397 Texts in Berber languages (General)
2399 History of Berber literature
Cushitic languages
General
2401 Collections
2404 General works
2405 Grammar
2409 Etymology
2413 Dictionaries. Glossaries, etc.
Special
Agau (Central Cushitic)
2425 General works
Dialects
2430 Bilin (Bogos)
2435 Hamir (Chamir)
2437 Hamta
2438 Kemant

Cushitic languages
Special
Agau (Central Cushitic)
Dialects -- Continued
2439 Quara (Khwara. Qwarasa)
2443 Falasha
Beja (Northern Cushitic)
2451 General works
Dialects
2453 Beni Amer
2455 Bishári
2457 Hadendoa
2459 Hallenga
Eastern Cushitic
2463 General works
2465 Afar. Saho (Table P-PZ15a)
Oromo (Galla)
Language
2471 General works
2471.12 Grammar
2471.4 Dictionaries
Literature
2471.5 History
2471.6 Collections
2471.9.A-Z Individual authors or works, A-Z
Dialects
2473 Bararetta
2475 Borana
2476 Harer
2477 Matštša
2478 Qottu
2479 Tulama
2485 Werizoid languages
Sidamo group. "Sidama Oriental"
2491 General works
Dialects
2497 Burji. Bambala
2501 Gedeo. Derasa
2503 Gudella (Hadya)
2509 Kambatta
2517 Sidamo
2521 Arbore
Somali group
2525 General
2527 Boni
2529 Rendile
2531-2534 Somali (Table P-PZ11)
Dialects
2535 Darod
2537 Hawiyya
2539 Sab
2545 Tunni (Table P-PZ15a)
Southern Cushitic

Cushitic languages
Special
Southern Cushitic -- Continued
2551 General works
Dialects
2554 Dahalo
2556 Iraqw
West Cushitic. Omotic
2561 General works
2564 Badditu
2570 Gimirra
2572 Gonga (Šinaša)
2578 Kaffa
2582 Kulla-Walamo
2586 Mocha
2594 Yemsa. Zendjero
Semitic philology
3001 Periodicals. Societies. Serials
3001.5 Congresses
Collections
Texts, sources, chrestomathies, see PJ3081+
Monographs. Studies
3002 Serials
3002.Z5A-Z Studies in honor of a particular person or institution, A-Z
3003.A-Z Individual authors, A-Z
3004 Encyclopedias. Dictionaries
3005 Philosophy. Theory. Method. Relations
3007 History of philology
3009 Biography
(3010) Bibliography. Bio-bibliography
see Z7049.S5
Study and teaching
3011 General works
3012.A-Z By region or country, A-Z
3013.A-Z By university, college, etc., A-Z
3014 Treatises
Including history of Semitic languages, etc.
3016 Compends
3017 Criticism, controversial discourses, reviews, etc.
3018 Popular. Lectures, addresses, pamphlets, etc.
Alphabet (Origin and development)
Cf. PJ1091+, Hieroglyphic
3019 General works
(3020) Transliteration
see P226
Grammar
3021 General works
3023 Phonology. Pronunciation
Morphology. Inflection. Accidence
3027 General works
3031 Word formation. Derivation. Suffixes, etc.
Parts of speech (Morphology and syntax)

Semitic philology
Grammar
Parts of speech (Morphology and syntax) -- Continued
3033 Noun. Adjective. Pronoun. Article. Numerals
3035 Verb
3041 Syntax
3051 Style. Composition. Rhetoric
3061 Prosody. Metrics. Rhythmics
3065 Etymology. Semantics
Lexicography
3071 Treatises
3075 Dictionaries
Particular groups
East Semitic (Akkadian or Assyro-Babylonian), see PJ3101 +
West Semitic (North and South Semitic), see PJ4101 +
North Semitic (Canaanite languages and Aramaic), see PJ4121 +
South Semitic (Arabic, South Arabic, Ethiopic), see PJ5901 +, PJ6950 +, PJ9001 +
3079 Linguistic geography. Dialects
Texts. Inscriptions
3081 Collections
3085 Particular groups
Cf. PJ3077.2 +
3087 Particular stories (of Semitic origin)
Includes Ahikar (Cf. PJ5209)
3091 Criticism. Commentaries, etc.
3095 Translations
3097 Semitic literature (History and criticism)
Cf. PJ601 +, Christian Oriental literature
Cf. PJ806 +, Mohammedan literature
East Semitic languages
Assyriology. Akkadian
"Assyriology" comprises the philological, archaeological, and historical study of the languages, culture, and history of Babylonia and Assyria. Treatises written mainly from the viewpoint of a given subject are classified by subject
Cf. DS67 +, History of Assyria and Babylonia
Periodicals
3101 International
3102 English and American
3103 French
3104 German
3105 Italian
3109 Other
Societies
3111 International
3112 English and American
3113 French

East Semitic languages
Assyriology. Akkadian
Societies -- Continued
3114 German
3115 Italian
3119 Other
3121 Congresses
Collections
Texts. Sources, etc , see PJ3701+
Monographs. Studies, etc.
3125 Serial
3126.A-Z Studies in honor of a particular person or institution, A-Z
3127 Individual authors
3131 Encyclopedias. Dictionaries
Philosophy. Theory. Methods
3135 General works
3137 Relations
History (of Assyriology)
Cf. PJ3197
3151 General
3152 General special
3153 Early period to ca. 1800/30
3155 19th and 20th centuries
3160.A-Z By region or country, A-Z
(3162) Bibliography
see Z7055
Cf. Z3036-Z3040
Biography. Memoirs. Correspondence
3163 Collective
3164.A-Z Individual, A-Z
Study and teaching (Curricula, etc.)
3165 General
3166 General special
3168.A-Z By region or country, A-Z
3169.A-Z By university, college, etc., A-Z
3171 General works
3181 Compends
3185 Popular
3189 Special philological-archaeological studies
Cuneiform writing
Treatises
3191 Through 1870
3193 1871-
3197 History (of the decipherment)
Cf. PJ3151+, History of Assyriology
3211 Origin and development
Special kinds
(3215) Sumerian
see PJ4010
(3216) Babylonian (New Babylonian)
see PJ3191-PJ3193

East Semitic languages
Assyriology. Akkadian
Cuneiform writing
Special kinds -- Continued
(3217) Assyrian (New Assyrian)
see PJ3191-PJ3193
(3218) "Cappadocian"
see PJ3591
(3221.1) Hittite
see P945
(3221.3) Elamite (Susian)
see P943
(3221.5) Chaldian (Vannic. Urartaean)
see P959
(3221.9) Persian
see PK6128-PK6129
3223 Collections of signs, ideograms, syllabaries, etc.
3225 Specimen lists, types, etc.
Language
Grammar
3231 Comparative
3241 Historical
3251 Descriptive
3259 Readers. Chrestomathies
3261 Phonology
Morphology. Inflection. Accidence
3271 General works
3281 Noun
3291 Verb
3302 Other. Miscellaneous
3311 Syntax
3401 Prosody. Metrics. Rhythmics
Etymology
3450 Treatises
3453 Dictionaries (exclusively etymological)
3455 Special elements
3457 Other special
3461 Semantics
3471 Synonyms
Cf. PJ3911, Scientific literature
Lexicography
3511 Treatises (History, etc.)
Dictionaries
Ancient vocabularies, see PJ3911
3523 Polyglot
3525 Assyro-Babylonian-English;
English-Assyro-Babylonian
3540 Dictionaries with definitions other than English
Special
3545 Names
3547 Technical, etc.
Linguistic geography. Dialects
3550 Treatises (General. General special)

East Semitic languages
Assyriology. Akkadian
Language
Linguistic geography. Dialects -- Continued
Babylonian
see PJ3231-PJ3550
3561-3569 New-Babylonian (Table P-PZ8)
3571-3579 Assyrian (Table P-PZ8)
For reference mainly, see PJ3231-PJ3550
"Cappadocian"
3591.A2 Collections of texts. By date
3591.A5-Z3 Treatises
3591.Z8 Glossaries. Indices, etc. By date
3595.A-Z Other dialects, A-Z
3595.A4 Alalakh dialect
3595.A48 Amurru
3595.E53 Emar
3595.N8 Nuzi dialect
3595.U34 Ugarit
Literature
History
3601 Treatises. Compends
By period
Early Babylonian
3611 General works
3621 Age of Hammurabi
3631 Assyrian
3641 Neo-Babylonian. Persian
3651 Poetry
3671 Special topics (not A-Z)
Texts: Inscriptions. Clay tablets, etc.
3701 General collections
3711 Museums. Institutions, etc.
3719 Minor collections (Private owners, etc.)
3721.A-Z By place where found, A-Z
3725 Selected texts (Prose, or Prose and poetry)
3728 Selections. Anthology
Prefer PJ3259
3730.A-Z Particular inscriptions, A-Z
Poetry
3751 Collections (General. Miscellaneous)
Epic
3761 General works
3771.A-Z Particular works, A-Z
e.g.
Gilgamesh
3771.G5 Editions. By date
3771.G5A-Z Translations. By language, age, A-Z
3771.G6 History and criticism
Lyric
3781 General. Miscellaneous
3785 Hymns. Psalms. Prayers
3791 Incantations. Magic. Omens, etc.

East Semitic languages
Assyriology. Akkadian
Literature
Texts: Inscriptions.
Clay tablets, etc. -- Continued
Prose
3801 General. Miscellaneous
Prefer PJ3725
By subject
History
3811 Collections. Selections
Inscriptions of kings and rulers
3815 General. Miscellaneous
Babylonian
Early to ca. 2200 B.C.
3824 General works
3825.A-Z Particular rulers, A-Z
Later, ca. 2200-1780 B.C.
3826 General works
3827.A-Z Particular rulers, A-Z
e.g.
3827.H3 Hammurabi
Kassite period, ca. 1780-689 B.C.
3828 General works
3829.A-Z Particular rulers, A-Z
Cf. PJ3884+, Letters
Neo-Babylonian. To ca. 100 B.C.
3831 General works
3833.A-Z Particular rulers, A-Z
e.g.
3833.N2 Nabonidus, fl. 555-538 B.C.
3833.N3 Nebuchadnezzar II, d. 561 B.C.
3834 Persian inscriptions (Babylonian translations)
Assyrian
3835 General works
3837.A-Z Particular rulers, A-Z
e.g.
3837.A5 Ashur-nasir-pal, fl. 885 B.C.
3837.A6 Assurbanipal, fl. 650 B.C.
3837.E7 Esarhaddon, fl. 668 B.C.
3837.S2 Sargon, fl. 722-705 B.C.
3837.S7 Sennacherib, d. 681 B.C.
3837.T8 Tukulti-Ninib I
3837.T9 Tukulti-Ninib II
Historical texts
3841 General. Miscellaneous
3845 Babylonian chronicles
Chronological lists
3851 Babylonian
3855 Assyrian
3861 Administration (Documents, etc.)
For legal documents, see subclass KL

East Semitic languages
Assyriology. Akkadian
Literature
Texts: Inscriptions. Clay tablets, etc.
Prose
By subject -- Continued
3870 Commerce, etc.
For legal documents, see subclass KL
Letters
Cf. PJ3815+, Inscriptions of kings and rulers
3881 Collections. Selections
3882 Early to ca. 2200 B.C.
3883 Later. Age of Hammurabi
Kassite period
3884 General works
Tell-el-Amarna tablets, ca. 1500 B.C.
3885 Editions
Subarrange by editor
3886.A-Z Translations. By language, A-Z
3887 Criticism
3889 Assyrian period
Including Harper, Waterman, etc.
3891 Neo-Babylonian and Persian period
Scientific literature
3911 Philology
Includes vocabularies (Cf. PJ3471) grammatical texts, paleography, bibliography, other
For syllabaries, see PJ3223
3921.A-Z Natural sciences, etc., A-Z
3921.A4 Agriculture
3921.A8 Astronomy
3921.B6 Botany
3921.D5 Divination
3921.G4 Geography. Topography
3921.M3 Magic
3921.M4 Mathematics
3921.M5 Medicine
3921.M6 Mineralogy
3921.Z6 Zoology
3931 Seals. Seal cylinders
Prefer CD5348, NK5563
3941 Moral literature
Including didactic treatises, fables, animal stories; Proverbs (Cf. PN6418.5.A8, Assyro-Babylonian)
Translations
3951 Collections
3953 Selections, etc.
(3959) Special works
see work, or subject
(3971.A-Z) By subject, A-Z

East Semitic languages -- Continued
Sumerian (Table P-PZ5)
4001-4007 Generalities: Periodicals. Societies, etc.
For publications not exclusively devoted to Sumerian, see PJ3101-PJ3137
4008 Treatises. Philological-archaeological studies
Cf. PJ3189, Assyriology. Akkadian
(4009) Writing
see PJ3191-PJ3225
Language
4010 Treatises (General. General special)
Including relation to other languages
Grammar
(4010.9) Ancient
see PJ3911
4011 Comparative. Historical
4013 Descriptive
4014 Readers. Chrestomathies
4015 Phonology
Cf. PJ3261, Assyriology. Akkadian
Cf. PJ3911+, Scientific literature (Assyriology)
4018 Alphabet. Transliteration
4019 Morphology. Inflection. Accidence
4021 Parts of speech (Noun, verb, etc.)
4025 Syntax
4031 Etymology
Dictionaries
(4034) Ancient
see PJ3911
4037.A-Z Other. By author, A-Z
4041 Dialects
Literature
4045 History (General)
4047 Special topics (not A-Z)
Texts
Class bilingual texts (Babylonian-Sumerian) with Babylonian literature
Collections
4051 General. Miscellaneous
4053.A-Z Special institutions, A-Z
Including museums, libraries, etc.
4054 By place where found
e. g. Drehem, Nippur, Telloh mound
4055 Minor (Private, etc.)
(4059) Selections. Anthologies
see PJ4014
Poetry
4061 Collections
4065 Particular works
Inscriptions
4070 Collections
4071 Particular inscriptions

East Semitic languages
Sumerian
Literature
Texts -- Continued
4075 Other texts (Documents, contracts, deeds, etc.)
For legal texts, see subclass KL
Translations
4081 Collections
4083 Selections. Anthologies
(4089) Special works
see work or subject
(4091.A-Z) By subject, A-Z
West and North Semitic languages
4101-4109 West Semitic (North and South Semitic) (Table P-PZ8)
Cf. PJ4121+, Northwest and North Semitic
Cf. PJ5901+, South Semitic languages
4121-4129 Northwest Semitic. North Semitic (Table P-PZ8)
Comprises the Canaanite and Aramaic languages
Cf. PJ4131+, Canaanite
Cf. PJ5201+, Aramaic
For inscriptions, see PJ3081
For inscriptions, see PJ3085
4131-4139 Canaanite (Table P-PZ8)
Comprises the ancient Canaanite (only known through the glosses in the Tell el-Amarna letters); Moabite; Phenician-Punic; Hebrew
4143 Ammonite (Table P-PZ15)
4145 Amorite
4147 Eblaite (Table P-PZ15)
4149 Moabite. The Moabite stone
4150 Ugaritic (Table P-PZ15)
4160 Proto-Sinaitic (Table P-PZ15)
Phenician-Punic
4171 General treatises
4173 Writing
Cf. P211, Linguistics
Cf. PJ4589+, Hebrew
Grammar
4175 General works
4177 Special
4181 Etymology
4185 Glossaries
4187 Punic in Plautus
If treated especially from the linguistic point of view
Cf. PA6568.P7
Texts
4191 Collections. General
Cf. PJ3081+, Semitic philology
4193 Particular inscriptions
4195 Punic inscriptions

West and North Semitic languages
Phenician-Punic
Texts -- Continued
4197 Neo-Punic inscriptions
Includes inscriptions dating after destruction of Carthage
Hebrew
Philology (Table P-PZ2)
Periodicals
4501 International. English. American
4502 German
4503 Other
4504 Annuals. Yearbook
Societies
4505 International. English. American
4506 German
4507 Other
4509 Congresses
Collections
Monographs. Studies
4513 Serial
4514.A-Z Studies in honor of a particular person or institution, A-Z
4515 Individual authors
4519 Encyclopedias
4520 Atlases. Maps. Charts, etc.
Cf. PJ4850, Linguistic geography
Cf. PJ5040, Poetry (Selections. Anthologies)
4521 Philosophy. Theory. Method
History of philology
Cf. BS1160+, English commentaries
Cf. PJ4823, Lexicography
4525 General
4526 General special
By period
4527 Early Middle Ages to 1500
Modern, 1500-
4528 General works
4529 19th and 20th centuries
4531.A-Z By country, A-Z
(4532) Bibliography. Bio-bibliography
see Z7070
Biography. Memoirs. Correspondence
4533 Collective
4534 Individual
Study and teaching
Including method, curricula, etc.
4535 General works
4536 General special
By period, see PJ4527+
4538.A-Z By country, A-Z
4539 By university, school, etc.
4541 General works

Hebrew -- Continued
Language (Biblical and Modern) (Table P-PZ2)
Cf. PJ4901+, Talmudic Hebrew
Treatises
4543 General
4544 General special
Includes Relation to other languages; Primality of Hebrew
4545 History (of language)
Grammar
4553 Theory. Methodology
Prefer PJ4521
4554 Terminology
(4555) History (of grammar)
see PJ4524-PJ4531
Treatises
4556 Hebrew
4557 Arabic
(4558) Other Oriental languages
(4559) Latin
see PJ4563
Western languages
4563 Early through 1870
4564 1871-
(4565) Comparative. Historical
see PJ4564
Textbooks
4566 Early through 1870
4567 1871-
Readers. Chrestomathies
4569 Primary
4571 Intermediate. Advanced
Phonology. Phonetics
4576 General works
4579 Pronunciation
4580 Pausals
4581 Accent. Pitch
4583 Orthography. Spelling
Alphabet. Writing. Script
Cf. P211, Linguistics
Cf. PJ3019, Semitic philology
4589 General works
4590 Punctuation. Masoretic points
Cf. BS718, Old Testament
4591 Transliteration
Cf. P226
4592 Vowels. Diphthongs
Cf. PJ4590, Punctuation
4593 Consonants
4595 Particular letters
4598 Syllabication
Morphology. Inflection. Accidence
4601 General works

Hebrew
Language (Biblical and Modern)
Grammar
Morphology. Inflection.
Accidence -- Continued
Special parts of speech, see PJ4619+
4611 Paradigms. Tables, etc.
Parts of speech (Morphology and syntax)
4619 Miscellaneous
4621 Noun
Adjective
4633 General works
4635 Numerals
4637 Article
4641 Pronoun
Verb
4645 General
4647 Special
Particle (Adverb, preposition, etc.)
4671 General works
4677 Preposition
Syntax
4701 General works
4707 General special
4711 Special
4731.A-Z Grammatical usage of particular authors, A-Z
4740 Style. Composition. Rhetoric
Prosody. Metrics. Rhythmics
4771 History
Treatises
4774 Early through 1800
4775 1801-
Etymology
4801 Treatises
4803 Names
4805 Dictionaries (exclusively etymological)
4807.A-Z Foreign elements, A-Z
e.g.
4807.A1 General
4807.A7 Aramaic
4810 Semantics
4815 Synonyms. Homonyms. Antonyms
4819 Particular words
Lexicography
4820 Collections
4823 General works (History, theory)
(4823.5) Biography of lexicographers
see PJ63-PJ64, PJ4533-PJ4534
4824 Criticism of particular dictionaries
Dictionaries
Ancient and medieval (to ca. 1500)
4825 Hebrew
Arabic, see PJ4837

Hebrew
Language (Biblical and Modern)
Lexicography
Dictionaries
Ancient and medieval (to ca. 1500) -- Continued
Greek, see PA4268.Z7+
Modern, ca. 1500-
4830 Hebrew (only)
4831 Polyglot
For dictionaries combining Hebrew, Biblical Aramaic (Chaldaic) and a modern language, see PJ4833+
For dictionaries with equivalent in Latin and English, see PJ4833
Bilingual
4833 Hebrew-English; English-Hebrew
4835.A-Z Other European languages, A-Z, by language
Yiddish, see PJ5117
4836 Hebrew-Slavic
Including Bohemian, Polish, Russian
4837 Hebrew-Oriental
Including Arabic, Persian, Syriac
Hebrew-Artificial languages, see PM8060+
4838 Picture dictionaries
Special dictionaries
Etymological, see PJ4805
Special periods. Post-Biblical, see PJ5001+
4839 Particular authors
4841 Names
4845 Special lists: Vocabularies, etc.
4847 Abbreviations
4850 Linguistic geography
Dialects. Provincialisms. Localisms
4855 General works
4860 Samaritan
Cf. BM920+, Language of the Samaritan Pentateuch
Cf. PJ5271+, Samaritan Aramaic
4865 Post-Biblical Hebrew (Table P-PZ15)
Talmudic (Mishnaic) Hebrew (Table P-PZ5)
4901 Periodicals. Societies. Serials
Collections
(4902) Texts, sources, etc.
see PJ4913
4903 Monographs. Studies
(4905.9) Bibliography
see Z7070
4906 Biography
4907 Study and teaching
4908 General works
4909 History of the language

Hebrew
Language (Biblical and Modern)
Talmudic (Mishnaic) Hebrew -- Continued
(4909.5) Script
see PJ4589-PJ4598
Grammar
4911 Comprehensive works. Compends (Advanced)
4912 Elementary. Introductory
4913 Readers. Chrestomathies
Prefer PJ4569-PJ4571
4913.A2 Primary
4913.A5-Z Intermediate. Advanced
4914 Conversation. Phrase books
4915 Phonology
4918 Vowels, etc.
4919 Morphology. Inflection. Accidence
Parts of speech (Morphology and syntax)
4920 Noun. Adjective. Pronoun. Article. Numerals
4921 Verb
4922 Particles (Adverb, preposition,etc.)
4923 Syntax
4925 Grammatical usage of particular authors
Style. Composition. Rhetoric
4927 General works
4928 Letter writing
4929 Prosody. Metrics. Rhythmics
Etymology
4931 General works
4932 Foreign elements
4933 Particular words
Lexicography
4934 Treatises
Dictionaries
4935 Hebrew (only)
4937 Other
4951-5000 Medieval Hebrew (Table P-PZ5)
Modern Hebrew, see PJ4543+
Literature
Literary history and criticism
5001 Periodicals. Serials
5002 Yearbooks
5003 Societies
5004 Congresses
Collections
5005.A1 Serials
5005.A2A-Z Collections in honor of a special person or institution, A-Z. Festschriften
5005.A3-Z Collected works, studies, essays, etc., of individual authors
5006 Encyclopedias. Dictionaries
5007 Study and teaching
5007.3 Criticism

Hebrew
Literature
Literary history and criticism -- Continued
5007.5.A-Z Biography of teachers, critics, and historians, A-Z
History
5008 General works
5009 Addresses, essays, etc.
Special aspects and topics
5010 Relations to history, civilization, culture, etc.
5011 Relations to other literatures
For relations to individual authors, see the author
5012.A-Z Treatment of special subjects, A-Z
5012.A3 Age groups
5012.D7 Dreams
5012.G3 Galilee
5012.H65 Holocaust, Jewish (1939-1945)
5012.I87 Israel-Arab War
5012.J3 Jaffa
5012.J4 Jerusalem
5012.N27 Nationalism
5012.N3 Nature
5012.P3 Palestine
5012.P64 Politics
5012.R4 Religion
5013.A-Z Treatment of special classes, races, etc. A-Z
e.g.
5013.C6 Children
5013.P7 Priests
Treatment of special persons and characters, see PN57.A+
5014 Biography of Hebrew authors (Collective)
Including memoirs and letters
For Individual biography, see PJ5050+
By period
(5015) Origins. Early to 700
Biblical literature, see BS701+
Apocrypha and Pseudepigrapha, see BS1691+
Aristeas' epistle
see BS744
Dead Sea Scrolls
see BM487
Elephantine papyri, see PJ5208.E4+
Talmudic, Midrashic, and Geonic literature, see BM495+
5016 Medieval (8th-17th centuries)
Modern
5017 General works
5018 1701-1820
5019 1821-1885
5020 1886-1945
5021 1946-

Hebrew
Literature
Literary history and criticism
History -- Continued
Special forms
Poetry
5022 General works
By period
Early
see BS1405+
5023 Medieval
5024 Modern
5025.A-Z Special forms of poetry, A-Z
Azharot, see BM670.A8
5025.C45 Children's poetry
5025.E45 Elegiac poetry
Piyutim, see BM670.P5
Drama
5026 General and modern
5027 Early
Prose. Fiction
5028 General, and medieval
5029 Modern
5030.A-Z Special topics, A-Z
5030.A7 Arabs
5030.C55 Children
5030.E45 Emigration and immigration
5030.E94 Expatriation
5030.G74 Grief
Immigration, see PJ5030.E45
Jews, Oriental, see PJ5030.O74
Jews, Yemenite, see PJ5030.Y45
5030.O74 Oriental Jews
5030.P64 Politics
5030.P65 Women
5030.Y45 Yemenite Jews
5030.Z55 Zionism
Other prose forms
5031 Letters
5032 Essays
5033 Wit and humor
5033.9 Miscellaneous
(5034) Folk literature
see subclass GR
Cf. GR98, Jewish folklore
Cf. GR285+, Folklore of Palestine and Israel
5034.2 Juvenile literature
By region or country, see PJ5049.A+
Inscriptions
5034.4 History and criticism
Collections
5034.5 General

Hebrew
Literature
Inscriptions
Collections -- Continued
5034.6 Museums. Institutions
5034.7 Private collections
5034.8.A-Z Special. By region or country, A-Z
5034.9 Individual inscriptions
Collections
5035 General collections
5036 Selections. Anthologies
By period
5037 Medieval
5038 Modern
By region or country, see PJ5049.A+
Special forms
Poetry
5039 General collections
5040 Selections. Anthologies
By period
Early
see BS1402+
5041 Medieval
5042 Modern
5043 Drama
Prose. Fiction
5044 General, and medieval
5045 Modern
Other prose forms
5046 Letters
5047 Essays
Wit and humor, see PN6231.J5
Proverbs (Book of the Bible), see BS1461+, PN6519.J5
5047.9 Miscellaneous
For Hasidic tales, see BM532
(5048) Folk literature
see GR
5048.7.A-Z By special sects, A-Z
e.g.
Under each (using three consecutive cutter numbers):
(1) General works
Including literary history and criticism, biography (Collective), etc.
(2) Collections
(3).A-Z Local, A-Z
Individual authors, see PJ5050+
5048.7.K3-K33 Karaites
Juvenile literature, see PZ39+

Hebrew
Literature -- Continued
5049.A-Z By region or country, A-Z
e.g.
Under each (using three successive cutter numbers):
1 *General works*
Including literary history and criticism, biography (Collective), etc.
2 *Collections*
3.A-Z *Local, A-Z*
Individual authors, see PJ5050+
Israel (Palestine)
History and criticism, see PJ5020, PJ5021
Collections, see PJ5038
Individual authors, see PJ5050+
Poland
5049.P6 General works
5049.P62 Collections
5049.P63A-Z Local, A-Z
e.g.
5049.P63W3 Warsaw
Individual authors and works, A-Z
For juvenile literature, see PZ39+
5050.A-Z Medieval through 1700
Including anonymous works
Subarrange each author by Table P-PZ40 unless otherwise specified
5050.A26 Abulafia, Todros, ha-Levi, b. 1247 (Table P-PZ40)
5050.B3 Barlaam and Joasaph (Table P-PZ40)
Hebrew version has title: Ben ha-melekh veha-nazir
5050.B4 Berechiah ben Natronai, 12th/13th cent. (Table P-PZ40)
5050.E4 Eleazar ben Jacob, ha-Bavli, ca. 1195-1250 (Table P-PZ40)
5050.H3 al-Ḥarizi, Judah ben Solomon, d. 1235 (Table P-PZ40)
5050.I18 Ibn Ezra, Abraham ben Meïr, 1092-1167 (Table P-PZ40)
5050.I185 Ibn Ezra, Isaac, b. ca. 1100 (Table P-PZ40)
5050.I2 Ibn Ezra, Moses ben Jacob, ca. 1060-ca. 1139 (Table P-PZ40)
5050.I3 Ibn Gabirol, Solomon ben Judah, ca. 1021-ca.1058 (Table P-PZ40)
5050.I35 Ibn Ghiyyat, Isaac, 1038-1089 (Table P-PZ40)
Ibn Khalfun, Isaac, 10th/11th cent , see PJ5050.I8
Ibn Zabara, Joseph ben Meir, b. 1140?, see PJ5050.J6
5050.I6 Immanuel ben Solomon, ca. 1265-ca. 1330 (Table P-PZ40)
5050.I8 Isaac Ibn Ḥalfon, fl. 970-1020 (Table P-PZ40)

Hebrew
Literature
Individual authors and works, A-Z
Medieval through 1700 -- Continued
5050.J33 Jagel, Abraham ben Hananiah dei Galicchi, 16th/17th cent. (Table P-PZ40)
5050.J6 Joseph ben Meir ibn Zabara, b. 1140? (Table P-PZ40)
5050.J6S4 Sefer sha' ashu' im (Table P-PZ40)
5050.J8 Judah, ha-Levi, 12th cent. (Table P-PZ40)
For Kitāb al-Ḥujjah, see BM550.J79
5050.J83 Judah ben Isaac ibu Shabbethai, 13th cent. (Table P-PZ40)
5050.K3 Kalonymus ben Kalonymus ben Meïr, b. 1286? (Table P-PZ40)
5050.L4 Leone da Modena, 1571-1648 (Table P-PZ40)
5050.M5 Mishle Sendabar (Table P-PZ40)
5050.N3 Najara, Israel ben Moses, 1555?-1625 (Table P-PZ40)
5050.S2 Sahula, Isaac ben Solomon, 13th cent. (Table P-PZ40)
5050.S23 Sa'id ben Bābshād, 10th/11th cent. (Table P-PZ40)
5050.S3 Samuel, ha-Nagid, 993-1056 (Table P-PZ40)
5050.S36 Santob, de Carrión de los Condes, ca. 1290-ca. 1369 (Table P-PZ40)
Shabazi, Shalem, 1619-1686, see PJ5050.S5
5050.S5 Shabazi, Shalom, 1619-1686 (Table P-PZ40)
5050.S54 Shawat, Fradji, 16th cent. (Table P-PZ40)
5050.Z29 Ẓaddik, Joseph ben Jacob Ibn, 1075-1149 (Table P-PZ40)
Modern, 1701-
By period
5051 1701-1820
Subarrange each author by Table P-PZ40 unless otherwise indicated
5051.A1A-Z Anonymous works. By title, A-Z
5051.B37 Benze'eb, Judah Loeb, 1764-1811 (Table P-PZ40)
5051.C6 Cohen, Salomon Jacob, 1772-1845 (Table P-PZ40)
5051.F7 Franco Mendes, David, 1713-1792 (Table P-PZ40)
5051.H3 Ḥayyim Abraham ben Aryeh Löb, 18th/19th cent. (Table P-PZ40)
Kats, Ḥayim Avraham ben Aryeh Leyb, 18th/19th cent , see PJ5051.H3
5051.L78 Luzzato, Ephraim, 1729-1792
Luzzato, Moses Ḥayyim, 1707-1747
5051.L8 Collected works. By date
5051.L8A2-L8A59 Translations (Collected)
5051.L8A6-L8A69 Selections. By editor (alphabetically)
5051.L8A7-L8Z4 Separate works, A-Z

	Hebrew
	Literature
	Individual authors and works, A-Z
	Modern, 1701-
	By period
	1701-1820
	Luzzato, Moses Ḥayyim, 1707-1747
	Separate works, A-Z -- Continued
5051.L8L3	La-yesharim tehilah
5051.L8M3	Ma'aseh Shimshon
(5051.L8M4)	Mesilat yesharim see BJ1287.L8L3
5051.L8M5	Migdal 'oz
5051.L8Z5-L8Z99	Biography and criticism
5051.P3	Pappenheim, Solomon, 1740-1814
5051.P4	Perl, Joseph, 1773-1839
5051.W4	Wessely, Naphthali Hirz, 1725-1805
5051.W65	Wolfssohn, Aaron, 1754-1835 (Table P-PZ40)
5052	1821-1885 Subarrange each author by Table P-PZ40 unless otherwise indicated
5052.A1A-Z	Anonymous works. By title, A-Z
	Abi-Ḥasira, Jacob ben Masoud, 1808-1880, see PJ5052.A9
5052.A9	Aviḥatsira, Jacob, 1808-1880 (Table P-PZ40)
5052.B43	Benjaminson, Abraham Loeb (Table P-PZ40)
5052.B67	Brandstädter, Mordecai David, 1844-1928 (Table P-PZ40)
	Brandstetter, M.D., 1844-1928, see PJ5052.B67
5052.G6	Gordon, Judah Loeb, 1830-1892 (Table P-PZ40)
5052.G63	Gottlober, Abraham Baer, 1811-1899 (Table P-PZ40)
	Guenzburg, Mordecai Aaron, 1795-1846, see PJ5052.G8
5052.G8	Günzburg, Mordeci Aaron, 1795-1846 (Table P-PZ40)
	Hacohen, Adam, 1794-1878, see PJ5052.L32
5052.L32	Lebensohn, Abraham Dob Baer, 1794-1878 (Table P-PZ40)
5052.L4	Levin, Judah Loeb, 1844-1925 (Table P-PZ40)
	Mapu, Abraham, 1808-1867
5052.M3	Collected works. By date
5052.M3A2-M3A59	Translations (Collected)
5052.M3A6-M3A69	Selections. By editor (alphabetically)
5052.M3A7-M3Z4	Separate works, A-Z
5052.M3A75	Ahavat Tsiyon
5052.M3A8	Ashmat Shomron
5052.M3A9	'Ayit tsavua'
5052.M3Z5-M3Z99	Biography and criticism
5052.M6	Morpurgo, Rahel (Luzzatto), 1790-1871 (Table P-PZ40)
5052.P4	Peretz, Isaac Loeb, 1851-1915 (Table P-PZ40)
5052.S314	Samoscz, David, 1789-1864 (Table P-PZ40)

Hebrew
Literature
Individual authors and works, A-Z
Modern, 1701-
By period
1821-1885 -- Continued

5052.S32 Schulman, Kalman, 1819-1899 (Table P-PZ40)
5052.S5 Smolenskin, Perez, 1842-1885 (Table P-PZ40)
5052.T65 Tour, N.W., d. 1885 (Table P-PZ40)
5052.W37 Weissbrem, Israel, 1839-ca. 1916 (Table P-PZ40)
Zamosc, David, 1789-1864, see PJ5052.S314
5053 1886-1945
Subarrange each author by Table P-PZ40 unless otherwise indicated
5053.A1A-Z Anonymous works. By title, A-Z
5053.A2 Abramowitz, Shalom Jacob, 1836-1917 (Table P-PZ40)
5053.A4 Agnon, Samuel Joseph, 1888- (Table P-PZ40)
Agnon, Shmuel Yosef, 1888-1970, see PJ5053.A4
5053.A43 Alper, Rebekah (Table P-PZ40)
Alper, Rivḳah, see PJ5053.A43
5053.A45 Alterman, Nathan, 1910- (Table P-PZ40)
5053.B3 Barash, Asher, 1889-1952 (Table P-PZ40)
5053.B3424 Bartana, Mordecai, 1910- (Table P-PZ40)
Ben Yiẓḥak, Avraham, 1883-1950, see PJ5053.S7
Berdichevsky, Micah Joseph, see PJ5053.B55
5053.B38 Berkowitz, Isaac Dob, 1885- (Table P-PZ40)
Berkowitz, Yitzḥak Dov, 1885-1967, see PJ5053.B38
5053.B5-B52 Bialik, Ḥayyim Haḥman 1873-1934 (Table P-PZ44)
5053.B52 Biography and criticism
Bikhovky, Elisheva, 1888-1949, see PJ5053.E5
5053.B55 Bin Gorion, Micha Joseph, 1865-1921 (Table P-PZ40)
5053.B63 Bluwstein, Rachel, 1890-1931 (Table P-PZ40)
Braudes, R. A. (Reuben Asher), 1851-1902, see PJ5053.B67
5053.B67 Braudes, Reuben Asher, 1851-1902 (Table P-PZ40)
Brenner, Joseph Ḥayyim, 1881-1921
5053.B7 Collected works. By date
5053.B7A2-B7A59 Translations (Collected) (Table P-PZ40)
5053.B7A6-B7A69 Selections. By editor (alphabetically)
5053.B7A7-B7Z4 Separate works, A-Z
5053.B7B4 Ben mayim le-mayim
5053.B7M3 Me-'emek 'akhor
5053.B7M4 Me-'ever li-gevulin
5053.B7M5 Mi-Kan umi-Kan
5053.B7S5 Shekol ve-kishalon
5053.B7Z5-B7Z99 Biography and criticism

Hebrew
Literature
Individual authors and works, A-Z
Modern, 1701-
By period
1886-1945 -- Continued
Cahan, Yaakov, 1881-1960, see PJ5053.K34
5053.D37 Deshe, Michael (Table P-PZ40)
Deshe, Mikha'el, see PJ5053.D37
Efros, Israel, 1891-1981, see PJ5053.E35
5053.E35 Efros, Israel Isaac, 1890- (Table P-PZ40)
5053.E5 Elisheva, 1888-1949 (Table P-PZ40)
5053.F37 Feigenberg-Eamri, Rachel, 1885-1972 (Table P-PZ40)
Feygenberg, Rakhel, 1885-1972, see PJ5053.F37
5053.F5 Fichman, Jacob, 1881- (Table P-PZ40)
5053.F514 Fichman, Josef, 1908- (Table P-PZ40)
Fikhman, Yosef, 1908- , see PJ5053.F514
Frischmann, David, 1859-1922, see PJ5053.F7
5053.F7 Frishman, David, 1865?-1922 (Table P-PZ40)
Gamzu, J.L., d. 1941, see PJ5053.G25
5053.G25 Gamzu, Judah Leib (Table P-PZ40)
5053.G4 Genessin, Uri Nissan, 1879?-1913 (Table P-PZ40)
5053.G5 Glusman, Sara (Table P-PZ40)
Gluzman, Śarah, see PJ5053.G5
Gnessin, Uri Nissan, d. 1913, see PJ5053.G4
Goṭfrid, Mordekhai, see PJ5053.G64
5053.G64 Gottfried, Markus (Table P-PZ40)
5053.H3 Hameiri, Avigdor, 1886- (Table P-PZ40)
5053.H32 Hanani, Joseph, 1908- (Table P-PZ40)
Ḥanani, Yosef, 1908- , see PJ5053.H32
Hochman, Chaim, see PJ5053.H58
5053.H58 Hokhman, Haim (Table P-PZ40)
Horovits, Ya'akov, 1901-1975, see PJ5053.H63
5053.H63 Horowitz, Jacob, 1901- (Table P-PZ40)
5053.I6 Imber, Naphtali Herz, 1856-1909 (Table P-PZ40)
5053.I9 Ivri, Isac (Table P-PZ40)
'Ivri, Yitsḥaḳ, 1900- , see PJ5053.I9
Kagan, Elieser, see PJ5053.K284
5053.K284 Kagan, Eliezer (Table P-PZ40)
5053.K34 Kahan, Jacob, 1881-1960 (Table P-PZ40)
5053.L364 Levin, Emma (Table P-PZ40)
5053.L412 Lewis, Abraham, 1838-1918 (Table P-PZ40)
5053.L5 Lisitzky, Ephram E., 1885- (Table P-PZ40)
5053.L54 Livne, Zvi, 1891- (Table P-PZ40)
Livneh, Tsevi, 1891- , see PJ5053.L54
Lurya, Avraham ben Me'ir, 1838-1918, see PJ5053.L412
Malets, D. (David), 1899-1981, see PJ5053.M3
5053.M3 Maletz, David, 1900- (Table P-PZ40)
Mordekhai, B., 1909- , see PJ5053.B3424

Hebrew
Literature
Individual authors and works, A-Z
Modern, 1701-
By period
1886-1945 -- Continued

5053.O64 Orenstein, Moses, 1839-1905 (Table P-PZ40)
5053.P38 Pen, Alexander, 1906-1972 (Table P-PZ40)
Penn, Alexander, 1906-1972, see PJ5053.P38
5053.R23 Rabinowitz, Shalom, 1859-1916 (Table P-PZ40)
Rachel, 1890-1931, see PJ5053.B63
5053.R4 Reubeni, Aaron, 1886- (Table P-PZ40)
Reuveni, A., 1886-1971, see PJ5053.R4
5053.R53 Rimon, Joseph Ziv, 1889-1958 (Table P-PZ40)
Rimon, Y. Zvi, 1889-1958, see PJ5053.R53
5053.R582 Rosen, Abraham, 1888- (Table P-PZ40)
Rosen, Avraham, 1889-1974, see PJ5053.R582
5053.S315 Salmon, Avraham, 1903- (Table P-PZ40)
5053.S34 Schoenberg, Isaac, 1901-1957 (Table P-PZ40)
Secco, M., 1876-1949, see PJ5053.S56
5053.S36 Sela, Isaac (Table P-PZ40)
Sela', Yitsḥak, see PJ5053.S36
Senesh, Hannah, 1921-1944, see PJ5053.S93
Shalmon, Avraham, 1903- , see PJ5053.S315
Shenhar, Yitzhak, see PJ5053.S34
5053.S4 Shimoni, David, 1886-1956 (Table P-PZ40)
5053.S45 Shlonsky, Abraham, 1900- (Table P-PZ40)
5053.S495 Silberschlag, Eisig, 1903- (Table P-PZ40)
5053.S5 Silkiner, Benjamin Nahum, 1882-1933 (Table P-PZ40)
5053.S56 Smilansky, Meir, 1876-1949 (Table P-PZ40)
5053.S57 Smilansky, Moshe, 1874-1953 (Table P-PZ40)
5053.S7 Sonne, Abraham, 1883-1950 (Table P-PZ40)
5053.S83 Steinberg, Jacob, 1887-1947 (Table P-PZ40)
5053.S85 Steinberg, Judah, 1863-1908 (Table P-PZ40)
5053.S93 Szenes, Hannah, 1921-1944 (Table P-PZ40)
Ṭabaḳai, Aryeh, d. 1982, see PJ5053.T2
5053.T2 Tabkai, Aryeh, 1910- (Table P-PZ40)
Talmi, Emma, see PJ5053.L364
Tan Pai, Yehoshu'a, 1914- , see PJ5053.T25
5053.T25 Tan-Pai, Yoshua, 1914- (Table P-PZ40)
5053.T3 Tchernichovski, Saul, 1875-1943 (Table P-PZ40)
5053.T75 Tsoref, Ephraim, 1903- (Table P-PZ40)
5053.W6 Wolfovsky, Menahem Zalman, 1893- (Table P-PZ40)
Wolfowski, Menahem Zalmen, 1893- , see PJ5053.W6
5053.Y55 Yizhar, S., 1916- (Table P-PZ40)
Zoref, Ephraim, 1903- , see PJ5053.T75
5054 1946-1990
Subarrange each author by Table P-PZ40 unless otherwise indicated

Hebrew
Literature
Individual authors and works, A-Z
Modern, 1701-
By period
1946-1990 -- Continued

5054.A1A-Z Anonymous works. By title, A-Z
'Adulah, see PJ5054.M426
5054.A4954 Agasi, Meir, 1947- (Table P-PZ40)
Agassi, Meir, 1947- , see PJ5054.A4954
5054.A4964 Albeg, Ezekiel H. (Table P-PZ40)
5054.A49755 Alon, Ya'el, 1943- (Table P-PZ40)
5054.A66 Amichal, Ada (Table P-PZ40)
Amichal Yeivin, Ada, see PJ5054.A66
Avivi, S , see PJ5054.A94
5054.A94 Avivi, Shmuel (Table P-PZ40)
Avnit, Hani, see PJ5054.Z48
5054.B24 Banai, Peretz (Table P-PZ40)
Bar-Yehoshu'a, 1912- , see PJ5054.B3
5054.B3 Bar-Yosef, Yehoshu'a, 1912- (Table P-PZ40)
Bar-Yossef, Yehoshua, 1912- , see PJ5054.B3
5054.B34 Baraḳ, Dodo (Table P-PZ40)
Barak, Dudu, see PJ5054.B34
5054.B366 Bassok, Iddo, 1950- (Table P-PZ40)
Bassok, Ido, see PJ5054.B366
Bat Ḥanah, Ahuvah, see PJ5054.B37
5054.B37 Bat-Hanna, Ahouva (Table P-PZ40)
Ben-Artsi, Shemu'el, 1914, see PJ5054.B4135
5054.B4135 Ben-Artzi, Shmuel, 1914- (Table P-PZ40)
Ben-Azar, Aviva, 1934- , see PJ5054.B7
Ben Gurion, Razia, see PJ5054.B4233
5054.B4233 Ben-Guryon, Raziyah (Table P-PZ40)
5054.B42356 Ben-Itzhak, Ruthi (Table P-PZ40)
5054.B42378 Ben-Ner, Asaf (Table P-PZ40)
5054.B4238 Ben-Ner, Isaac, 1937- (Table P40)
Ben-Ner, Yitzhak, 1937- , see PJ5054.B4238
Ben-Tsevi, Tseviyah Katsenelson, see PJ5054.K338
5054.B466 Ben-Yehudah, Y. (Table P-PZ40)
Ben-Yishai, Sh, see PJ5054.B4665
5054.B4665 Ben-Yishai, Shalom (Table P-PZ40)
Ben-Yosef Ginor, Tseviyah, see PJ5054.B4672
5054.B4672 Ben-Yoseph Ginor, Zvia, 1942- (Table P-PZ40)
Benyoëtz, Elazar, 1937- , see PJ5054.B47
5054.B47 Benyoez, Elazar (Table P-PZ40)
5054.B475 Bernstein, Ori (Table P-PZ40)
Bernstein, Ory, see PJ5054.B475
Beser, Yaacov, see PJ5054.B49
5054.B49 Beser, Ya'akov (Table P-PZ40)
5054.B67 Brandwein, Chaim, 1921- (Table P-PZ40)
Brandwein, Naftali Chaim, 1921- , see PJ5054.B67

Hebrew
Literature
Individual authors and works, A-Z
Modern, 1701-
By period
1946-1990 -- Continued

5054.B7 Broshi, Avivah, 1934 (Table P-PZ40)
5054.C3 Carmel, Shelomo (Table P-PZ40)
5054.C355 Carmi Laniado, Meira (Table P-PZ40)
5054.C42 Chalfi, Abraham, 1904- (Table P-PZ40)
Chen, Yael, 1943- , see PJ5054.A49755
Cohen, Joseph, 1943- , see PJ5054.C588
5054.C585 Cohen, Shlomit (Table P-PZ40)
5054.C588 Cohen, Yosef, 1943- (Table P-PZ40)
Cohen-Assif, Shlomit, see PJ5054.C585
Dafnah, see PJ5054.L55
5054.D2195 Dagan, Avigdor, 1912- (Table P-PZ40)
David, Sandou, see PJ5054.D3
5054.D3 David, Sandu (Table P-PZ40)
5054.D63 Dotan, Naomi (Table P-PZ40)
Dror-Banay, Perets, see PJ5054.B24
5054.E4 Eitan, Eitan, 1940- (Table P-PZ40)
El-Beg, Yeḥezḳel Ḥai, see PJ5054.A4964
Eliraz, Aleks, see PJ5054.E487
5054.E487 Eliraz, Alex (Table P-PZ40)
Eliraz, Israel, see PJ5054.E488
5054.E488 Eliraz, Yisrael, 1936- (Table P-PZ40)
5054.E5 El'or, Tsiporah (Table P-PZ40)
5054.E6 Epstein, Beinish (Table P-PZ40)
Epstein, Benzion, 1912- , see PJ5054.E6
Etan, Shulamit, see PJ5054.E92
Eytan, Eytan, 1940- , see PJ5054.E4
5054.E92 Eytan, Shula (Table P-PZ40)
5054.F17 Fadlun-Peled, Daṿid (Table P-PZ40)
Fischl, Viktor, 1912- , see PJ5054.D2195
5054.G27 Gafni, Sheraga (Table P-PZ40)
Gafni, Shraga, see PJ5054.G27
5054.G28 Gal, Benjamin (Table P-PZ40)
Gal, Binyamin, see PJ5054.G28
5054.G2813 Gal, Daliyah, 1940- (Table P-PZ40)
Gal Elgal, Daliyah, 1940- , see PJ5054.G2813
Galai, Binyamin, 1921- , see PJ5054.G3
5054.G3 Gallay, Benjamin, 1921- (Table P-PZ40)
Ganan, M , see PJ5054.G3525
5054.G3525 Ganan, Mosheh (Table P-PZ40)
Gar, Tsafrirah, 1926- , see PJ5054.G36
5054.G36 Gar, Zafrira, 1926- (Table P-PZ40)
5054.G393 Geldman,Mordekhai, 1946- (Table P-PZ40)
Geldmann, Mordechay, 1946- , see PJ5054.G393
5054.G394 Genosar, Vardah (Table P-PZ40)
Genosar-Arest, Vardah, 1943- , see PJ5054.G394
Geranot, Yosh, see PJ5054.G72

Hebrew
Literature
Individual authors and works, A-Z
Modern, 1701-
By period
1946-1990 -- Continued

	Gilboa, Shulamit, see PJ5054.G51434
5054.G51434	Gingold-Gilboa, Shulamit (Table P-PZ40)
5054.G54	Glaser, Lea, 1942- (Table P-PZ40)
	Granatstein, Yechiel, see PJ5054.G67
5054.G67	Granatsztajn, Jechiel (Table P-PZ40)
5054.G72	Granoth, Yehoshu a (Table P-PZ40)
5054.H155	Ḥabib, Yifraḥ, 1930- (Table P-PZ40)
	Hadar, Tania, see PJ5054.H184
5054.H184	Hadar, Ṭanyah (Table P-PZ40)
	Ḥaimi-Selilat, Tami, see PJ5054.S587
	Hakak, Herzl, 1948- , see PJ5054.H226
5054.H226	Hakkak, Herzl, 1948- (Table P-PZ40)
	Haleṿi, Bar-Mazal Yeḥi'el, 1935 or 6, see PJ5054.Y418
	Halevi, Mania, see PJ5054.H2269
5054.H2269	Halevi, Manyah (Table P-PZ40)
	Ḥalfi, Avraham, see PJ5054.C42
	Ḥanokh, L., 1912-1980, see PJ5054.L4
	Harekhavi, Hedva, see PJ5054.H29315
5054.H29315	Harkavy, Hevda (Table P-PZ40)
	Ḥaviv, Yifraḥ, see PJ5054.H155
	Heler-El'or, Tsiporah, see PJ5054.E5
	Herts, Daliyah, see PJ5054.H47
5054.H47	Hertz, Dalia, 1942- (Table P-PZ40)
5054.H49	Hilel, O. (Table P-PZ40)
5054.H54	Hirsh, Mikhal (Table P-PZ40)
	Hirsh-Noi, Mikhal, see PJ5054.H54
5054.H58	Hittin, Ronit Yochel (Table P-PZ40)
	Hokhler, Pasyah, see PJ5054.H632
5054.H632	Hokhler, Pesyah (Table P-PZ40)
5054.H65	Horwitz, Yair (Table P-PZ40)
	Hurvitz, Ya'ir, see PJ5054.H65
5054.J6	Josifor, David (Table P-PZ40)
5054.K3117	Kadouri, Ruth Shtreit (Table P-PZ40)
	Kaduri, Rut Shṭraiṭ, see PJ5054.K3117
	Kafri, Yudith, see PJ5054.K312
5054.K312	Kafry, Yudith (Table P-PZ40)
	Ḳal, Ester, see PJ5054.K315
5054.K315	Kal, Esther (Table P-PZ40)
5054.K32	Kalo, Shelomoh (Table P-PZ40)
	Kalo, Shlomo, see PJ5054.K32
	Karmel, Shelomoh, see PJ5054.C3
	Katan, Dina, see PJ5054.K33655
5054.K33655	Katan Ben-Cijon, Dina (Table P-PZ40)
5054.K338	Katsenelson, Tsivyah (Table P-PZ40)
	Kohen-Or, Yitsḥaḳ, see PJ5054.O66
5054.L362	Lerman, Israel, 1923- (Table P-PZ40)

Hebrew
Literature
Individual authors and works, A-Z
Modern, 1701-
By period
1946-1990 -- Continued

	Lerman, Yisra'el, see PJ5054.L362
	Lev, Igal, see PJ5054.L366
5054.L366	Lev, Yig'al (Table P-PZ40)
	Levin, David, see PJ5054.L42
5054.L38	Levin, Hanoch (Table P-PZ40)
5054.L4	Levin, Ḥanokh (Table P-PZ40)
5054.L42	Levine, David (Table P-PZ40)
5054.L428	Levit, Anat, 1958- (Table P-PZ40)
5054.L443	Lidsky, Zvi (Table P-PZ40)
5054.L45	Lifshitz, Aryeh (Table P-PZ40)
5054.L485	Lipavski-Halifi, Isaac (Table P-PZ40)
	Lipshitz, Ayre, 1901, see PJ5054.L45
5054.L55	Litvinovski, Dafna (Table P-PZ40)
5054.M273	Maller, Amos (Table P-PZ40)
5054.M322	Mark, Moshe (Table P-PZ40)
	Me-'Ami, No'omi, see PJ5054.D63
	Meller, Amos, see PJ5054.M273
5054.M426	Meseg, Sabina (Table P-PZ40)
	Miriam, Rivka, see PJ5054.R58
	Mish'ol, Agi, see PJ5054.R496
5054.M565	Mittwoch, Edna (Table P-PZ40)
	Miṭvokh-Meler, Èdnah, see PJ5054.M565
	Mossenson, Yigal, 1917-
5054.M6	Collected works. By date
5054.M6A2-M6A59	Translations (Collected) (Table P-PZ40)
5054.M6A6-M6A69	Selections. By editor (alphabetically)
5054.M6A7-M6Z4	Separate works, A-Z
5054.M6A7	Adam beli shem
5054.M6B4	Be-'arvot ha-Negev
5054.M6D4	Derek gever
5054.M6D5	ha-Derekh li-Yeriḥo
5054.M6I5	'Im yesh tsedek
5054.M6M5	Mi amar she-hu shaḥor
5054.M6T3	Tamar eshet 'Er
5054.M6Z5-M6Z99	Biography and criticism
5054.N24	Nadel, Baruch, 1926- (Table P-PZ40)
	Nadel, Barukh, see PJ5054.N24
5054.N42	Negev, Rachel (Table P-PZ40)
	Negev, Raḥel, see PJ5054.N42
	Nitsan, Shelomoh, see PJ5054.N53
5054.N53	Nitzan, Shlomo (Table P-PZ40)
5054.O47	Olifant, Arye (Table P-PZ40)
	Olifanṭ, Aryeh, see PJ5054.O47
	Omer, Hillel, 1926- , see PJ5054.H49
	Or, Meira, see PJ5054.C355
5054.O66	Or, Yitzhak (Table P-PZ40)
	Oren, Miriam, see PJ5054.O69

Hebrew
Literature
Individual authors and works, A-Z
Modern, 1701-
By period
1946-1990 -- Continued

5054.O69 Oren, Miryam (Table P-PZ40)
Oren, Y., 1918- , see PJ5054.O7
5054.O7 Oren, Yitsḥak (Table P-PZ40)
Orion, Ezra, 1934- , see PJ5054.B42378
Peled, Daṿid Fadlun, see PJ5054.F17
Prager, Moshe, 1909- , see PJ5054.M322
Preǐgerson, 1900-1969, see PJ5054.P69
5054.P69 Preǐgerzon, Grigoriĭ Izraĭlevich, 1900-1969 (Table P-PZ40)
5054.P75 Priver, Ida (Table P-PZ40)
Priver, Idah, see PJ5054.P75
Puts'u, 1930- , see PJ5054.W53
5054.R263 Rabi, David, 1938- (Table P-PZ40)
Ratsabi, Shalom, see PJ5054.R3384
5054.R3384 Ratzbi, Shalom (Table P-PZ40)
5054.R4 Reshef, Chaim (Table P-PZ40)
Reshef, Haim, see PJ5054.R4
Revi'a, Daṿid, see PJ5054.R263
5054.R49 Ribner, Tuvia (Table P-PZ40)
5054.R496 Rimon-Mish'ol, Agi, 1946- (Table P-PZ40)
5054.R58 Rochman, Rivka Miryam, 1952- (Table P-PZ40)
5054.R614 Ron, Mordecai (Table P-PZ40)
Ron, Mordekhai, see PJ5054.R614
5054.R618 Rosen, Shemuel (Table P-PZ40)
5054.R6295 Roth, Hana (Table P-PZ40)
Roth-Pasca, Hana, see PJ5054.R6295
5054.R673 Roussek, Suzie (Table P-PZ40)
Rubi, Avraham, 1931- , see PJ5054.R82
5054.R82 Ruby, Abraham Abba, 1931- (Table P-PZ40)
Ruebner, Tuvia, 1924- , see PJ5054.R49
Rusen, Shmulik, see PJ5054.R618
Russek-Osherov, Suzie, see PJ5054.R673
5054.S18 Sach, Nathan (Table P-PZ40)
5054.S212 Sagi, Yaacov (Table P-PZ40)
Sagy, Jacob, see PJ5054.S212
Samid, Shalom, see PJ5054.S249
5054.S2234 Saporta, Raphael, 1913- (Table P-PZ40)
Saporṭah, Refa'el, 1913- , see PJ5054.S2234
5054.S225 Schiff, Mejdad, 1918- (Table P-PZ40)
Segal, Bath Sheva Sherif, see PJ5054.S453
5054.S249 Semid, Shalom (Table P-PZ40)
5054.S3 Shamam, Nathan (Table P-PZ40)
5054.S4 Shamir, Moshe, 1921- (Table P-PZ40)
Shapira Elboim, Devorah, 1917- , see PJ5054.S4424

Hebrew
Literature
Individual authors and works, A-Z
Modern, 1701-
By period
1946-1990 -- Continued

5054.S4424 Shapiro Elbaum, Devora, 1917- (Table P-PZ40)
Shem-Ur, Anat Levit, 1958- , see PJ5054.L428
5054.S4493 Shenhar, 'Alizah (Table P-PZ40)
Shenhar-Alroy, Aliza, see PJ5054.S4493
5054.S453 Sheriff, Bat-Sheva (Table P-PZ40)
Sherira, Shoshanah, see PJ5054.S47
Shif, Medad, 1918- , see PJ5054.S225
5054.S4537 Shifman, Shifra (Table P-PZ40)
Shifrah, S , see PJ5054.S4537
5054.S462 Shnaid-Ofzaiher, Miryam (Table P-PZ40)
Shnaid-Ofzeher, Miryam, see PJ5054.S462
5054.S47 Shrira, Shoshanah, 1917- (Table P-PZ40)
Shṭendel, Yiśrael,1904- , see PJ5054.S745
(5054.S5) Silberschlag, Eisig, 1903- see PJ5053.S495
Silberstein, Zev W , see PJ5054.Z5
5054.S587 Slilat, Tammi (Table P-PZ40)
Smilansky, Izhar, 1916- , see PJ5053.Y55
5054.S745 Stendel, Israel, 1904- (Table P-PZ40)
5054.S85 Sulamy, Tuvya, 1939- (Table P-PZ40)
Ṭaharlev, Yoram, see PJ5054.T37
Tammuz, Benjamin, 1919- , see PJ5054.T317
5054.T317 Tamuz, Benjamin, 1919- (Table P-PZ40)
Taran, Lea, see PJ5054.G54
5054.T37 Ṭeharlev, Yoram (Table P-PZ40)
5054.T7 Trainin, Abner (Table P-PZ40)
Trainin, Avner, see PJ5054.T7
Tsivion, Abraham, 1925- , see PJ5054.T8
5054.T8 Tsivyon, Abraham (Table P-PZ4)
5054.T9 Twersky, Jochanan, 1904- (Table P-PZ40)
Uriel, Gila, see PJ5054.U73
5054.U73 Uriel, Gilah (Table P-PZ40)
Vinberger, Ḥayim, see PJ5054.W42
5054.V484 Viner, Shelomoh (Table P-PZ40)
Vinner, Shlomo, see PJ5054.V484
5054.W3 Wallenrod, Reuben (Table P-PZ40)
5054.W42 Weinberger, Haim, 1919- (Table P-PZ40)
5054.W53 Wisler, Israel Menahem, 1930- (Table P-PZ40)
Yanai, Yitsḥak, see PJ5054.Y25
5054.Y25 Yanay, Yitsḥak (Table P-PZ40)
5054.Y415 Yeḥezkel, Y. (Table P-PZ40)
Yehezkel, Yosef, see PJ5054.Y415
5054.Y418 Yeḥi'el, Bar-Mazal (Table P-PZ40)
5054.Y45 Yerushalmi, Aharon, 1914- (Table P-PZ40)
Yerushalmi, Aron, see PJ5054.Y45

Hebrew
Literature
Individual authors and works, A-Z
Modern, 1701-
By period
1946-1990 -- Continued
Yevi, see PJ5054.B466
Yishai, Ortsiyon, 1936- , see PJ5054.Y497
5054.Y497 Yishai, Zion, 1936- (Table P-PZ40)
Yitsḥaḳi, Ruti, see PJ5054.B42356
Yochel Hittin, Ronit, see PJ5054.H58
5054.Y65 Yonatan, Nathan (Table P-PZ40)
Yonathan, Nathan, see PJ5054.Y65
Yosefsberg, B. (Barukh), 1929- , see PJ5054.Y677
5054.Y677 Yosefsberg, Barukh (Table P-PZ40)
Yosif'or, Daṿid, see PJ5054.J6
Zach, Nathan, see PJ5054.S18
5054.Z48 Zilberman, Hana (Table P-PZ40)
5054.Z5 Zilbershtein, Ze'ev (Table P-PZ40)
5054.Z53 Ziman, Rachel (Table P-PZ40)
Ziman-Coral, Rachel, see PJ5054.Z53
5055.1-51 1991-
Subarrange each author by Table P-PZ40 unless otherwise indicated
The author number is determined by the second letter of the name, unless otherwise specified
5055.1.A-Z Anonymous works. By title, A-Z
5055.12 A
Subarrange each author by Table P-PZ40
The author number is determined by the second letter of the name
5055.13 B - Bar
Subarrange each author by Table P-PZ40
The author number is determined by the third letter of the name
5055.14 Bar (compound name)
Subarrange each author by Table P-PZ40
The author number is determined by the next portion of the name
5055.15 Bara - Ben
Subarrange each author by Table P-PZ40
The author number is determined by the second letter of the name
5055.16 Ben (compound name)
Subarrange each author by Table P-PZ40
The author number is determined by the next portion of the name
5055.17 Bena - Bz
Subarrange each author by Table P-PZ40
The author number is determined by the second letter of the name

Hebrew
Literature
Individual authors and works, A-Z
Modern, 1701-
By period
1991- -- Continued

5055.18 C
Subarrange each author by Table P-PZ40
The author number is determined by the second letter of the name

5055.19 D
Subarrange each author by Table P-PZ40
The author number is determined by the second letter of the name

5055.2 E
Subarrange each author by Table P-PZ40
The author number is determined by the second letter of the name

Elazar, Natan, see PJ5055.2.L35

5055.2.L35 Elazar-Natko, Natan (Table P-PZ40)

5055.21 F
Subarrange each author by Table P-PZ40
The author number is determined by the second letter of the name

5055.22 G
Subarrange each author by Table P-PZ40
The author number is determined by the second letter of the name

5055.23 H
Subarrange each author by Table P-PZ40
The author number is determined by the second letter of the name

5055.24 I
Subarrange each author by Table P-PZ40
The author number is determined by the second letter of the name

5055.25 J
Subarrange each author by Table P-PZ40
The author number is determined by the second letter of the name

5055.26 K - Kohem
Subarrange each author by Table P-PZ40
The author number is determined by the second letter of the name

Ḳarolevits, Shelomoh, see PJ5055.28.R65

5055.27 Kohen
Subarrange each author by Table P-PZ40
The author number is determined by the first letter of the forename

5055.28 Kohen (compound name) - Kz
Subarrange each author by Table P-PZ40
The author number is determined by the second letter of the name

Hebrew
Literature
Individual authors and works, A-Z
Modern, 1701-
By period
1991-
Kohen (compound name) - Kz -- Continued
5055.28.R465 Ḳrisfal, Yif'at (Table P-PZ40)
Ḳrispel, Yif'at, see PJ5055.28.R465
5055.28.R65 Ḳrolevits, Shelomoh (Table P-PZ40)
5055.29 L - Levh
Subarrange each author by Table P-PZ40
The author number is determined by the second letter of the name
5055.3 Levi
Subarrange each author by Table P-PZ40
The author number is determined by the first letter of the forename
5055.31 Levi- (compound name)
Subarrange each author by Table P-PZ40
The author number is determined by the next portion of the name
5055.32 Levia - Leviz
Subarrange each author by Table P-PZ40
The author number is determined by the fifth letter of the name
5055.33 Levj - Lz
Subarrange each author by Table P-PZ40
The author number is determined by the second letter of the name
5055.34 M
Subarrange each author by Table P-PZ40
The author number is determined by the second letter of the name
Moradi, Refa'el, see PJ5055.34.U73
5055.34.U73 Muradi, Refa'el (Table P-PZ40)
5055.35 N
Subarrange each author by Table P-PZ40
The author number is determined by the second letter of the name
5055.36 O
Subarrange each author by Table P-PZ40
The author number is determined by the second letter of the name
5055.37 P
Subarrange each author by Table P-PZ40
The author number is determined by the second letter of the name
5055.38 Q
Subarrange each author by Table P-PZ40
The author number is determined by the second letter of the name

Hebrew
Literature
Individual authors and works, A-Z
Modern, 1701-
By period
1991- -- Continued

5055.39 R
Subarrange each author by Table P-PZ40
The author number is determined by the second letter of the name

5055.4 S - Sg
Subarrange each author by Table P-PZ40
The author number is determined by the second letter of the name

5055.41 Sh
Subarrange each author by Table P-PZ40
The author number is determined by the third letter of the name

5055.41.A73 Shar'abi-Zlotnik, Le'ah, 1959- (Table P-PZ40)

5055.42 Si - Sz
Subarrange each author by Table P-PZ40
The author number is determined by the second letter of the name

5055.43 T - Tr
Subarrange each author by Table P-PZ40
The author number is determined by the second letter of the name

5055.44 Ts
Subarrange each author by Table P-PZ40
The author number is determined by the third letter of the name

5055.45 Tt - Tz
Subarrange each author by Table P-PZ40
The author number is determined by the second letter of the name

5055.46 U
Subarrange each author by Table P-PZ40
The author number is determined by the second letter of the name

5055.47 V
Subarrange each author by Table P-PZ40
The author number is determined by the second letter of the name

5055.48 W
Subarrange each author by Table P-PZ40
The author number is determined by the second letter of the name

5055.49 X
Subarrange each author by Table P-PZ40
The author number is determined by the second letter of the name

Hebrew
Literature
Individual authors and works, A-Z
Modern, 1701-
By period
1991- -- Continued
5055.5 Y
Subarrange each author by Table P-PZ40
The author number is determined by the second letter of the name
5055.51 Z
Subarrange each author by Table P-PZ40
The author number is determined by the second letter of the name
Zlotnik, Lea, 1959- , see PJ5055.41.A73
5059-5060 Translations from Hebrew literature into foreign languages (Table P-PZ30)
Other languages used by Jews
5061-5069 General (Table P-PZ8)
Special
5071-5079 Judeo-Arabic (Table P-PZ8a)
5081-5089 Judeo-Persian (Table P-PZ8)
5089.2 Judeo-Tajik (Table P-PZ16)
5089.297 Judeo-Tat (Table P-PZ16)
(5089.3) Judeo-French
see PC3151+
(5089.5) Judeo-Italian
see PC1784
(5091) Ladino (Judeo-Spanish)
see PC4813
(5095) Judeo-Portuguese
see PC5423
Yiddish (Judeo-German)
5111 Periodicals. Societies. Collections
Biography
5111.4 Collective
5111.5.A-Z Individual, A-Z
5112 Study and teaching
5113 General works. History, etc.
Grammar
5115 Treatises
Special
5116 General works
5116.5 Readers. Chrestomathies
5116.7 Style. Composition. Rhetoric
5117 Dictionaries (by author)
5118 Other works
5119.A-Z Special regions or countries, A-Z
Literature
History
5120.A1-A4 Periodicals. Societies. Collections
5120.A5 Study and teaching
5120.A6-Z General works. Compends

Hebrew
Other languages used by Jews
Special
Yiddish (Judeo-German)
Literature
History -- Continued
5120.5 Addresses,essays, lectures
5120.7.A-Z Special topics, A-Z
5120.7.H64 Holocaust, Jewish (1939-1945)
5120.7.L33 Labor
5121 Biography (Collective)
5122 Poetry
5123 Drama
5124 Other (including fiction)
Collections
5125 General
5126 Poetry
5127 Drama
5128 Other (including fiction)
5129.A1A-Z Anonymous works. By title, A-Z
5129.A15-Z Individual authors, A-Z
Including translations
e.g.
Subarrange each author by Table P-PZ40 unless otherwise specified
Aaronson, M. (Michael), b. 1879, see PJ5129.A16
5129.A16 Aaronson, Michael, 1879- (Table P-PZ40)
5129.A2 Abramowitz, Shalom Jacob, 1836-1917 (Table P-PZ40)
5129.A5 Adler, Jacob, b. 1877 (Table P-PZ40)
Aichenrand, L , see PJ5129.A56
5129.A56 Ajchenrand, Lajzer (Table P-PZ40)
5129.A62 Aksel'rod, Zelig (Table P-PZ40)
Almi, A., 1892-1963, see PJ5129.S432
5129.A7 Alpersohn, Marcos (Table P-PZ40)
Altman, Moishe, 1890- , see PJ5129.A72
5129.A72 Altman, Moses, 1890- (Table P-PZ40)
An-Ski, S., 1863-1920, see PJ5129.R3
5129.A75 Anohi, Zalman Isaac, 1876-1947 (Table P-PZ40)
Anokhi, Zalman Yiẓḥak, 1876-1947, see PJ5129.A75
Arnshṭeyn, Mark, d. 1942 or 3, see PJ5129.A777
5129.A777 Arnstein, Marc, 1879- (Table P-PZ40)
5129.A94 Austri-Dunn, Isaias (Table P-PZ40)
Austridan, Yeshayahu, 1912- , see PJ5129.A94
Axelrod, Selik, 1904-1941, see PJ5129.A62
Ayznman, Tsevi, 1920- , see PJ5129.E5325
5129.B34 Baumwoll, Rokhl, 1913- (Table P-PZ40)
For Baumwoll's Russian works, see PG3476.B336
5129.B377 Beḳerman, Simeon (Table P-PZ40)

Hebrew
Other languages used by Jews
Special
Yiddish (Judeo-German)
Literature
Individual authors, A-Z -- Continued

5129.B42 Ben-Moshe, Michael, 1911- (Table P-PZ40)
Ben Mosheh, M., 1911- , see PJ5129.B42
Ben-Yaơ akov, 1889-1929, see PJ5129.Z545
Berdichevsky, Micah Joseph, see PJ5129.B563
5129.B4745 Berliner, Isaac (Table P-PZ40)
Berliner, Yiẓḥak, 1899-1957, see PJ5129.B4745
5129.B563 Bin Gorion, Micha Joseph, 1865-1921 (Table P-PZ40)
5129.B57 Birnbaum, Martin, 1904- (Table P-PZ40)
Birnboym, Martin, see PJ5129.B57
5129.B5715 Birshtein, Yosl, 1920- (Table P-PZ40)
Birstein, Yossel, see PJ5129.B5715
5129.B575 Blaustein, Auser, 1840-1898 (Table P-PZ40)
Blei, Relly, see PJ5129.B5762
5129.B5762 Blei, Rely (Table P-PZ40)
Botoshansky, Jacob, 1895- , see PJ5129.B677
5129.B677 Botoshansky, Jacobo, 1895- (Table P-PZ40)
Boymvol, Rachel, 1913- , see PJ5129.B34
5129.B7 Brahinsky, Mani Leib, 1883-1953 (Table P-PZ40)
5129.B7353 Bregstone, Philip P. (Philip Pollack) (Table P-PZ40)
5129.B792 Burstein-Finer, Jacques (Table P-PZ40)
5129.C52 Chesler, Samuel, 1904- (Table P-PZ40)
5129.D22 Daixel, Samuel (Table P-PZ40)
Dayḳsel, Sh. (Shemu'el), see PJ5129.D22
Daymondshteyn, B. (Boris), 1892- , see PJ5129.D47
Der Nister, 1884-1950, see PJ5129.K27
Der Tunkler, 1881-1949, see PJ5129.T8
5129.D47 Dimondstein, Boris, 1892?- (Table P-PZ40)
5129.D5 Dinesohn, Jacob, 1856-1919 (Table P-PZ40)
Dubelman, A.J., 1908- , see PJ5129.D78
5129.D78 Dubelman, Abraham Josef (Table P-PZ40)
5129.E35 Edelstadt, David, 1866-1892 (Table P-PZ40)
5129.E5325 Eisenman, Zvi (Table P-PZ40)
5129.E5425 Elinas, Mejaris, 1910- (Table P-PZ40)
5129.E55 Elkin, Mendl, 1874- (Table P-PZ40)
5129.F32 Fedler, Chaye (Table P-PZ40)
Fedler, Ḥayah, d. 1953, see PJ5129.F32
Finer, Y. (Yitsḥaḳ), 1908- , see PJ5129.B792
5129.F75 Frishman, David, 1865?-1922 (Table P-PZ40)
Fuchs, A.M , see PJ5129.F8
5129.F8 Fuchs, Abraham Moses, 1890- (Table P-PZ40)
5129.G523 Glantz, Jacob (Table P-PZ40)

Hebrew
Other languages used by Jews
Special
Yiddish (Judeo-German)
Literature
Individual authors, A-Z -- Continued

	Glantz, Yaacov, see PJ5129.G523
5129.G533	Glasserman, Samuel, 1898- (Table P-PZ40)
	Glazerman, Shemu'el, 1898-1952, see PJ5129.G533
5129.G567	Good, Edward, b. 1885 (Table P-PZ40) For Good's English works, see PR6013.O47
5129.G6	Gordin, Jacob, 1853-1909 (Table P-PZ40)
	Granaṭshṭeyn, Perets, 1907- , see PJ5129.G69
5129.G69	Granatstein, Perez, 1907- (Table P-PZ40)
	Granitstein, M. (Moses), 1897-1956, see PJ5129.G7
5129.G7	Granitstein, Moses, 1897-1956 (Table P-PZ40)
	Guiser, M.D. (Moisés David), 1893-1952, see PJ5129.G82
5129.G82	Guiser, Moisés David, 1893-1952 (Table P-PZ40)
5129.H4416	Herz, Joseph, 1776-1828 (Table P-PZ40)
5129.H45	Hirsch, H., 1880-1931 (Table P-PZ40)
	Hirsh, H., 1880-1931, see PJ5129.H45
	Hornczyk, Sz., 1889-1939, see PJ5129.H65
5129.H65	Horontchik, Simon, 1889-1939 (Table P-PZ40)
	Hosid, M. (Mordekhai), 1909- , see PJ5129.H84
5129.H8	Hurwitz, Samuel, 1862-1943 (Table P-PZ40)
5129.H84	Husid, M. (Table P-PZ40)
5129.I15	Ianasovich, Isaac, 1909- (Table P-PZ40)
5129.K27	Kahanovitch, Pinchas, 1884-1950 (Table P-PZ40)
5129.K2788	Kaplan, Israel (Table P-PZ40)
	Ḳaplan, Yiśra'el, see PJ5129.K2788
5129.K315	Karpinovitsh, A (Table P-PZ40)
	Karpinowitz, Abraham, see PJ5129.K315
5129.K46	Khaikina, Dora, 1913- (Table P-PZ40)
	Khayḳine, Dore, 1913- , see PJ5129.K46
5129.K59	Korenchandler, Chaskiel, 1899- (Table P-PZ40)
	Ḳornhendler, Yeḥesḳel, 1899- , see PJ5129.K59
	Kovner, B., b. 1877, see PJ5129.A5
5129.K665	Kreitman, Esther (Table P-PZ40)
	Ḳreyṭman, Ester, 1891-1954, see PJ5129.K665
	Kupershmid, Leibl, see PJ5129.K773
5129.K773	Kuperszmidt, Lejb (Table P-PZ40)
5129.K82	Kviatkovski-Pinchasik, Rivka (Table P-PZ40)
	Kwiatkowski-Pinchasik, Rivka, see PJ5129.K82
	Leib, Mani, 1883-1953, see PJ5129.B7
	Levi, Yosef Hilel, see PJ5129.L466

Hebrew
Other languages used by Jews
Special
Yiddish (Judeo-German)
Literature
Individual authors, A-Z -- Continued

5129.L4448 Levin, Ali, 1893- (Table P-PZ40)
Levinski, Yitsḥaḳ, ha-Levi, see PJ5129.L457
5129.L457 Levinsky, I.H. (Table P-PZ40)
5129.L466 Levy, Joseph Hillel, 1891- (Table P-PZ40)
Liptsin, Sem, 1893- , see PJ5129.L55
5129.L55 Liptzin, Samuel, 1893- (Table P-PZ40)
Litvin, A., 1862-1943, see PJ5129.H8
5129.L595 Lokiec, M. (Table P-PZ40)
Lokiec, Moshe, 1911- , see PJ5129.L595
5129.M19 Ma-Yafith, Israel, 1897-1930 (Table P-PZ40)
Mah-Yafit, Yiśra'el, 1897-1930, see PJ5129.M19
Maltinski, Chaim, see PJ5129.M238
5129.M238 Mal'tinskiĭ, Khaim (Table P-PZ40)
Maltz, Saul, 1908- , see PJ5129.M24
5129.M24 Maltz, Sol, 1908- (Table P-PZ40)
5129.M313 Margolin, Arn, 1892-1959 (Table P-PZ40)
Melamud, Ḥayim, 1907- , see PJ5129.M423
5129.M423 Melamud, Khaim Gershkovich (Table P-PZ40)
Mendele Mokher Sefarim, 1835-1917, see PJ5129.A2
Miler, L., 1889- , see PJ5129.M595
5129.M595 Miller, Louis, 1889- (Table P-PZ40)
Minkus, M., b. 1891, see PJ5129.M663
5129.M663 Minkus, Moses, 1891- (Table P-PZ40)
5129.N436 Neugroeschel, Max, 1903-1965 (Table P-PZ40)
Neugröschel, Mendl, see PJ5129.N436
Nister, 1884-1950, see PJ5129.K27
Olevski, Buzi, 1908- , see PJ5129.O52
5129.O52 Olievsky, Buzi (Table P-PZ40)
Olitsky, L , see PJ5129.O524
5129.O524 Olitzky, Leib, 1894- (Table P-PZ40)
5129.O525 Olitzky, Mates (Table P-PZ40)
Orzhitzer, A.M. (Abraham Mordecai), 1913- , see PJ5129.O73
5129.O73 Orzhitzer, Abraham Mordecai, 1913- (Table P-PZ40)
Oyved, Moysheh, b. 1885, see PJ5129.G567
5129.P32 Papiernikow, Joseph 1899- (Table P-PZ40)
Papyernikov, Yosef, see PJ5129.P32
5129.P4 Peretz, Isaac Loeb, 1851-1915 (Table P-PZ40)
Perle, Iehoshua, 1888-1943, see PJ5129.P413
5129.P413 Perle, Joshua, 1888- (Table P-PZ40)
5129.P47 Pinchevskiĭ, Moiseĭ, 1894-1955 (Table P-PZ40)
Pinski, David, see PJ5129.P5
5129.P5 Pinsky, David, 1872-1959 (Table P-PZ40)

Hebrew
Other languages used by Jews
Special
Yiddish (Judeo-German)
Literature
Individual authors, A-Z -- Continued
Pinṭshevsḳi, M. (Mosheh), 1894-1955, see PJ5129.P47
Polakiewicz, S , see PJ5129.P576
5129.P576 Polakiewicz, Symcha (Table P-PZ40)
5129.P58 Polianker, Hershl (Table P-PZ40)
Polyanker, Hirsh, 1911- , see PJ5129.P58
5129.R2 Rabinowitz, Shalom, 1859-1916 (Table P-PZ40)
Radzher, Moris, see PJ5129.R572
5129.R3 Rappoport, Solomon, 1863-1920 (Table P-PZ40)
Razumni, Mark, see PJ5129.R36
5129.R36 Razumny, Mark, 1899- (Table P-PZ40)
Reisen, Abraham, 1876-1953, see PJ5129.R37
5129.R37 Reisin, Abraham, 1876-1953 (Table P-PZ40)
5129.R394 Reubeni, Aaron, 1886- (Table P-PZ40)
Reuveni, A., 1886-1971, see PJ5129.R394
5129.R42 Richter, Moses, 1874-1939 (Table P-PZ40)
Roden, David, 1893- , see PJ5129.L4448
5129.R572 Roger, Maurice (Table P-PZ40)
5129.R5736 Rollansky, Samuel, 1902- (Table P-PZ40)
Rosenfarb, Chawa, 1923- , see PJ5129.R597
5129.R597 Rosenfarb, Eva (Table P-PZ40)
5129.R6 Rosenfeld, Morris, 1862-1923 (Table P-PZ40)
Rozshansḳi, Shemu'el, 1902- , see PJ5129.R5736
5129.R79 Rubin, Moisés, 1856- (Table P-PZ40)
Rus, Rivḳah, see PJ5129.R89
5129.R89 Russ, Rivka (Table P-PZ40)
5129.S2917 Schneersohu, Fischel, 1887-1958 (Table P-PZ40)
5129.S293 Schudrich, Jacob (Table P-PZ40)
5129.S3218 Schwartz, Selwyn S. (Table P-PZ40)
Schwartz, Shloime, see PJ5129.S3218
Segal, Meyer, see PJ5129.S3734
5129.S3734 Segal, Myer (Table P-PZ40)
5129.S376 Segalowicz, Zusman, 1884-1949 (Table P-PZ40)
Segalowitch, Zusman, 1884-1949, see PJ5129.S376
Sh. B. (Shim'on Beḳerman), see PJ5129.B377
5129.S414 Shaikewitz, Nahum Meir, 1849-1905 (Table P-PZ40)
Shargel, I.Z , see PJ5129.S43135
5129.S43135 Shargel, Iaacov Zvi (Table P-PZ40)
Shayḳeviṭsh. N.M. (Nahum Meir), 1849-1905, see PJ5129.S414
Shechtman, Eli, 1908- , see PJ5129.S4316
5129.S4316 Shekhtman, Elye (Table P-PZ40)
Shene'urson, Fishl, d. 1958, see PJ5129.S2917

Hebrew
Other languages used by Jews
Special
Yiddish (Judeo-German)
Literature
Individual authors, A-Z -- Continued

5129.S432 Sheps, Elias, 1892- (Table P-PZ40)
Sherman, J.M., 1885-1958, see PJ5129.S4335
5129.S4335 Sherman, Jacob Max, 1885- (Table P-PZ40)
Shkli'ar, Mosheh, 1920- , see PJ5129.S883
Shleṿin, B. (Binyamin), 1913-1981, see PJ5129.S437
5129.S437 Shlewin, Benjamin (Table P-PZ40)
5129.S4378 Shmuelzohn, M., 1871- (Table P-PZ40)
Sholem Aleichem, see PJ5129.R2
Shomer, 1849-1905, see PJ5129.S414
5129.S443 Shraĭbman, Iekhiel (Table P-PZ40)
Shraybman, Yekhiel, 1913- , see PJ5129.S443
Shternberg, Yakov, 1890-1973, see PJ5129.S768
Shṭuker-Payuḳ, Mashe, see PJ5129.S795
5129.S46 Siegalovsky, Noah, 1901- (Table P-PZ40)
Sigaloṿsḳi, N. (Noah), see PJ5129.S46
5129.S485 Sinay, M. Hacohen (Table P-PZ40)
Sinay, Miguel H , see PJ5129.S485
5129.S653 Sochachewsky, Jehiel Meir, 1889- (Table P-PZ40)
Sokhaṭsheṿsḳi, Ben-A. (Ben-Avraham), 1889-1958, see PJ5129.S653
Spiegel, Isaiah, 1906- , see PJ5129.S6812
5129.S6812 Spiegel, Jeshajahu, 1906- (Table P-PZ40)
Stern, Manachem, 1912- , see PJ5129.S7677
5129.S7677 Stern, Menahem, 1912- (Table P-PZ40)
5129.S768 Sternberg, Iacob, 1890- (Table P-PZ40)
5129.S795 Stuker de Paiuk, Martha (Table P-PZ40)
5129.S883 Szklar, Mosze (Table P-PZ40)
Ṭambur, Ṿolf, see PJ5129.T347
5129.T347 Tamburu, Vladimir (Table P-PZ40)
5129.T38 Teitelbaum, Dora (Table P-PZ40)
Teitelboim, Dora, see PJ5129.T38
5129.T385 Telesin, Zinoviĭ L'avovich (Table P-PZ40)
Telessin, Ziame, 1912- , see PJ5129.T385
5129.T43 Tenenbaum, Shea, 1910- (Table P-PZ40)
Ṭenenboym, Shie, 1908- , see PJ5129.T43
Treister, L , see PJ5129.T7
5129.T7 Treister, Leizer, 1903- (Table P-PZ40)
Tsanin, M. (Mordekhai), 1906- , see PJ5129.T773
5129.T773 Tsanin, Mordecai, 1906- (Table P-PZ40)
Tsesler, Shemu'el, 1904- , see PJ5129.C52
5129.T8 Tunkel, Joseph, 1881-1949 (Table P-PZ40)
Ṿasertsug, Zalman, 1904- , see PJ5129.W38
5129.V4 Veviorka, Abram, 1887-1935 (Table P-PZ40)
Vieṿiorḳa, Avraham, 1887-1935, see PJ5129.V4

Hebrew
Other languages used by Jews
Special
Yiddish (Judeo-German)
Literature
Individual authors, A-Z -- Continued
Vinokur, Grigory, 1903- , see PJ5129.W413
V̦olk̦enshṭeyn, D. (David), 1891- , see PJ5129.W64
5129.W315 Wajc, Abraham (Table P-PZ40)
5129.W38 Wasertzug, Salomón, 1904- (Table P-PZ40)
5129.W413 Weinrauch, Herschel Henry (Table P-PZ40)
5129.W48 Weprinsky, Rashel (Table P-PZ40)
Weprinsky, Roshelle, see PJ5129.W48
Wietz, A , see PJ5129.W315
5129.W64 Wolkenstein, David, 1891- (Table P-PZ40)
Yanasowicz, Itzhak, 1909- , see PJ5129.I15
Yelin, Meir, 1910- , see PJ5129.E5425
Yofe, Yudl, ca. 1882-1941, see PJ5129.Y6
5129.Y6 Yoffe, Yudl,1882- (Table P-PZ40)
Yungman, M., 1922- , see PJ5129.Y78
5129.Y78 Yungman, Moses (Table P-PZ40)
Zaretski, Hinde, 1899- , see PJ5129.Z38
5129.Z38 Zaretsky, Hinde, 1899- (Table P-PZ40)
5129.Z453 Zelik̦ovitsh, Getsl, 1863-1926 (Table P-PZ40)
5129.Z542 Zigelboym, Feivel (Table P-PZ40)
Ziper, Ya'akov, see PJ5129.Z55
5129.Z545 Zingman, Kalman, 1889-1929 (Table P-PZ40)
5129.Z55 Zipper, Jacob (Table P-PZ40)
Zygielbaum, Faivel, 1908- , see PJ5129.Z542
Zychlinska, Rajzel, 1910- , see PJ5129.Z96
5129.Z96 Zychlinsky, R., 1910- (Table P-PZ40)
Local
Europe
Soviet Union
History
5140.A1 Periodicals. Societies. Collections
5140.A2-Z General works. Compends
5140.1 General special
5140.15 Biography (Collective)
5140.2 Poetry
5140.3 Drama
5140.4 Other
Collections
5140.5 General
5140.6 Poetry
5140.7 Drama
5140.8 Other
5140.9.A-Z Local, A-Z
e.g.
5140.9.W45 White Russia
Poland

Hebrew
Other languages used by Jews
Special
Yiddish (Judeo-German)
Literature
Local
Europe
Poland -- Continued
History
5141.A1 Periodicals. Societies. Collections
5141.A2-Z General works. Compends
5141.1 General special
5141.15 Biography (Collective)
5141.2 Poetry
5141.3 Drama
5141.4 Other
Collections
5141.5 General
5141.6 Poetry
5141.7 Drama
5141.8 Other
5141.9.A-Z Local, A-Z
Lithuania
History
5142.A1 Periodicals. Societies. Collections
5142.A2-Z General works. Compends
5142.1 General special
5142.15 Biography (Collective)
5142.2 Poetry
5142.3 Drama
5142.4 Other
Collections
5142.5 General
5142.6 Poetry
5142.7 Drama
5142.8 Other
5142.9.A-Z Local, A-Z
Germany
History
5143.A1 Periodicals. Societies. Collections
5143.A2-Z General works. Compends
5143.1 General special
5143.15 Biography (Collective)
5143.2 Poetry
5143.3 Drama
5143.4 Other
Collections
5143.5 General
5143.6 Poetry
5143.7 Drama
5143.8 Other
5143.9.A-Z Local, A-Z
France

Hebrew
Other languages used by Jews
Special
Yiddish (Judeo-German)
Literature
Local
Europe
France -- Continued
History

5144.A1	Periodicals. Societies. Collections
5144.A2-Z	General works. Compends
5144.1	General special
5144.15	Biography (Collective)
5144.2	Poetry
5144.3	Drama
5144.4	Other
	Collections
5144.5	General
5144.6	Poetry
5144.7	Drama
5144.8	Other
5144.9.A-Z	Local, A-Z
	Great Britain
	History
5145.A1	Periodicals. Societies. Collections
5145.A2-Z	General works. Compends
5145.1	General special
5145.15	Biography (Collective)
5145.2	Poetry
5145.3	Drama
5145.4	Other
	Collections
5145.5	General
5145.6	Poetry
5145.7	Drama
5145.8	Other
5145.9.A-Z	Local, A-Z

Hebrew
Other languages used by Jews
Special
Yiddish (Judeo-German)
Literature
Local
Europe -- Continued

5149.A-Z Other European regions or countries, A-Z

Under each country, if applicable:

.A1-.4	*History*
.A1	*Periodicals. Societies. Collections*
.A2-.Z	*General works. Compends*
.1	*General special*
.15	*Biography (Collected)*
.2	*Poetry*
.3	*Drama*
.4	*Other*
.5-.8	*Collections*
.5	*General*
.6	*Poetry*
.7	*Drama*
.8	*Other*
.9.A-Z	*Local, A-Z*

America

5150 General works

United States

History

5151.A1 Periodicals. Societies. Collections
5151.A2-Z General works. Compends
5151.1 General special
5151.15 Biography (Collective)
5151.2 Poetry
5151.3 Drama
5151.4 Other

Collections

5151.5 General
5151.6 Poetry
5151.7 Drama
5151.8 Other
5151.9.A-Z Local, A-Z

Canada

History

5152.A1 Periodicals. Societies. Collections
5152.A2-Z General works. Compends
5152.1 General special
5152.15 Biography (Collective)
5152.2 Poetry
5152.3 Drama
5152.4 Other

Collections

5152.5 General
5152.6 Poetry

Hebrew
Other languages used by Jews
Special
Yiddish (Judeo-German)
Literature
Local
America
Canada
Collections -- Continued
5152.7 Drama
5152.8 Other
5152.9.A-Z Local, A-Z
Mexico
History
5153.A1 Periodicals. Societies. Collections
5153.A2-Z General works. Compends
5153.1 General special
5153.15 Biography (Collective)
5153.2 Poetry
5153.3 Drama
5153.4 Other
Collections
5153.5 General
5153.6 Poetry
5153.7 Drama
5153.8 Other
5153.9.A-Z Local, A-Z
5154.A-Z Other North American regions or countries, A-Z
Apply table at PJ5149.A-Z
South America and Spanish America
5155 General works
Argentina
History
5156.A1 Periodicals. Societies. Collections
5156.A2-Z General works. Compends
5156.1 General special
5156.15 Biography (Collective)
5156.2 Poetry
5156.3 Drama
5156.4 Other
Collections
5156.5 General
5156.6 Poetry
5156.7 Drama
5156.8 Other
5156.9.A-Z Local, A-Z
5159.A-Z Other South American regions or countries, A-Z
Apply table at PJ5149.A-Z
Asia
5160 General works

Hebrew
Other languages used by Jews
Special
Yiddish (Judeo-German)
Literature
Local
Asia -- Continued
Palestine. Israel
History
5161.A1 Periodicals. Societies. Collections
5161.A2-Z General works. Compends
5161.1 General special
5161.15 Biography (Collective)
5161.2 Poetry
5161.3 Drama
5161.4 Other
Collections
5161.5 General
5161.6 Poetry
5161.7 Drama
5161.8 Other
5161.9.A-Z Local, A-Z
5162.A-Z Other regions or countries, A-Z
Apply table at PJ5149.A-Z
Africa
5163 General works
South Africa
History
5164.A1 Periodicals. Societies. Collections
5164.A2-Z General works. Compends
5164.1 General special
5164.15 Biography (Collective)
5164.2 Poetry
5164.3 Drama
5164.4 Other
Collections
5164.5 General
5164.6 Poetry
5164.7 Drama
5164.8 Other
5164.9.A-Z Local, A-Z
5165.A-Z Other regions or countries, A-Z
Apply table at PJ5149.A-Z
Oceania
5166 General works
Australia
History
5167.A1 Periodicals. Societies. Collections
5167.A2-Z General works. Compends
5167.1 General special
5167.15 Biography (Collective)
5167.2 Poetry
5167.3 Drama

Hebrew
Other languages used by Jews
Special
Yiddish (Judeo-German)
Literature
Local
Oceania
Australia
History -- Continued
5167.4 Other
Collections
5167.5 General
5167.6 Poetry
5167.7 Drama
5167.8 Other
5167.9.A-Z Local, A-Z
5168.A-Z Other regions or countries, A-Z
Apply table at PJ5149.A-Z
5191-5192 Translations. From Yiddish into other languages (Table P-PZ30)
For translations of works of individual authors, see PJ5129.A1+
Aramaic
Aramaic (General: Old West and East Aramaic)
5201-5207 General works (Table P-PZ8)
Texts: Inscriptions. Papyri, etc.
5208.A2 Collections. Selections. By date
5208.A5 Inscriptions
Texts by place where found
Elephantine (Assuan) papyri, ostraka, etc.
5208.E4 Editions. By date
5208.E5A-Z Translations. By language, A-Z, and date
5208.E6 Criticism
5209 Individual texts
Including Story of Ahikar (Fragments)
Including Behistum inscription (Aramaic version)
Cf. PJ3087, Semitic philology
West Aramaic
General and Old Aramaic, see PJ5201+
5211-5219 Biblical Aramaic (Chaldaic) (Table P-PZ8a)
Including language of the Aramaic portions of the Old Testament (Ezra and Daniel)
Cf. BS1351+, Ezra (1st Esdras of the Vulgate)
Cf. BS1551+, Daniel
Cf. PJ4837, Hebrew-Oriental
Palmyrene inscriptions
Cf. PJ3081+, Semitic philology
5229.A1 Editions. By date
5229.A5-Z Criticism

Aramaic
West Aramaic -- Continued
Nabataean inscriptions
Including the "Sinaitic" inscriptions, i.e. inscriptions in the Nabataean dialect found in the Sinaitic Peninsula
Cf. PJ3081+, Semitic philology
5239.A1 Editions. By date
5239.A5-Z Criticism
5241-5249 Christian Palestinian Aramaic (Palestinian Syriac) (Table P-PZ8)
Including language of the Melchites
5251-5259 Jewish Palestinian Aramaic (Table P-PZ8)
Includes language of the Targums of Onkelos (Pentateuch) and Jonathan (Prophets), of the Palestinian Talmud (Jerusalem Talmud) and of the Midrashim
Cf. BM500+, Babylonian Talmud
Cf. BM510+, Midrash
5271-5279 Samaritan Aramaic (Table P-PZ8)
Including language of the Samaritan Targum
Cf. BM930+, Samaritan Targum
Cf. PJ4860, Samaritan Pentateuch
5281-5289 Neo-Aramaic dialects (Table P-PZ8)
Including modern dialects in Malula and a few other villages of the Antilibanus (near extinction)
Cf. PJ5801+, Neo-Syriac dialects
East Aramaic
General, see PJ5201+
5301-5309 Language of the Babylonian Talmud (Table P-PZ8)
e.g.
5302.S3 Schlesinger, Satzlehre der aramäischen sprache des babylonischen Talmuds, 1928
5321-5329 Mandaean (Table P-PZ8a)
Syriac
Philology (Table P-PZ4)
5401 Periodicals. Societies. Serials
Collections
Texts. Sources, etc , see PJ5601+
Minor. Chrestomathies, see PJ5425, PJ5613
5403 Monographs. Studies
5407 History of philology
(5408) Bibliography
see Z6605.S9, Z7094
(5409) Biography
see PJ63-PJ64, PJ3009
5411 Study and teaching
Language (Table P-PZ4)
5414 Treatises (General and General special)
5417 Script (Estrangelo; Serto; Nestorian)
Grammar
5419 Treatises in Syriac

Syriac
Language
Grammar -- Continued
Treatises in other languages. Compends (Advanced)
5420 Early to 1800
5421 1801-
5423 Elementary. Introductory
5425 Readers. Chrestomathies
Cf. PJ5613, Syriac literature
Phonology
Cf. PJ5417, Script
5428 General works
5431 Pronunciation
5432 Accent
Morphology. Inflection. Accidence
5439 General works
5440 Word formation. Derivation. Suffixes, etc.
Noun. Verb, etc , see PJ5449+
5447 Tables. Paradigms
Parts of speech (Morphology and syntax)
5449 Miscellaneous
5451 Noun
5453 Adjective
5459 Pronoun
5461 Verb
5467 Particle. Adverb
5471 Syntax
5473 Grammatical usage of particular authors
5475 Style. Rhetoric
5481 Prosody. Metrics. Rhythmics
For Syriac authors, see PJ5671.A+
5483 Etymology
Lexicography
Dictionaries
5490 Polyglot
Bilingual
5491 Syriac-English; English-Syriac
5493.A-Z Other, A-Z
Literature
Cf. PJ601+, Christian Oriental
History
Treatises
5601 General
5603 General special
5604 Poetry
5605 Prose
5606.A-Z Other special forms, A-Z
5607.A-Z Special topics, A-Z
Collections
5611 General

Syriac
Literature
Collections -- Continued
5613 Selections. Chrestomathies
Cf. A. Baumstark, Geschichte der syrischen literatur, 1922, p. 5, Note 2
Prefer PJ5425
5615 Inscriptions
5617 Poetry
5619 Prose
By subject
Theology
5621 General. Miscellaneous
(5625) Bible. Apocryphal books
see BS
5627 Liturgies
5629 Church history. Biographies
5631 Martyrologies. Legends
5632.A-Z Individual saints, or persons, A-Z
5635 Nestorians
5637 Monophysites. Jacobites
5638 Other
Including Melchites (Cf. PJ5241-PJ5249); Maronites; Gnostics; etc.
(5639) Law. Canonical law
see subclass KL
5641 Philosophy
5643 History. Chronology. Biography
Cf. PJ5629, Church history
Science
5645.A4 Agriculture
5645.A6 Alchemy. Chemistry
5645.A8 Astronomy. Astrology
5645.M8 Medicine
5647 Other (Superstition, folklore, etc.)
5670 Anonymous works (Single)
5671.A-Z Individual authors, A-Z
Subarrange each author by Table P-PZ40 unless otherwise specified
Translations into foreign languages
Syriac into foreign languages
5691.A2 Arabic
5691.A5 Armenian
5691.C6 Coptic
5691.E7 Ethiopian
5691.G7 Greek
5691.L3 Latin
5691.S5 Church Slavic
Modern languages. By language and date
5693.E5 English. Prefer subject
5693.F7 French
5693.G4 German

Syriac
Literature
Translations
Syriac into foreign languages
Modern languages.
By language and date -- Continued
5695 Slavic
Cf. PJ5691.S5, Church Slavic
5701-5709 East Syriac (Nestorian) (Table P-PZ8)
Cf. PJ5601+, Syriac literature
5711-5719 West Syriac (Jacobite) (Table P-PZ8)
Cf. PJ5601+, Syriac literature
5801-5809 Neo-Syriac dialects (Modern Syriac) (Table P-PZ8)
Including dialects spoken by Syrians in the villages surrounding Mosul (Olkosh, Tur Abdin, etc.) in the mountains of Kurdistan and in the districts of Urumiah and Salmasin in Persia
5901-5909 South Semitic languages (Table P-PZ8)
Arabic
Philology
6001 Periodicals
Cf. PJ1+, Oriental philology
6011 Societies
Cf. PJ1+, Oriental philology
6021 Congresses
Cf. PJ20+, Oriental philology
Collections
Monographs. Studies
6023 Serial
6023.5 Several authors
6024.A-Z Studies in honor of a particular person or institution, A-Z
6025.A-Z Individual authors, A-Z
6031 Encyclopedias. Dictionaries
6033 Atlases. Maps. Charts. Tables
6035 Philosophy. Theory. Method
6037 Relations
History of philology
6051 General
6052 General special
By period
6053 Early. Middle Ages
6057 Modern (including 19th and 20th centuries)
6060.A-Z By region or country, A-Z
Biography. Memoirs. Correspondence, etc.
Cf. PJ63+, Oriental philology
6063 Collective
6064.A-Z Individual, A-Z
Study and teaching
6065 General
6066 General special
By period, see PJ6053+
6068.A-Z By region or country, A-Z

Arabic
Philology
Study and teaching -- Continued
6069 By university, college, etc.
General works
6070 Early through 1800
6071 1801-
Language
6073 Treatises (General)
6074 General special
Including relation to other languages
6075 History (of the language)
6095 Popular
Grammar, etc.
Oriental languages
Class translations with original language
Arabic
6101 Treatises to ca. 1800
May be subdivided (successive cutter numbers):
(1) Texts. By date (of imprint)
(2).A-Z Translations. By language, A-Z, and date
(3) Commentaries in Oriental languages
(4) Commentaries in Western languages
(5) Indexes, glossaries, etc.
6106 Treatises, 1801-
6111 Textbooks
6115 Conversation and phrase books
6119 Chrestomathies. Readers
6119.5 Technical Arabic
6120 Examination questions, etc.
Phonology
6121 General works
6121.35 Phonetics
Writing. Alphabet
Cf. BP189.65.A47, Symbolism of the alphabet in Sufism
6123 General works
6124 Paleography
Cf. Z115X
6126 Calligraphy
6127 Orthography
6131 Morphology. Inflection. Accidence
Parts of speech (Morphology and syntax)
6141 General works
6141.5 Parsing
Noun
6142 General works
6142.2 Gender
6143 Adjective. Adverb
Including numerals

Arabic
Language
Grammar, etc.
Oriental languages
Arabic
Parts of speech (Morphology and syntax) -- Continued

6143.5	Adverbials
6144	Article
6144.5	Pronoun
6145	Verb
	Particles
6148	General works
6148.5.A-Z	Special, A-Z
6148.5.C65	Conditionals
6148.5.N44	Negatives
6148.5.P73	Prepositions
6151	Syntax
6161	Rhetoric
6166	Choice of words. Vocabulary, etc.
6167	Idioms. Errors
6170	Translating
6171	Metrics. Rhythmics. Versification
	Etymology
6172	Treatises
6173	Names
6174	Dictionaries
6175.A-Z	Special elements. By language, A-Z
6175.A3	Foreign elements (General)
6184	Semantics
6190	Synonyms. Antonyms
6191	Paronyms
6192	Homonyms
6199	Particular words
6199.5	Lexicology
	Dictionaries, see PJ6622
	Persian
6201	Treatises Apply table at PJ6101
6203	Textbooks
6204	Chrestomathies. Readers
6207	Versification
6208	Etymology
6209	Dictionaries
	Turkish
6231	Treatises Apply table at PJ6101
6233	Textbooks
6234	Chrestomathies. Readers
6237	Versification
6238	Etymology
6239	Dictionaries

PJ

Arabic
Language
Grammar, etc.
Oriental languages -- Continued
Other
Including languages of Africa, the Pacific, etc.
6271 Treatises
Apply table at PJ6101
6273 Textbooks
6274 Chrestomathies. Readers
6277 Versification
6278 Etymology
6279 Dictionaries
Western languages
Class translations with original language
6301 Treatises, through 1870
6303 Treatises, 1871-
6305 Textbooks, through 1870
6307 Textbooks, 1871-
6308 Self-instructors
6309 Conversation and phrase books
6311 Chrestomathies. Readers
6313 Examination questions, etc.
Phonology
6315 General works
6316 Phonetics
6317 Pronunciation
6318 Accent. Accentuation
Writing. Alphabet
6321 General works
6325 Transliteration
6327 Orthography
6331 Morphology. Inflection. Accidence
6341 Word formation. Derivation. Suffixes, etc.
6351 Parts of speech (Morphology and syntax)
6381 Syntax
6395 Other special
6400 Particular authors and works
e.g.
Koran, see PJ6696.A6+
6400.M3 Maimonides
6403 Translating
6405 Metrics. Rhythmics. Versification
Etymology
6571 Treatises
6576 Names
6582.A-Z Foreign elements. By language, A-Z
6583 Other special
6585 Semantics
6591 Synonyms. Antonyms
6599.A-Z Particular words, A-Z
6599.Q3 Qalb

Arabic
Language -- Continued
Lexicography
6601 Collections
Treatises
6611 General. History (of lexicography)
6617 Criticism of particular dictionaries
Dictionaries
Arabic only
6620 Classical authors through 1800
6622 1801-
Polyglot
6633 Arabic-Oriental languages
6635 Arabic-Western languages
Bilingual
6636.A-Z Arabic-Oriental. By language, A-Z
Arabic-Hebrew, see PJ4837
6637 Arabic-Latin; Latin-Arabic
6640 Arabic-English; English-Arabic
6645.A-Z Other Western languages. By language, A-Z
Particular periods
Pre-Islamic, see PJ6695.Z8
6650 Other
Particular authors or works
6655 General works
Koran, see PJ6696.Z8
6660 Names
6670 Foreign words
6680 Special (Technical, etc.)
Ancient Arabic (North Arabic)
6690.A-Z Inscriptions of Northern Arabia. By author or editor, A-Z
Including "Proto-Arabic"; Safaitic; Thamudic; Lihyanic
Cf. PJ6953
Pre-Islamic
Class here works restricted to that period exclusively
6695.A6-Z3 General works. Grammar, etc.
6695.Z4 Chrestomathies. Readers
6695.Z8 Glossaries. Indexes, etc.
Language of the Koran
For general works about the Koran, see BP130+
For subject dictionaries, concordances, indexes, etc., see BP133
For texts and translations of the Koran, see BP100+
6696.A6-Z3 General works. Grammar, etc.
6696.Z5A-Z Special topics, A-Z
6696.Z5A36 Adverb
6696.Z5A4 Alphabet. Script
6696.Z5E45 Emphasis
6696.Z5F5 Figures of speech

Arabic
Language
Language of the Koran
Special topics, A-Z -- Continued
6696.Z5I54 Inflection
6696.Z5I57 Interrogative
6696.Z5N4 Negatives
6696.Z5P28 Parsing
6696.Z5P3 Particles
6696.Z5P48 Phonology
6696.Z5P64 Polysemy
6696.Z5P73 Prepositions
6696.Z5R45 Rhetoric
6696.Z5S3 Saj'
6696.Z5V45 Verb
6696.Z6A-Z Individual sūrahs, A-Z
6696.Z6A4 Āl 'Imrān
6696.Z6F36 Fātiḥah
6696.Z8 Glossaries, vocabularies, etc.
Language of the Hadīth
6697.A6-Z3 General works. Grammar, etc.
6697.Z5A-Z Special topics, A-Z
6697.Z5A36 Adverb
6697.Z5A4 Alphabet. Script
6697.Z5E45 Emphasis
6697.Z5F5 Figures of speech
6697.Z5I54 Inflection
6697.Z5I57 Interrogative
6697.Z5N4 Negatives
6697.Z5P28 Parsing
6697.Z5P3 Particles
6697.Z5P48 Phonology
6697.Z5P73 Prepositions
6697.Z5R45 Rhetoric
6697.Z5S3 Saj'
6697.Z5V45 Verb
6697.Z6A-Z Individual sūrahs, A-Z
6697.Z8 Glossaries, vocabularies, etc.
Modern Arabic dialects (North Arabic)
General
6701 Collections
6703 Atlases. Maps. Charts
6707 Study and teaching
6709 General works
(6710) Script. Transliteration
see P211
6713 Grammar
6714 Chrestomathies. Readers
6715 Phonology. Phonetics
6719 Morphology. Inflection. Accidence
6721 Parts of speech (Morphology and syntax)
6723 Syntax
6731 Etymology

Modern Arabic dialects (North Arabic)
General -- Continued
6737 Dictionaries. Glossaries, etc.
Spain (Table P-PZ8a)
6751.A1-A5 Collections
6751.A6-Z General works
(6752) Script. Transliteration
see P211, P226, PJ6321
Grammars. Treatises. Textbooks
6753 Western
6754 Oriental
6755 Chrestomathies. Readers. Exercises
Dictionaries
6756 Western
6757 Oriental
6758 Texts
6759 Other special
6760.A-Z Local, A-Z
6761-6769 North Africa (Table P-PZ8a)
Morocco
6770.22 General works
6770.23 Grammar
6770.24 Readers. Exercises
6770.25 Phonology. Phonetics
6770.26 Dictionaries
6770.27 Texts
6770.28.A-Z Local, A-Z
Algeria
6770.32 General works
6770.33 Grammar
6770.34 Readers. Exercises
6770.35 Phonology. Phonetics
6770.36 Dictionaries
6770.37 Texts
6770.38.A-Z Local, A-Z
Tunisia
6770.42 General works
6770.43 Grammar
6770.44 Readers. Exercises
6770.45 Phonology. Phonetics
6770.46 Dictionaries
6770.47 Texts
6770.48.A-Z Local, A-Z
Libya
6770.52 General works
6770.53 Grammar
6770.54 Readers. Exercises
6770.55 Phonology. Phonetics
6770.56 Dictionaries
6770.57 Texts
6770.58.A-Z Local, A-Z
Egypt
6771 Periodicals. Societies. Collections

Modern Arabic dialects (North Arabic)
Egypt -- Continued
6773 General treatises
6775 Study and teaching
6776 Treatises in Oriental languages
Grammar
6777 Treatises (Advanced)
Textbooks. Exercises. Readers
6779 General works
(6780) Script. Transliteration
see P211, P226, PJ6321
6781 Phonology. Phonetics
6782 Morphology. Inflection. Accidence
6783 Special parts of speech (Morphology and Syntax)
6785 Syntax
6791 Etymology
6795 Dictionaries
6798 Texts
6799.A-Z Local dialects. By region, place, etc., A-Z
Sudan
6801.2 General works
6801.3 Grammar
6801.4 Readers. Exercises
6801.5 Phonology. Phonetics
6801.6 Dictionaries
6801.7 Texts
6801.8.A-Z Local, A-Z
Jordan
6803.2 General works
6803.3 Grammar
6803.4 Readers. Exercises
6803.5 Phonology. Phonetics
6803.6 Dictionaries
6803.7 Texts
6803.8.A-Z Local, A-Z
Palestine and Israel
6805 General works
6806 Grammar
6806.4 Readers. Exercises
6806.5 Phonology. Phonetics
6807 Dictionaries
6808 Texts
6809.A-Z Local, A-Z
Lebanon
6810.2 General works
6810.3 Grammar
6810.4 Readers. Exercises
6810.5 Phonology. Phonetics
6810.6 Dictionaries
6810.7 Texts
6810.8.A-Z Local, A-Z
Syria
6811.A1-A5 Collections

Modern Arabic dialects (North Arabic)
Syria -- Continued
6811.A6-Z General works
Grammars. Treatises. Textbooks
6813 Western languages
6814 Oriental languages
6815 Readers. Exercises
Dictionaries
6816 Western languages
6817 Oriental languages
6818 Texts
6819 Other special
6820.A-Z Local, A-Z
Iraq
6821.A1-A5 Collections
6821.A6-Z General works
Grammars. Treatises. Textbooks
6823 Western languages
6824 Oriental languages
6825 Readers. Exercises
Dictionaries
6826 Western languages
6827 Oriental languages
6828 Texts
6829 Other special
6830.A-Z Local, A-Z
Arabian Peninsula
6830.2 General works
6830.3 Grammar
6830.4 Readers. Exercises
6830.5 Phonology. Phonetics
6830.6 Dictionaries
6830.7 Texts
Saudi Arabia
6841.A1-A5 Collections
6841.A6-Z General works
(6842) Script. Transliteration
see PJ6123, PJ6321
Grammars. Treatises. Textbooks
6843 Western languages
6844 Oriental languages
6845 Readers. Exercises
Dictionaries
6846 Western languages
6847 Oriental languages
6848 Texts
6849 Other special
6850.A-Z Local, A-Z
Gulf States
6851.A1-A5 Collections
6851.A6-Z General works
Grammars. Treatises. Textbooks
6853 Western languages

Modern Arabic dialects (North Arabic)
Arabian Peninsula
Gulf States
Grammars. Treatises. Textbooks -- Continued
6854 Oriental languages
6855 Readers. Exercises
Dictionaries
6856 Western languages
6857 Oriental languages
6858 Texts
6859 Other special
Bahrain
6862.2 General works
6862.3 Grammar
6862.4 Readers. Exercises
6862.5 Phonology. Phonetics
6862.6 Dictionaries
6862.7 Texts
6862.8.A-Z Local, A-Z
Kuwait
6863.2 General works
6863.3 Grammar
6863.4 Readers. Exercises
6863.5 Phonology. Phonetics
6863.6 Dictionaries
6863.7 Texts
6863.8.A-Z Local, A-Z
Oman
6864.2 General works
6864.3 Grammar
6864.4 Readers. Exercises
6864.5 Phonology. Phonetics
6864.6 Dictionaries
6864.7 Texts
6864.8.A-Z Local, A-Z
Qatar
6865.2 General works
6865.3 Grammar
6865.4 Readers. Exercises
6865.5 Phonology. Phonetics
6865.6 Dictionaries
6865.7 Texts
6865.8.A-Z Local, A-Z
United Arab Emirates
6866.2 General works
6866.3 Grammar
6866.4 Readers. Exercises
6866.5 Phonology. Phonetics
6866.6 Dictionaries
6866.7 Texts
6866.8.A-Z Local, A-Z
Yemen
6871.A1-A5 Collections

	Modern Arabic dialects (North Arabic)
	Arabian Peninsula
	Yemen -- Continued
6871.A6-Z	General works
	Grammars. Treatises. Textbooks
6873	Western languages
6874	Oriental languages
6875	Readers. Exercises
	Dictionaries
6876	Western languages
6877	Oriental languages
6878	Texts
6879	Other special
6880.A-Z	Local, A-Z
6891	Maltese (Table P-PZ15a)
6901.A-Z	Other, A-Z
(6901.B34)	Bahrain
	see PJ6862.2-8
6901.C35	Central Asian
6901.C45	Chad
6901.C9	Cypriote
	Cyrenaic, see PJ6770.52+
(6901.J67)	Jordanian
	see PJ6803.2-8
(6901.L5)	Libyan
	see PJ6770.52-58
6901.M37	Mauritanian
6901.N53	Nigerian
6901.S5	Sicilian
6901.S68	South African
(6901.S8)	Sudanese
	see PJ6801.2-8
6901.T8	Turkish
6901.Z35	Zanzibar
	South Arabian
	Ancient
6950-6954	General works (Table P-PZ9)
	Particular languages and dialects
6956	Minaean
6958	Sabaean
6965	Himyaritic
6971	Hadramaut
	Cf. PJ6871+, South Arabian Peninsula
6981	Kataban (Qataban)
	Modern
7051-7055	General works (Table P-PZ9)
	Particular dialects
7111-7114	Mahri (Mehri) (Table P-PZ11)
7121-7124	Šhauri (Table P-PZ11)
7131-7134	Sokotri (Table P-PZ11)
7141-7144	Ḥarsūsī (Table P-PZ11)
	Arabic literature
	History and criticism

Arabic literature
History and criticism -- Continued
7501 Periodicals. Societies. Serials
7503 Collections
7505 Study and teaching
Biography of critics, historians, etc.
7505.4 Collective
7505.5.A-Z Individual, A-Z
7507 Criticism
7510 General works
7515 Miscellaneous
7517 General special
Relations to other languages
7518 General works
7518.5 Translations
7519.A-Z Special, A-Z
7519.A49 Alexander, the Great, 356-323 B.C. Dhū al-Qarnayn
7519.A5 Animals
7519.A72 Architecture. Buildings
7519.A9 Autobiography
Buildings, see PJ7519.A72
7519.C5 Christianity
7519.C6 Clouds
7519.C67 Country life
7519.C7 Crime
7519.D48 Devil. Satan. Iblis
Dhū al-Qarnayn, see PJ7519.A49
7519.E4 Egypt
7519.E76 Erotic literature
7519.E87 Europe. Europeans
7519.E94 Eye
7519.F37 Fate and fatalism
7519.F45 Femininism
7519.F6 Food
7519.H33 Hallāj, al-Ḥusayn ibn Manṣūr, 858 or 9-922
7519.H4 Heroes
7519.H59 Ḥiṭṭin, Battle of, 1187
7519.H67 Horses
Iblis, see PJ7519.D48
7519.I58 Intifada, 1987-
7519.I7 Iraq
7519.I72 Iraq-Kuwait Crisis, 1990-1991
7519.I84 Islam
7519.J4 Jewish-Arab relations
7519.J5 Jinn
7519.L55 Lizards
7519.L6 Love
7519.M35 Majnūn Laylá. Laylá and Majnūn as a theme in literature
Man. Manhood, see PJ7519.M44
7519.M38 Mawlid al-Nabī
7519.M44 Men. Man. Manhood

Arabic literature
History and criticism
Special, A-Z -- Continued

7519.M56 Mirrors
7519.M6 Mothers
7519.M76 Muḥammad, Prophet, d. 632
7519.M9 Mythology
7519.N27 Nasser, Gamal Abdel, 1918-1970
7519.N3 Nationalism
7519.N33 Nawrūz (Persian New Year)
7519.N6 Nostalgia. Homesickness
7519.O38 Oaths. Qasam
7519.P27 Paganism
7519.P3 Palms. Palm trees
7519.P32 Parasitism (Social sciences)
7519.P33 Patronage of literature
7519.P35 Peace
7519.P4 Peasants
7519.P58 Poets
7519.P6 Politics
7519.P64 Poor
7519.P74 Prisons
Qasam, see PJ7519.O38
7519.R3 Rain
7519.R46 Revolutionary literature. Revolution in literature
Cf. PJ7542.R44, Revolutionary poetry
7519.R63 Rogues. Vagabonds. Scoundrels
Satan, see PJ7519.D48
Scoundrels, see PJ7519.R63
7519.S4 Sex
7519.S45 Shiites
7519.S48 Shu'ūbījah
7519.S84 Suicide
7519.S9 Symbolism
7519.T7 Travel
7519.U85 Utopias
Vagabonds, see PJ7519.R63
7519.W5 Wine
7519.W66 Women

Biography
7521 Collective
7525.A-Z Individual, A-Z
7525.2 Women authors. Literary relations of women

Other classes of authors, A-Z
7525.4.C53 Circassian authors
7525.4.H35 Harranians
7525.4.K83 Kudyah authors
7525.4.P45 Physicians

By period
7526 Pre-Islamic. Early to 622 A.D.
7527 622-660
666-1258

PJ

Arabic literature
History and criticism
By period
666-1258 -- Continued
7528 General works
7529 660-750. Omayyad period
750-1258. Abbasid period
7530 General works
7531 750-846
7532 846-946
7533 946-1055
7534 1055-1258
1258-1800
7535 General works
7536 1258-1517. Mamlūk (Mameluke) period
7537 1517-1800. Turkish period
7538 Modern, 1801-
Special forms
Poetry
7541 General works
7542.A-Z Special, A-Z
7542.A23 Abdūlhamid II, Sultan of the Turks, 1842-1918
7542.A27 Abu Jihad
7542.A32 Aesthetics
7542.A34 Afghanistan
Aged, see PJ7542.O43
7542.A45 Alienation (Social psychology)
7542.A47 Ambiguity
7542.A52 Animals
7542.A58 Anxiety
7542.A7 Arabs
7542.A9 Autobiography
7542.B37 Barmecides
7542.B57 Blame
7542.C47 Children's poetry
7542.C5 Christianity. Christian authors
7542.C56 Cities and towns
7542.C6 Coffee
7542.C64 Communication
7542.C65 Conflict (Psychology)
7542.C67 Costume
7542.C75 Crucifixion
7542.D35 Dancers. Dancing
7542.D43 Death
7542.D53 Dialect poetry
7542.E38 Egypt
7542.E4 Elegiac poetry. Rithā
7542.E54 Emigration and immigration
7542.E6 Epic poetry
7542.E65 Ethics
7542.E8 Eulogy. Madīḥ
7542.E85 Exiles
7542.E9 Eye. Vision

Arabic literature
History and criticism
Special forms
Poetry
Special, A-Z -- Continued

7542.F35 Faisal, King of Saudi Arabia, 1906-1975
7542.F66 Food
7542.G35 Generosity
7542.G4 Ghazal
7542.H4 Heroes. Heroism
Hijā, see PJ7542.S3
7542.H6 Homosexuality
7542.H65 Horses
7542.H78 Hunting
7542.H79 Ḥusayn, Ṣuddām
7542.H8 al-Ḥusayn ibn Alī, d. 680
7542.I24 Ibn Sa'ūd, King of Saudi Arabia, 1880-1953
Immigration, see PJ7542.E54
7542.I58 Intifada, 1987-
7542.I73 Iran-Iraq War, 1980-1988
7542.I8 Islam. Islamic religious poetry
7542.I85 Israel-Arab War, 1967
7542.I86 Israel-Arab War, 1973
7542.J48 Jewish-Arab relations
7542.K35 Karam, Yūsuf, 1823-1889
7542.K47 Kharijites
7542.L34 Lanterns
7542.L42 Lebanon
7542.L6 Love
Madīḥ, see PJ7542.E8
7542.M34 Majnūn Laylá. Laylá and Majnūn
7542.M35 Mannerism
7542.M37 Mawlid al-Nabī
7542.M65 Mongols
7542.M74 Mu'āraḍāt
7542.M75 Muḥummad, the prophet
7542.M8 Muwashshah
Cf. PQ6056, Moorish-Spanish literature
7542.M9 Mythology
7542.N27 Narrative poetry
7542.N3 Nasser, Gamal Abdul, pres., United Arab Republic, 1918-1970
7542.N32 Nationalism
7542.N33 Nature
7542.N4 Negro poetry. Negro authors
Odor, see PJ7542.S58
7542.O43 Old age. Aged
7542.O5 Onager
7542.P35 Palestine
7542.P47 Persian Gulf War, 1991
7542.P49 Pigeons
7542.P53 Plagiarism
7542.P54 Pleiades

Arabic literature
History and criticism
Special forms
Poetry
Special, A-Z -- Continued

7542.P64 Politics
7542.Q3 Qasidas
7542.R34 Rajaz poetry
7542.R42 Realism
7542.R43 Religion
7542.R44 Revolutionary poetry
Rithā, see PJ7542.E4
7542.R6 Romances
7542.R63 Romanticism
7542.S3 Satire. Hijā'
7542.S35 Sayf al-Dawlah al-Ḥamdānī, 'Alī ibn 'Abd Allāh, 915 or 6-967
7542.S42 Sea
7542.S45 Self
7542.S52 Shiites
7542.S53 Sinbad the sailor
7542.S58 Smell. Odor
7542.S6 Spring
7542.S67 Stars
7542.S9 Sufism
7542.S95 Symbolism
7542.T3 Taste
7542.T5 Time
7542.T6 Touch
7542.T87 Turks
7542.V34 Values
Vision, see PJ7542.E9
7542.W3 War poetry
7542.W5 Wine. Wine songs
7542.W64 Wolves
7542.W65 Women
7542.Y68 Youth
7542.Z3 Zajal

By period
7543 Pre-Islamic. Early to 622 A.D.
7545 622-660
660-1258
7551 General works
7552 660-750. Omayyad period
750-1258. Abbasid period
7553 General works
7554 750-846
7555 846-946
7556 946-1055
7557 1055-1258
1258-1800
7558 General works
7559 1258-1517. Mamlūk (Mameluke) period

Arabic literature
History and criticism
Special forms
Poetry
By period
1258-1800 -- Continued
7560 1517-1800. Turkish period
7561 Modern, 1801-
7565 Drama
Prose. Fiction
7571 General works
7572.A-Z Special, A-Z
7572.D47 Deserts
7572.E37 East and West
7572.E95 Exiles
7572.M3 Maqamah
7572.M94 Mythology
7572.N37 Narration
7572.P64 Politics
7572.S24 Saj'
7572.T54 Time
7572.W37 War
By period
7573 Pre-Islamic. Early to 622 A.D.
7574 622-660
7575 660-1258
7576 1258-1800
7577 Modern, 1801-
7577.5 Oratory
7578 Wit and humor
Cf. PN6222.A+, Collections
(7580) Folk literature
see subclass GR
7585 Children's literature (General)
For special genres, see the genre
Inscriptions. Papyri
7593 History and criticism
Collections
7595 General
7596 Museums. Institutions
7597 Private collections
7599.A-Z Special. By region or country, A-Z
e.g.
7599.S7 Spain
7600 Special inscriptions. By author
Collections
7601 General
7604.A-Z Special, A-Z
7604.A49 Alexander, the Great, 356-323 B.C. Dhū al-Qarnayn
7604.A5 Animals
7604.A72 Architecture. Buildings
Buildings, see PJ7604.A72

Arabic literature
Collections
Special, A-Z -- Continued

7604.C5	Christianity
7604.C6	Clouds
7604.C67	Country life
7604.C7	Crime
7604.D48	Devil. Satan. Iblis
	Dhū al-Qarnayn, see PJ7604.A49
7604.E4	Egypt
7604.E87	Europe. Europeans
7604.F45	Feminism
7604.F6	Food
7604.H33	Ḥallāj, al-Ḥusayn ibn Manṣūr, 858 or 9-922
7604.H4	Heroes
7604.H54	Ḥiṭṭin, Battle of, 1187
7604.H67	Horses
	Iblis, see PJ7604.D48
7604.I58	Intifada, 1987-
7604.I7	Iraq
7604.I72	Iraq-Kuwait Crisis, 1990-1991
7604.I84	Islam
7604.J4	Jewish-Arab relations
7604.J5	Jinn
7604.L55	Lizards
7604.L6	Love
7604.M35	Majnūn Laylá. Laylá and Majnūn as a theme in literature
	Man. Manhood, see PJ7604.M44
7604.M38	Mawlid al-Nabī
7604.M44	Men. Man. Manhood
7604.M6	Mothers
7604.M76	Muḥammad, Prophet, d. 632
7604.M9	Mythology
7604.N3	Nationalism
7604.N33	Nawrūz (Persian New Year)
7604.N6	Nostalgia. Homesickness
7604.O38	Oaths. Qasam
7604.P27	Paganism
7604.P3	Palms. Palm trees
7604.P32	Parasitism (Social sciences)
7604.P33	Patronage of literature
7604.P35	Peace
7604.P4	Peasants
7604.P58	Poets
7604.P6	Politics
7604.P64	Poor
	Qasam, see PJ7604.O38
7604.R3	Rain
7604.R46	Revolutionary literature. Revolution in literature Cf. PJ7542.R44, Revolutionary poetry
7604.R63	Rogues. Vagabonds. Scoundrels

	Arabic literature
	Collections
	Special, A-Z -- Continued
	Satan, see PJ7604.D48
	Scoundrels, see PJ7604.R63
7604.S4	Sex
7604.S45	Shiites
7604.S48	Shu'ūbījah
7604.S9	Symbolism
7604.T7	Travel
7604.U85	Utopias
	Vagabonds, see PJ7604.R63
7604.W5	Wine
7604.W66	Women
	Translations, see PJ7694+
7611	By period
7613	Pre-Islamic. Early to 622 A.D.
	622-660
7615	660-1258
7616	General works
	660-750. Omayyad period
7617	750-1258. Abbasid period
7618	General works
7619	750-846
7620	846-946
7621	946-1055
	1055-1258
7622	1258-1800
7623	General works
7624	1258-1517. Mamlūk (Mameluke) period
7625	1517-1800. Turkish period
	Modern, 1801-
	Special forms
7631	Poetry
7632.A-Z	General
7632.A23	Special, A-Z
7632.A34	Abdūlhamid II, Sultan of the Turks, 1842-1918
	Afghanistan
7632.A45	Aged, see PJ7632.O43
7632.A52	Alienation (Social psychology)
7632.A58	Animals
7632.A7	Anxiety
7632.A9	Arabs
7632.B37	Autobiography
7632.B57	Barmecides
7632.C47	Blame
7632.C5	Children's poetry
7632.C56	Christianity. Christian authors
7632.C6	Cities and towns
7632.C64	Coffee
7632.C65	Communication
7632.C67	Conflict (Psychology)
7632.D35	Costume
	Dancers. Dancing

Arabic literature
Collections
Special forms
Poetry
Special, A-Z -- Continued

7632.D43 Death
7632.D53 Dialect poetry
7632.E38 Egypt
7632.E4 Elegiac poetry. Rithā
7632.E54 Emigration and immigration
7632.E6 Epic poetry
7632.E65 Ethics
7632.E8 Eulogy. Madīh
7632.E85 Exiles
7632.E9 Eye. Vision
7632.F35 Faisal, King of Saudi Arabia, 1906-1975
7632.F66 Food
7632.G4 Ghazal
7632.H4 Heroes. Heroism
Hijā, see PJ7632.S3
7632.H6 Homosexuality
7632.H65 Horses
7632.H78 Hunting
7632.H79 Ḥusayn, Ṣuddām
7632.H8 al-Ḥusayn ibn Alī, d. 680
7632.I24 Ibn Sa'ūd, King of Saudi Arabia, 1880-1953
Immigration, see PJ7632.E54
7632.I58 Intifada, 1987-
7632.I73 Iran-Iraq War, 1980-1988
7632.I8 Islam. Islamic religious poetry
7632.I85 Israel-Arab War, 1967
7632.I86 Israel-Arab War, 1973
7632.J48 Jewish-Arab relations
7632.K35 Karam, Yūsuf, 1823-1889
7632.K47 Kharijites
7632.L34 Lanterns
7632.L42 Lebanon
7632.L6 Love
Madīḥ, see PJ7632.E8
7632.M34 Majnūn Laylá. Laylá and Majnūn
7632.M35 Mannerism
7632.M37 Mawlid al-Nabī
7632.M65 Mongols
7632.M74 Mu'āraḍāt
7632.M75 Muḥummad, the prophet
7632.M8 Muwashshah
Cf. PQ6056, Moorish-Spanish literature
7632.M9 Mythology
7632.N27 Narrative poetry
7632.N3 Nasser, Gamal Abdul, pres., United Arab Republic, 1918-1970
7632.N32 Nationalism
7632.N33 Nature

Arabic literature
Collections
Special forms
Poetry
Special, A-Z -- Continued
7632.N4 Negro poetry. Negro authors
Odor, see PJ7632.S58
7632.O43 Old age. Aged
7632.O5 Onager
7632.P35 Palestine
7632.P47 Persian Gulf War, 1991
7632.P53 Plagiarism
7632.P54 Pleiades
7632.P64 Politics
7632.Q3 Qasidas
7632.R34 Rajaz poetry
7632.R42 Realism
7632.R44 Revolutionary poetry
Rithā, see PJ7632.E4
7632.R6 Romances
7632.R63 Romanticism
7632.S3 Satire. Hijā'
7632.S35 Sayf al-Dawlah al-Ḥamdānī, 'Alī ibn 'Abd Allāh, 915 or 6-967
7632.S42 Sea
7632.S45 Self
7632.S52 Shiites
7632.S53 Sinbad the sailor
7632.S58 Smell. Odor
7632.S6 Spring
7632.S67 Stars
7632.S9 Sufism
7632.S95 Symbolism
7632.T3 Taste
7632.T5 Time
7632.T6 Touch
7632.V34 Values
Vision, see PJ7632.E9
7632.W3 War poetry
7632.W5 Wine. Wine songs
7632.W64 Wolves
7632.W65 Women
7632.Y68 Youth
7632.Z3 Zajal
Translations, see PJ7694+
By period
Pre-Islamic. Early to 622 A.D.
7633 General works
Special anthologies
Subarrange each by Table P-PZ41
7641 Hamāsa (Table P-PZ41)
7642 Mu'allaḳāt (Table P-PZ41)
7643 Mufaḍḍalīyāt (Table P-PZ41)

Arabic literature
Collections
Special forms
Poetry
By period
Pre-Islamic. Early to 622 A.D.
Special anthologies -- Continued
7645.A-Z Other, A-Z
Subarrange each by Table P-PZ43
7648 622-660
660-1258
7650 General works
7651 660-750. Omayyad period
750-1258. Abbasid period
7653 General works
7654 750-846
7655 846-946
7656 946-1055
7657 1055-1258
1258-1800
7658 General works
7659 1258-1517. Mamlūk (Mameluke) period
7660 1517-1800. Turkish period
7661 Modern, 1801-
7665 Drama
Prose. Fiction
7671 General
Translations, see PJ7694+
By period
7673 Pre-Islamic. Early to 622 A.D.
7674 622-660
7675 660-1258
7676 1258-1800
7677 Modern, 1801-
(7680) Folk literature
see subclass GR
7694-7695 Translations (Table P-PZ30)
Individual authors or works
Subarranged by Table P40 or P41
7695.8 Anonymous works of unknown date
7696 Pre-Islamic. Early to 622 A.D.
7696.A25 'Abd Allāh ibn Rawāhah, d. 629 or 30 (Table P-PZ40)
7696.A254 'Abid ibn al-Abraṣ (Table P-PZ40)
7696.A257 Abū Dhu'ayb al'Hudhaylī, Khuwaylid ibn Khālid, 7th cent. (Table P-PZ40)
7696.A44 Aktham ibn Ṣayfī, d.630-31 (Table P-PZ40)
7696.A468 'Amr ibn Kulthūm, fl. 6th cent. (Table P-PZ40)
7696.A47 'Amr ibn Ma'dīkarib al-Zubaydī, d. 641? (Table P-PZ40)
7696.A5 'Amr ibn Qamī'ah (Table P-PZ40)
7696.A52 'Amr ibn Sha's al'Asadī, 7th cent. (Table P-PZ40)
7696.A53 'Antarah ibn Shaddād, al-'Absī (Table P-PZ40)

Arabic literature
Individual authors or works
Pre-Islamic. Early to 622 A.D. -- Continued

7696.A8 al-A'shá, Maymūn ibn Qays, d. ca. 629 (Table P-PZ40)
7696.A93 Aws ibn Ḥajar, 6th cent. (Table P-PZ40)
7696.D48 Dhū al-Iṣba 'al-'Adwānī, Ḥurthān ibn Muḥarrith, d. ca. 600 (Table P-PZ40)
7696.D498 Dirār ibn al-Khaṭṭab al-Fihrī, 7th cent. (Table P-PZ40)
7696.D85 Durayd ibn al-Ṣimmah, d. ca. 630 (Table P-PZ40)
7696.H25 al-Ḥādirah, Quṭbah ibn Aws (Table P-PZ40)
7696.H34 Ḥātim al-Ṭa'ī (Table P-PZ40)
7696.I5 Imru' al-Qays, fl. 530 (Table P-PZ40)
7696.J5 Jirān al-'Awd al-Numayrī, 'Amir ibn al-Ḥārith (Table P-PZ40)
7696.K5 Khansā' bint 'Amr, d. ca. 645 (Table P-PZ40)
7696.L3 Labīd ibn Rabī'ah, ca. 560-ca. 661 (Table P-PZ40)
7696.M74 Muhalhil (Table P-PZ40)
7696.M76 Musayyab ibn 'Alas, 6th cent. (Table P-PZ40)
7696.M8 Muthaqqib al-'Abdī, 'A'idh ibn Miḥṣan, 6th cent. (Table P-PZ40)
7696.N25 Nābighah al-Dhubyānī, 6th cent. (Table P-PZ40)
7696.N27 Nābighah al-Ja'dī, 7th cent. (Table P-PZ40)
7696.N3 Namir ibn Tawlab, d. ca. 635 (Table P-PZ40)
7696.Q16 al-Qaṣīdah al-yatimah (Table P-PZ40)
7696.Q27 Qays ibn Zuhayr, d. 631 or 2 (Table P-PZ40)
7696.Q8 Quss ibn Sā'idah (Table P-PZ40)
7696.S35 Samaw'al, ca. 560 (Table P-PZ40)
7696.S5 'al-Shanfará (Table P-PZ40)
7696.S94 Sulayk ibn al-Sulakah, 6th cent. (Table P-PZ40)
7696.T25 Ta'abbaṭa Sharran, Thābiṭ ibn Jābir, d. ca. 540 (Table P-PZ40)
7696.T3 Ṭarafah ibn al-'Abd (Table P-PZ40)
7696.U4 Umayyah ibn Abī al-Ṣalt, ca. 534-623? (Table P-PZ40)
7696.U7 'Urwah ibn al-Ward, 6th cent. (Table P-PZ40)
7696.Y3 al-Yashkurī, Suwayd ibn Abī Kāhil, 7th cent. (Table P-PZ40)
7696.Z8 Zuhayr ibn Abī Sulmá (Table P-PZ40)
7698 622-660
7698.A23 Abū al-Aswad al-Du'alī, d. 688? (Table P-PZ40)
7698.A24 Abū Bakr, Caliph, d. 634 (Table P-PZ40)
7698.A3 Abū Mihjan al-Thaqafī, fl. 629-637 (Table P-PZ40)
7698.A5 'Alī ibn Abī Tālib, caliph, 600-ca. 661 (Table P-PZ40)
7698.H3 Ḥassān ibn Thābit, d. 674 (Table P-PZ40)
7698.H8 Ḥuṭay'ah, Jarwal ibn Aws, d. 650 (Table P-PZ40)
7698.I2 Ibn Muqbil, Tamīm ibn Ubayy, 7th cent. (Table P-PZ40)
7698.K28 Ka'b ibn Malik, d. 670 or 71 (Table P-PZ40)
7698.U7 'Urwah, ibn Ḥizām, 7th cent. (Table P-PZ40)

Arabic literature
Individual authors or works
622-660 -- Continued
7698.Z3 Zayd al-Khayl, 7th cent. (Table P-PZ40)
7700 Omayyad period, 660-750
Subarranged by Table P40 or P41
7700.A2 'Abd al-Ḥamīd ibn Yaḥyá, d. 749 or 50 (Table P-PZ40)
7700.A26 Abū al-Najm al-Faḍl ibn Qudāmah al-'Ijlī, d. 747 or 8 (Table P-PZ40)
7700.A3 Abū Ḥanīfah, d. 767 or 8 (Table P-PZ40)
7700.A32 Abū Ṣakhr al-Hudhalī, 'Abd Allāh ibn Salmah, d. ca. 700 (Table P-PZ40)
7700.A33 'Adī ibn al-Riqā' al-'Āmilī, d. 714 (Table P-PZ40)
7700.A35 Aḥwaṣ al-Anṣārī, 'Abd Allah bin Muḥammad, ca. 655-728 or 9 (Table P-PZ40)
7700.A38 'Ajjāj, 'Abd Allāh ibn Ru'bah, ca. 646-ca. 715 (Table P-PZ40)
7700.A42 Akhḍar al-Lahabī, al-Faḍl ibn al-'Abbš, d. 714 (Table P-PZ40)
7700.A43 al-Akhṭal, ca. 640-ca. 710 (Table P-PZ40)
7700.D5 Dhū al-Rummah, Ghaylān ibn 'Uqbah, 696-735 (Table P-PZ40)
7700.F3 Farazdaq, ca. 641-ca. 728 (Table P-PZ40)
7700.H33 Hajjaj ibn Yūsuf, 661-714 (Table P-PZ40)
7700.H37 Ḥasan al-Baṣrī, 641 or 2-726 or 7 (Table P-PZ40)
7700.I125 Ibn Abī Àtīq, Àbd Allāh, 8th cent. (Table P-PZ40)
7700.I14 Ibn Harmah, Ibrāhīm ibn 'Ali, 709-792 or 3 (Table P-PZ40)
7700.I158 Ibn Mu'awiyah, 'Abd Allāh, d. 748? (Table P-PZ40)
7700.I16 Ibn Mufarrigh al-Ḥimarī, Yazīd ibn Ziyād, d. 688 or 9 (Table P-PZ40)
7700.I18 Ibn al-Muqaffa', d. ca. 760 (Table P-PZ40)
7700.I2 Ibn Qays al-Ruqayyāt, 'ubayd Allāh, fl. 657-704 (Table P-PZ40)
7700.I34 Ibn al-Dumaynah, 'Abd Allāh ibn 'Ubayd Allāh, d. ca. 747 (Table P-PZ40)
7700.J27 Jamīl ibn 'Abd Allāh al-'Udhrī, d. 701 or 2 (Table P-PZ40)
7700.J3 Jarīr ibn 'Aṭīhah, d. 728? (Table P-PZ40)
7700.K2 Ka'b ibn Zuhayr (Table P-PZ40)
7700.K78 al-Kamayt ibn Zayd, 679 or 80-743 or 4 (Table P-PZ40)
7700.M312 Majnūn Laylá (Table P-PZ40)
7700.M73 Mu'āwiyah ibn Abī Sufyān, Caliph, d. 680 (Table P-PZ40)
7700.N24 Nābighah al-Shaybānī, Àbd Allāh ibn al-Makhāriq, d. 742 or 3 (Table P-PZ40)
7700.Q34 Qays ibn Dharḥ, d. 688 (Table P-PZ40)
7700.R3 al-Rā'ī al-Numayrī, 'Ubayd ibn Ḥuṣayn, d. 708 or 9 (Table P-PZ40)

Arabic literature
Individual authors or works
Omayyad period, 660-750 -- Continued
7700.R8 Ru'bah ibn al-'Ajjāj, d. 762? (Table P-PZ40)
7700.S52 Shamardal ibn Sharīk, 8th cent. (Table P-PZ40)
7700.T33 al-Taymī, 'Umar ibn Laja', d. ca. 724 (Table P-PZ40)
7700.T55 al-Ṭirimmāḥ ibn Ḥakīm al-Ṭā'ī, 8th cent. (Table P-PZ40)
7700.U4 'Umar ibn Abī Rabī'ah, 643 or 4-711 or 12 (Table P-PZ40)
7700.W27 Waḍḍāḥ al-Yaman, 'Abd al-Raḥmān ibn Ismā'īl, d. ca. 708 (Table P-PZ40)
7700.W3 Walīd ibn Yazīd, Caliph, d. 744 (Table P-PZ40)
7700.Y3 Yazīd ibn al-Ṭathrīyah, d. 743 or 4 (Table P-PZ40)
7700.Z58 Ziyād ibn Salmá al-A'jam, 7th/8th cent. (Table P-PZ40)
First Abbasid period, 750-846
7701 A - Abd
Subarranged by Table P40 or P41
7701.A117 al-'Abbās ibn al-Aḥnaf, b. ca. 750 (Table P-PZ40)
7701.1 'Abd al-
Cutter A-Z by letter following "'Abd al-"
Subarranged by Table P40 or P41
7701.2 'Abd Allāh
e.g.
Cutter A-Z by letter following "'Abd Allāh"
Subarranged by Table P40 or P41
7701.2.I2 'Abd Allāh ibn Wahb, d. ca. 812 (Table P-PZ40)
7701.3 'Abd B - 'Abd Z
Cutter A-Z by letter following "'Abd"
Subarranged by Table P40 or P41
7701.4 'Abda - 'Abdz
Cutter A-Z by letter following "'Abd"
Subarranged by Table P40 or P41
7701.5 'Abe - 'Abū
Cutter A-Z by letter following "Ab"
Subarranged by Table P40 or P41
7701.6 'Abū
Including all authors of this period whose names begin with this word. Cutter under the next portion of their names
Subarranged by Table P40 or P41
7701.6.A45 'Abū al-'Atāhiyah, Ismā'īl ibn al-Qāsim, 747 or 8-826? (Table P-PZ40)
7701.6.H3 'Abū Ḥayyah al-Numayrī, al-Haytham ibn al-Rabī' (Table P-PZ40)
7701.6.N8 'Abū Nuwās, ca. 756-ca. 810 (Table P-PZ40)
7701.6.S3 'Abū Sa'd al-Makhzūmī, 'Isa ibn Khālid, d. 845 (Table P-PZ40)
7701.6.S34 'Abū al-Shamaqmaq, d. ca. 815 (Table P-PZ40)

Arabic literature
Individual authors or works
First Abbasid period, 750-846
Abū -- Continued
7701.6.T35 'Abū Tammān Ḥabīb ibn 'Aws al-Ṭā'ī, fl. 808-842 (Table P-PZ40)
7701.7 Abū - 'Alī
Subarranged by Table P40 or P41
7701.8 'Alī
Including all authors of this period whose names begin with this word. Cutter under the next portion of their names
Subarranged by Table P40 or P41
7701.8.I22 Alī ibn al-Jahm, ca. 804-863 (Table P-PZ40)
7701.9 'Alī - An
Subarranged by Table P40 or P41
7702 Antar (Romance) (Table P-PZ41)
7703 Ant - Ara
Subarrange individual authors by Table P-PZ40
Subarrange individual works by Table P-PZ43
Arabian nights
Arabic texts
7711 Comprehensive
Minor
7712.A1A-Z Selections. By editor, A-Z
7712.A3-Z Individual tales, A-Z
Translations
For juvenile works, see PZ8, etc.
Baltic, see PJ7729.B8+
English
7715 Comprehensive
Minor
7716.A1A-Z Selections. By translator, A-Z
7716.A3-Z Individual tales, A-Z
Dutch
7719.A1 Comprehensive
7719.A2A-Z Selections. By translator, A-Z
7719.A3-Z Individual tales, A-Z
French
7721 Comprehensive
Minor
7722.A1A-Z Selections. By translator, A-Z
7722.A3-Z Individual tales, A-Z
German
7723 Comprehensive
Minor
7724.A1A-Z Selections. By translator, A-Z
7724.A3-Z Individual tales, A-Z
Hebrew
7724.5.A1 Comprehensive
7724.5.A2A-Z Selections. By translator, A-Z
7724.5.A3-Z Individual tales, A-Z
Italian

Arabic literature
Individual authors or works
First Abbasid period, 750-846
Arabian nights
Translations
Italian -- Continued

7725.A1 Comprehensive
7725.A2A-Z Selections. By translator, A-Z
7725.A3-Z Individual tales, A-Z

Portuguese

7726.A1 Comprehensive
7726.A2A-Z Selections. By translator, A-Z
7726.A3-Z Individual tales, A-Z

Scandinavian

Danish

7727.D3 Comprehensive
7727.D32A-Z Selections. By translator, A-Z
7727.D33A-Z Individual tales, A-Z

Icelandic

7727.I3 Comprehensive
7727.I32A-Z Selections. By translator, A-Z
7727.I33A-Z Individual tales, A-Z

Norwegian

7727.N6 Comprehensive
7727.N62A-Z Selections. By translator, A-Z
7727.N63A-Z Individual tales, A-Z

Swedish

7727.S8 Comprehensive
7727.S82A-Z Selections. By translator, A-Z
7727.S83A-Z Individual tales, A-Z

Slavic and Baltic

Bulgarian

7729.B8 Comprehensive
7729.B82A-Z Selections. By translator, A-Z
7729.B83A-Z Individual tales, A-Z

Czech

7729.C95 Comprehensive
7729.C952A-Z Selections. By translator, A-Z
7729.C953A-Z Individual tales, A-Z

Latvian

7729.L3 Comprehensive
7729.L32A-Z Selections. By translator, A-Z
7729.L33A-Z Individual tales, A-Z

Lithuanian

7729.L5 Comprehensive
7729.L52A-Z Selections. By translator, A-Z
7729.L53A-Z Individual tales, A-Z

Polish

7729.P6 Comprehensive
7729.P62A-Z Selections. By translator, A-Z
7729.P63A-Z Individual tales, A-Z

Russian

7729.R8 Comprehensive

Arabic literature
Individual authors or works
First Abbasid period, 750-846
Arabian nights
Translations
Slavic and Baltic
Russian -- Continued

7729.R82A-Z Selections. By translator, A-Z
7729.R83A-Z Individual tales, A-Z
Serbo-Croatian
7729.S4 Comprehensive
7729.S42A-Z Selections. By translator, A-Z
7729.S43A-Z Individual tales, A-Z
Slovak
7729.S6 Comprehensive
7729.S62A-Z Selections. By translator, A-Z
7729.S63A-Z Individual tales, A-Z
Slovenian
7729.S7 Comprehensive
7729.S72A-Z Selections. By translator, A-Z
7729.S73A-Z Individual tales, A-Z
Sorbian
7729.S75 Comprehensive
7729.S752A-Z Selections. By translator, A-Z
7729.S753A-Z Individual tales, A-Z
Spanish
7730.A1 Comprehensive
7730.A2A-Z Selections. By translator, A-Z
7730.A3-Z Individual tales, A-Z
7733.A-Z Oriental languages, A-Z

Under each language:

.x	*Comprehensive*
.x2A-Z	*Selections. By translator, A-Z*
.x3A-Z	*Individual tales, A-Z*

7735.A-Z Other languages, African, Oceanic, etc., A-Z
Apply table at PJ7733.A-Z
7737 History and criticism
7741.A-Z Other authors or works, A-Z
Subarrange by Table P40 or P41
7741.A8 'Attābī, Kulthūm ibn 'Amr, d. 835? (Table P-PZ40)
7741.B3 Bashshār ibn Burd, d. 783 or 4 (Table P-PZ40)
7741.B5 Bīdpaī. Arabic versions. Kalilah wa-Dimnah, etc. (Table P-PZ40)
Cf. PK3792, Sanskrit
Cf. PK6451.B5, Persian
Cf. PQ6321.C16, Spanish
For popular works in modern translations, see PN989.I5B4+
7741.B58 Bishr ibn al-Mu'tamir, d. 825 (Table P-PZ40)
7741.D55 Dīk al-Jinn, 'Abd al Salām ibn Raghbān, 778?-850? (Table P-PZ40)

Arabic literature
Individual authors or works
First Abbasid period, 750-846
Other authors or works, A-Z -- Continued
7741.G52 Ghazāl, Yahyá ibn al-Ḥakam, 772 or 3-864 or 5 (Table P-PZ40)
7741.H85 al-Ḥusayn ibn al-Ḍaḥḥāk, d. ca. 865 (Table P-PZ40)
7741.I147 Ibn Abī Ṣubḥ, 'Abd Allāh ibn 'Amr, 8th cent. (Table P-PZ40)
7741.I185 Ibn al-Zayyāt, Muḥammad ibn 'Abd al-Malik, d. 847 (Table P-PZ40)
Kalilah wa-Dimnah, see PJ7741.B5
7741.K52 Khuzā'ī, Di'bil ibn 'Alī, 765 or 6-860 or 61 (Table P-PZ40)
7741.K56 Kitāb Bilawhar wa-Būdhāsaf (Table P-PZ40)
Koran, see BP100+
7741.L8 Luqmān (Table P-PZ40)
7741.M28 Ma'mun, Caliph, 786-833 (Table P-PZ40)
7741.M37 Mawqifī, Muḥammad ibn 'Āṣim, d. 830 (Table P-PZ40)
Mu'allaḳāt, see PJ7642
7741.M796 Muslim ibn al-Walīd, d. 823 or 4 (Table P-PZ40)
7741.N33 Namarī, Manṣūr ibn al-Zibriqān, d. ca. 805 (Table P-PZ40)
7741.R35 Raqqī, Rabī'ah ibn Thābit, d. 813 (Table P-PZ40)
7741.R59 Riyāshī, Muḥammad ibn Yasīr, d. 825 (Table P-PZ40)
7741.S17 Sahl ibn Hārūn, d. 830 or 31 (Table P-PZ40)
7741.S46 al-Shāfi'ī, Muḥammad ibn Idrīs, 767 or 8-820 (Table P-PZ40)
7741.S94 Ṣūlī, Ibrāhīm ibn al-'Abbās, 792-857 (Table P-PZ40)
7741.U48 'Ulayyah bint al-Mahdī, 776 or 7-825 or 6 (Table P-PZ40)
7741.W3 Warrāq, Maḥmūd ibn Ḥasan, d. ca. 844 (Table P-PZ40)
7745 Second Abbasid period, 846-946
Subarrange by Table P40 or P41
7745.A17 Abū al-'Aynā', Muhammad ibn al Qāsim, d. 896 (Table P-PZ40)
7745.B8 Buḥturī, al-Walīd ibn 'Ubayd, ca. 821-897 or 8 (Table P-PZ40)
7745.D54 Dīnawarī, Abū Ḥanīfah Ahmad ibn Dāwūd, d. ca. 895 (Table P-PZ40)
7745.F35 Faqīh, Manṣūr ibn Ismā'īl,d. 918 (Table P-PZ40)
7745.H3 al-Ḥallāj, al-Ḥusayn ibn Mansūr, 858 or 9-922 (Table P-PZ40)
7745.I15 Ibn 'Abd Rabbih, Aḥmad ibn Muḥammad, 860-940 (Table P-PZ40)

Arabic literature
Individual authors or works
Second Abbasid period, 846-946 -- Continued

7745.I155 Ibn al-Marzubān, Muḥammad ibn Khalaf, d. 921 or 2 (Table P-PZ40)
7745.I16 Ibn al-Mu'tazz, 'Abd Allāh, 861-908 (Table P-PZ40)
7745.I165 Ibn al-Rūmī, 836-896 (Table P-PZ40)
7745.I17 Ibn Durayd, Muḥummad ibn al-Ḥasan, 837 or 8-933 (Table P-PZ40)
7745.I19 Ibn Ḥumayd, Saīd, 9th cent. (Table P-PZ40)
7745.I28 Ibn Shirshīr al-Nāshi' Abd Allāh ibn Muḥammad, d. 906 (Table P-PZ40)
7745.J3 Ibn Jāḥiẓ, d. 868 or 9 (Table P-PZ40)
7745.K54 Khālid ibn Yazīd al-Kātib al-Tamīmī, d. ca. 883 (Table P-PZ40)
7745.K8 Kushājim, Maḥmūd ibn al-Husayn, 10th cent. (Table P-PZ40)
7745.S2 al-Ṣanawbarī, Muḥammad ibn Aḥmad, d. 946 (Table P-PZ40)
7745.S77 Ṣūlī, Muḥammad ibn Yaḥyá, d. ca. 947 (Table P-PZ40)
7745.W37 Washshā', Muḥammad ibn Isḥāq ibn Yaḥyā, d. 936 (Table P-PZ40)
7750 Third Abbasid period, 946-1055
Subarrange by Table P40 or P41
7750.A25 Abū al-'Alā', al-Ma'arrī, 973-1057 (Table P-PZ40)
7750.A257 Abū Firās al-Ḥamdānī, al-Ḥārith ibn Sa'īd, 932-968 (Table P-PZ40)
7750.A26 Abū Hayyān al-Tawhīdī, 'Alī ibn Muḥammad, 10th cent. (Table P-PZ40)
7750.A27 Abū Ishāq al-Ilbīrī Ibrāhīm ibn Mas'ūd, d. ca. 1067 (Table P-PZ40)
7750.B294 Babbaghā', 'Abd al-Wāḥid ibn Naṣr, d. 1007 (Table P-PZ40)
7750.B3 Badī' al-Zamān al-Hamadhānī, 969-1008 (Table P-PZ40)
7750.B34 al-Bākharzī, 'Alī ibn al-Ḥasan, d. 1075 (Table P-PZ40)
7750.B35 al-Bayhaqī, Ibrāhīm ibn Muḥammad, 10th cent. (Table P-PZ40)
7750.B87 Bustī, 'Alī ibn Muḥammad, d. 1010 (Table P-PZ40)
7750.F39 Fazārī, Muḥammad ibn 'Amir, d. 956 (Table P-PZ40)
7750.G45 Ghazzī, Sulaymān ibn Ḥasan, 10th/11th cent. (Table P-PZ40)
7750.H37 Ḥātimī, Abū 'Alī Muḥammad ibn al-Ḥasan, d. 998 (Table P-PZ40)
7750.H54 Ḥimyarī, Ismā'il ibn 'Āmir, d. ca. 1048 (Table P-PZ40)
7750.H8 Ḥuṣrī, Ibrāhīm ibn 'Alī, d. 1022 (Table P-PZ40)

Arabic literature
Individual authors or works
Third Abbasid period, 946-1055 -- Continued

7750.I15 Ibn Abī Ḥuṣaynah al-Ḥasan ibn 'Abd-Allāh, 998?-1065 (Table P-PZ40)

7750.I17 Ibn Darrāj, Aḥmad ibn Muḥammad, 958-1030 (Table P-PZ40)

7750.I19 Ibn Ghalbūn al-Sūrī, 'Abd al-Muḥsin ibn Muḥammad, 950 or 51-1028 (Table P-PZ40)

7750.I196 Ibn Ḥajjāj, al-Ḥusayn ibn Aḥmad, d. 1001 (Table P-PZ40)

7750.I2 Ibn Hānī al-Andalusī, Abū al-Qāsim Muḥammad, 937?-972 (Table P-PZ40)

7750.I23 Ibn Ḥayyūs, Muḥammad ibn Sulṭān, 1003-1801 (Table P-PZ40)

7750.I253 Ibn Hudhayl, Yaḥyá ib Hudhayl, 917-999 (Table P-PZ40)

7750.I255 Ibn Lankak, Muḥammad ibn Muḥammad, d. ca. 970 (Table P-PZ40)

7750.I27 Ibn Rashīq al-Qayrawānī al-Ḥasan, c. 1064? (Table P-PZ40)

7750.I2716 Ibn Shahīd, Abū 'Āmīr Ḥamad, 992 or 3-1034 or 5 (Table P-PZ40)

Ibn Shuhayd al-Andalūsī, Abū 'Amīr Ahmad ibn 'Abd al-Malik, 992 or 3-1035, see PJ7750.I2716

7750.I276 Ibn Wakī, 'al-Tinnīsī, al-Ḥasan ibn 'Alī, d. 1003 (Table P-PZ40)

7750.I28 Ibn Zaydūn, Ahmad ibn 'Abd Allāh, 1003 or 4-1071 (Table P-PZ40)

7750.J37 Jazīrī, 'Abd al Malik ibn Idrīs, d. 1003 or 4 (Table P-PZ40)

7750.J87 Jurjānī, Alī ibn al-'Azīz, d. 1002 (Table P-PZ40)

7750.K456 al-Khabbāz al-Baladī, Muḥammad ibn Aḥmad, 10th cent. (Table P-PZ40)

7750.K53 Khuwārizmīm Muḥammad ibn al-'Abbās, 934 or 5-993 or 4 (Table P-PZ40)

7750.M5 Mihyar ibn Marzawayh al-Daylamī, d. 1037 (Table P-PZ40)

7750.M54 Mīkālī, 'Ubayd Allāh ibn Aḥmad, d. 1044 or 5 (Table P-PZ40)

7750.M8 al-Mutanabbī, Abū al-Ṭayyib Aḥmad ibn al-Ḥusayn, 915 or 16-965 (Table P-PZ40)

7750.N28 Nashalī, 'Abd al-Karīm, d. 1014 (Table P-PZ40)

7750.S263 al-Salāmī, Muḥammad ibn 'Abd Allāh, 948-1004 (Table P-PZ40)

7750.S285 al-Sarīyal Raffā', Abū al-Ḥasan ibn Aḥmad, 10th cent. (Table P-PZ40)

7750.S5 al-Sharīf al-Raḍī, Muḥammad ibn al-Husayn, 969 or 70-1016 (Table P-PZ40)

7750.S94 Suhayl ibn 'Abbād (Table P-PZ40)

7750.T35 Tamīm ibn al-Mu'izz, 948-984 (Table P-PZ40)

Arabic literature
Individual authors or works
Third Abbasid period, 946-1055 -- Continued
7750.T5 Tha ālibī, Abd al-Malik ibn Muḥammad, 961 or 2-1037 (Table P-PZ40)
7750.W3 al-Wa'wa' al Dimashqī, Muḥammad ibn Aḥmad, 10th cent. (Table P-PZ40)
7750.W35 Wazir al-Maghribi, al-Husayn ibn 'Ali, 981-1027 (Table P-PZ40)
7755 Fourth Ạbbasid period, 1055-1258
Subarrange by Table P40 or P41
7755.A117 'Abd al-Qādir al-Jīlānī, d. 1166 (Table P-PZ40)
7755.A12 'Abd Allāh ibn Ḥamzah ibn Sulaymān, d. 1217 or 18 (Table P-PZ40)
7755.A14 al-Abīwardī, Muḥammad ibn Aḥmad, d. 1113 (Table P-PZ40)
7755.A33 Abu al-Ṣalt Umayyah ibn 'Abd al-'Azīz, 1067 or 8-1134 (Table P-PZ40)
7755.A5 al-Andalusī, 'Abd al-Raḥmān Yakhlaftan ibn Aḥmad (Table P-PZ40)
7755.A54 al-'Aqīlī, 'Alī ibn al-Husayn, 11th cent. (Table P-PZ40)
7755.A72 'Arrajānī, Aḥmad ibn Muḥammad, 1067 or 8-1149 or 50 (Table P-PZ40)
7755.B32 al-Balansī, Muḥammad ibn Ghālib, d. 1177? (Table P-PZ40)
7755.B8 al-Buṣīrī, 1213?-1296 (Table P-PZ40)
7755.F37 Fāriqī, al-Ḥasan ibn Asad, d. 1074 (Table P-PZ40)
7755.H27 Ḥamawī, Muslim ibn al-Khiḍr, d. 1146 (Table P-PZ40)
7755.H3 Ḥarīrī, 1054-1122 (Table P-PZ40)
7755.H35 Ḥayṣa Bayṣ, Sa'd ibn Muḥammad, d. 1179 (Table P-PZ40)
7755.H87 al-Ḥuṣrī, Abū al-Ḥasan 'Alī ibn 'Abd al-Ghanī, d. 1095 (Table P-PZ40)
7755.I175 Ibn al-'Arabī, 1165-1240 (Table P-PZ40)
7755.I176 Ibn al-'Ashtarkūnī, Muḥammad ibn Yūsuf, d. 1143 (Table P-PZ40)
7755.I177 Ibn al-'Athīr, Ḍiyā' al-Dīn Naṣr Allāh ibn Muḥammad, 1163-1239 (Table P-PZ40)
7755.I18 Ibn al-Fāriḍ, 'Umar ibn 'Alī, 1181 or 2-1235 (Table P-PZ40)
7755.I1834 Ibn al-Haddād, Muḥammad ibn Aḥmad, d. 1087 or 8 (Table P-PZ40)
7755.I1847 Ibn al-Jannān, Muḥammad ibn Muḥammad, 13th cent. (Table P-PZ40)
7755.I185 Ibn al-Jawzī, Abū al-Faraj 'Abd al-Raḥmān ibn 'Alī, ca. 1116-1201 (Table P-PZ40)
7755.I192 Ibn al-Muqarrab, 'Alī, 1176 or 7-1231 or 2 (Table P-PZ40)
7755.I193 Ibn al-Nabīh, 'Alī Muḥammad, d. 1222 (Table P-PZ40)

Arabic literature
Individual authors or works
Fourth Abbasid period, 1055-1258 -- Continued

7755.I1933 Ibn al-Qaysarānī, Muḥammad ibn Naṣr, 1085-1154 (Table P-PZ40)

7755.I1936 Ibn al-Qaysarani, Muḥammad ibn Ṭāhir, 1056-1113 (Table P-PZ40)

7755.I195 Ibn al-Zaqqāq, 'Alī ibn 'Aṭiyah, d. 1133 (Table P-PZ40)

7755.I198 Ibn Daftarkhān, 'Alī ibn Muḥammad, 1193-1257 (Table P-PZ40)

7755.I2 Ibn Ḥamdīs, 'Abd al-Jabbār ibn Abī Bakr, 1055 or 6-1132 or 3 (Table P-PZ40)

7755.I213 Ibn Ḥimyar, Muḥammad, d. 1253 (Table P-PZ40)

7755.I214 Ibn Hutaymal, al-Qāsim ibn'Alī, 13th cent. (Table P-PZ40)

7755.I217 Ibn Jubayr, Muḥammad ibn Aḥmad, 1145-1217 (Table P-PZ40)

7755.I22 Ibn Khafājah al-Andalūsī, Ibrahīm ibn Abī al-Fatḥ, 1058 or 9-1138 or 9 (Table P-PZ40)

7755.I223 Ibn Labbāl, 'Alī ibn Aṃad, 1114-1187 (Table P-PZ40)

7755.I225 Ibn Marj al-Kuḥl, Muḥammad ibn Idrīs, 1159-1236 (Table P-PZ40)

7755.I23 Ibn Matrūh, Yaḥyá ibn 'Isá, 1196-1251 (Table P-PZ40)

7755.I245 Ibn Qalāqis, Naṣr ibn 'Abd Allāh, 1137-1172 (Table P-PZ40)

7755.I25 Ibn Quzmān, Muḥammad ibn 'Abd al-Malik, ca. 1080-1160 (Table P-PZ40)

7755.I293 Ibn Sahl al-Isrā'īlī, Ibrāhīm, d. 1251 or 2 (Table P-PZ40)

7755.I2935 Ibn Sa'īd, Aḥmad ibn 'Abd al-Malik, d. 1163 (Table P-PZ40)

7755.I294 Ibn Sanā' al Mulk, Hibat Allāh ibn Ja'far, d. 1212 (Table P-PZ40)

7755.I297 Ibn 'Unayn, Muḥammad ibn Naṣr, 1154-1232 (Table P-PZ40)

7755.I3 Ibn Yakhluftan, Àbd al-Raḥmān, d. 1229 or 30 (Table P-PZ40)

7755.I33 Ibn Zuhr, Muḥammad ibn 'Abd al-Malik, ca. 1113-1198 or 9 (Table P-PZ40)

7755.K37 Kātib al-Iṣfahānī, 'Imād al-Dīn Muḥammad ibn Muḥammad, 1125-1201 (Table P-PZ40)

7755.M27 Makhzūmī, 'Alī ibn Muḥammad, 1156-1225 (Table P-PZ40)

7755.M8 al-Mu'tamid, King of Seville, 1039-1095 (Table P-PZ40)

7755.N73 Nubāhī, 'Abd Allāh ibn Ibrāhīm, d. 1160 (Table P-PZ40)

7755.Q27 Qāḍī al-Muhadhdhab, al-Ḥasan ibn 'Alī, d. 1166 (Table P-PZ40)

Arabic literature
Individual authors or works
Fourth Abbasid period, 1055-1258 -- Continued
7755.Q37 al-Qarṭājannī, Ḥāzim ibn Muḥammad, 1211 or 12-1285 (Table P-PZ40)
7755.R86 al-Rundī Abū al-Baqā, Sāliḥ ibn 'Alī, 1204-1285 or 6 (Table P-PZ40)
7755.S34 Satālī, Aḥmad ibn Sa'id, 1188-1277 or 8 (Table P-PZ40)
7755.S45 Shushtarī, Alī ibn 'Abd Allāh, 1213 or 14-1269 (Table P-PZ40)
7755.T37 Tarābulusī, Aḥmad ibn Munīr, 1080 or 81-1153 (Table P-PZ40)
7755.T8 al-Ṭughrā'ī, al-Ḥusayn ibn 'Alī, 1061 or 2-1121? (Table P-PZ40)
7755.Z3 Ẓāfir ibn al-Qāsim al-Ḥaddād, d. 1134 (Table P-PZ40)
7755.Z35 Zamakhsharī, Maḥmūd ibn Ùmar, 1075-1144 (Table P-PZ40)
7760 Mamlūk (Mameluke) period, 1258-1517
Subarrange by Table P40 or P41
7760.A36 Aḥmad ibn Mājid al-Sa'dī, fl. 1462-1498 (Table P-PZ40)
7760.A54 'Āmir ibn 'Āmir al-Baṣrī (Table P-PZ40)
7760.B28 Bahrām' shāh, al-Malik al-Amjad, d. 1321 (Table P-PZ40)
7760.B36 Basṭi, Muḥammad ibn 'Abd al-Karīm, 15th cent. (Table P-PZ40)
7760.H5 al-Hillī, Safī al-Dīn 'Abd al-'Azīz ibn Sārāya, b. 1278 (Table P-PZ40)
7760.I13 Ibn 'Abd al-Ẓāhir, Muḥyī al-Dīn, 223-1292 (Table P-PZ40)
7760.I134 Ibn Abī Ḥajalah, Aḥmad ibn Yaḥyá, 1325-1374 or 5 (Table P-PZ40)
7760.I14 Ibn al-Jayyāb, Abū al-Ḥasan 'Ali ibn Muḥammad, 1274-1349 (Table P-PZ40)
7760.I146 Ibn al-Khalūf, Aḥmad ibn Muhammad, 1425-1494 (Table P-PZ40)
7760.I15 Ibn al-Khaṭīb, d. 1374 (Table P-PZ40)
7760.I152 Ibn al-Muqrî, Ismāīl ibn Abī Bakr, 1354-1433 or 4 (Table P-PZ40)
7760.I154 Ibn al-Qilā'ī, Jibrā'il, 1447-1516 (Table P-PZ40)
7760.I16 Ibn al-Ṣayqal, Shams al-Dīn Ma'add ibn Muḥammad Naṣr Allāh, d. 1301 (Table P-PZ40)
7760.I174 Ibn al-Wardi, Zayn al-Din Umar ibn al-Muzaffar, d. 1349 (Table P-PZ40)
7760.I185 Ibn Dānīyāl, Muḥammad, 1249 or 50-1310 or 11 (Table P-PZ40)
7760.I217 Ibn Habīb al-Halabī, Badr al-Dīn al-Hasan ibn 'Umar, 1332-1377 (Table P-PZ40)
7760.I2443 Ibn Iyās, 1448-ca. 1524 (Table P-PZ40)

Arabic literature
Individual authors or works
Mamlūk (Mameluke)
period, 1258-1517 -- Continued

7760.I2454 Ibn Khātimah, Aḥmad ibn 'Alī, 1324-ca. 1369 (Table P-PZ40)

7760.I246 Ibn Nubātah, Muḥammad ibn Muḥammad, 1287-1366 (Table P-PZ40)

7760.I265 Ibn Sayyid al-Nās, Muḥammad ibn Muḥammad, 1273?-1334 (Table P-PZ40)

7760.I275 Ibn Sūdūn al-Bashbughāwī, 'Alī, 1407 or 8-1464 (Table P-PZ40)

7760.I3 Ibn Zumruk, Muḥammad ibn Yuṣaf, 14th cent. (Table P-PZ40)

7760.N25 Nabahānī, Sulaymān ibn Sulaymān ibn Muẓaffar, d. ca. 1505 (Table P-PZ40)

7760.S48 Sīrat al-Ẓāhir Baybars (Table P-PZ40)

7760.S5 Sīrat Sauf ibn Dhī Yazan (Table P-PZ40)

7760.S89 Suyūṭī, 1445-1505 (Table P-PZ40)

7760.T54 Tilimsānī, Afīf al-Dīn Sulaymān ibn 'Ali, d. 1291 (Table P-PZ40)

7765 Turkish period, 1517-1800
Subarrange by Table P40 or P41

7765.B39 Barakāt ibn Mubārak, d. 1615 (Table P-PZ40)

7765.B45 Bilfaqīh, 'Abd al-Raḥmān ibn 'Abd Allāh, d. ca. 1749 (Table P-PZ40)

7765.F36 Fatḥ Allāh, 'Abd al-Laṭīf, 1766-1844 (Table P-PZ40)

7765.G45 Ghurāb, 'Ali ibn Muḥammad, d. 1770? (Table P-PZ40)

7765.H27 Habal, al-Hasan ibn 'Alī, 1639-1668 (Table P-PZ40)

7765.H52 Ḥifẓī, Aḥmad ibn 'Abd al-Qādir, 1732-1818 (Table P-PZ40)

7765.H54 al-Hilālī, Muḥammad ibn Najm al-Dīn, 1549 or 50-1603 or 4 (Table P-PZ40)

7765.I28 Ibn al-Naḥḥās, Fatḥ Allāh ibn 'Abd Allāh, d. 1642 or 3 (Table P-PZ40)

7765.I3 Ibn Rāzigah, 'Abd Allāh ibn Muhammad, ca. 1650-1731 (Table P-PZ40)

7765.J34 Jalāl al-Yamanī, al-Ḥasan ibn Aḥmad, 1605-1673 (Table P-PZ40)

7765.K43 Khalāwī, Rāshid, 17th/18th cent. (Table P-PZ40)

7765.L37 Lawwāḥ al-Kharūṣī, Sālim ibn Ghassān, 1489 or 90-1573 or 4 (Table P-PZ40)

7765.M34 Ma'ūlī, Muḥammad ibn 'Abd Allāh (Table P-PZ40)

7765.N32 Nābulusī, 'Abd al-Ghanī ibn Ismā'īl, 1641-1731 (Table P-PZ40)

7765.R59 Riyāḥī, Ibrāhīm ibn 'Abd al-Qādir, 1766 or 7-1849 or 50 (Table P-PZ40)

7765.S58 Shuway'ir, Ḥamīdān, 18th cent. (Table P-PZ40)

7765.S64 Sidi Cheikh, 1533 or 4-1616 (Table P-PZ40)

7765.T34 Ṭāluwī, Darwīsh Muḥammad ibn Aḥmad, 1543 or 4-1606 (Table P-PZ40)

Arabic literature
Individual authors or works
Turkish period, 1517-1800 -- Continued
7765.W37 Warghi, Muḥammad ibn Aḥmad, d. 1776 (Table P-PZ40)
Modern, 1801-
7800 Anonymous works
7802 A - 'Abd
Subarranged by Table P40 or P41
7804 'Abd al-
e.g.
Cutter A-Z by letter following "'Abd al-"
Subarranged by Table P40 or P41
7804.B3 'Abd-al Bāqī Samīr (Table P-PZ40)
7804.Q4 'Abd-al Qādir ibn Muḥyī al-Dīn, Amir of Mascara, 1807?-1883 (Table P-PZ40)
7805 'Abd Allāh
e.g.
Cutter A-Z by letter following "'Abd Allāh"
Subarranged by Table P40 or P41
7805.F3 'Abd Allāh, Fāris (Table P-PZ40)
7805.6 'Abd B - 'Abd Z
e.g.
Cutter A-Z by letter following "'Abd"
Subarranged by Table P40 or P41
7805.6.R3 'Abd Rabbih, 'Abd al-Azīz (Table P-PZ40)
7805.8 'Abda - 'Abdz
e.g.
Cutter A-Z by letter following "'Abd"
Subarranged by Table P40 or P41
7805.8.U4 'Abduh, Ibrāhīm (Table P-PZ40)
7806 'Abe - 'Abt
e.g.
Cutter A-Z by letter following "'Ab"
Subarranged by Table P40 or P41
7806.I3 'Abid, 'Izrā Minashshī (Table P-PZ40)
7808 Abū
e.g.
Including all authors of this period whose last names are some form of this word. Cutter under the next portion of their names
Subarranged by Table P40 or P41
7808.A37 Abū al-Hudā al-Sayyādī, Muḥammad ibn Ḥasan, 1850-1909 or 10 (Table P-PZ40)
7810 Abua - 'Alh
e.g.
Subarranged by Table P40 or P41
Adūnīs, 1930- , see PJ7862.A519
7810.I8 'A'ishah al-Taymūrīyah, 1840-1902 (Table P-PZ40)

Arabic literature
Individual authors or works
Modern, 1801- -- Continued
7812 'Ali
Class here authors of this period whose last names consist of the single word "Ali." Cutter under the next portion of their name
Subarranged by Table P40 or P41
7813 'Ali A - 'Ali Z
Class here authors of this period who have compound names beginning with the word "Ali." Cutter under the second part of the name using an additional digit for the author's first name
Subarranged by Table P40 or P41
7814 'Alia - Az
Subarranged by Table P40 or P41
7816 B
e.g.
Subarranged by Table P40 or P41
7816.A457 al-Bājī al-Mas'ūdī, Abū 'Abd Allāh Muḥammad, 1810 or 11-1880 (Table P-PZ40)
7818 C
Subarranged by Table P40 or P41
7818.H6 Choukri, Mohamed, 1935- (Table P-PZ40)
7820 D
Subarranged by Table P40 or P41
7820.A54 Danqal, Amal (Table P-PZ40)
Dunqul, Amal, d. 1983, see PJ7820.A54
7822 E
Subarranged by Table P40 or P41
7824 F
Subarranged by Table P40 or P41
7826 G
Subarranged by Table P40 or P41
7828 H - Hasam
e.g.
7828.D228 al-Ḥaddād, Najīb ibn Sulaymān, 1867-1899 (Table P-PZ40)
7828.D6 al-Ḥadramī, Sa'īd ibn 'Ubayd, 1799-1873 (Table P-PZ40)
7828.F5 Ḥāfiẓ Ibrāhīm, Muḥammad, 1872?-1932 (Table P-PZ40)
7830 Hasan
Including all authors of this period whose last names are some form of this word. Cutter under the next portion of their names
Subarranged by Table P-PZ40 or P-PZ41
7832 Hasana - Hz
e.g.
Subarranged by Table P-PZ40 or P-PZ41
(7832.U7125) Ḥusayn, Ṭāhā
see PJ7864.A35

Arabic literature
Individual authors or works
Modern, 1801- -- Continued

7834 I - Ibm
Subarranged by Table P40 or P41

7836 Ibn
e.g.
Subarrange individual authors by Table P-PZ40
Subarrange individual works by Table P-PZ43
Including all authors of this period whose last names are some form of this word. Cutter under the next portion of their names

7836.L33 Ibn La'būn, Muḥummad ibn Ḥamad, d. 1831 or 32 (Table P-PZ40)

7836.M84 Ibn Muḥummad, Muḥammad al. Bashīr, 1789 or 90-1872 or 3 (Table P-PZ40)

7836.R89 Ibn Ruzayq, Ḥamīd ibn Muḥammad, d. 1873 (Table P-PZ40)

7836.U43 Ibn 'Udayyim, Nāṣir ibn Sālim, d. 1916 (Table P-PZ40)

7836.U85 Ibn 'Uthaymīn, Muḥammad ibn 'Abd Allāh, 1853 or 4-1944 (Table P-PZ40)

7838 Ibna - Iz
Subarranged by Table P40 or P41

7840 J
e.g.
Subarranged by Table P40 or P41

7840.A385 Jalāl, Muḥammad 'Uthmān, 1829-1898 (Table P-PZ40)

7840.U34 Judayy, Salīm Naṣr Allāh, 1869-1895 (Table P-PZ40)

7842 K
e.g.
Subarranged by Table P40 or P41

7842.A87 Al-Kāẓimī, 'Abd al-Muḥsin, 1865-1935 (Table P-PZ40)

7844 L
Subarranged by Table P40 or P41

7846 M - Muḥammad
Subarranged by Table P40 or P41

7848 Muḥammad
Includes Mahomet, Mehemet, Mohammed, etc.
Including all authors of this period whose last names are some form of this word. Cutter under the next portion of their names
Subarranged by Table P40 or P41

Arabic literature
Individual authors or works
Modern, 1801- -- Continued

7849 Muḥammad A - Muḥammad Z
e.g.
Including authors of this period who have compound names beginning with this word. Cutter under the second part of the name using an additional digit for the author's first name
Subarranged by Table P40 or P41

7849.A42 Muḥammad 'Ali, 'Abbu (Table P-PZ40)

7850 Muhammae -Mz
e.g.
Subarranged by Table P40 or P41

7850.U87 Muṭran, Khalil, 1872-1949 (Table P-PZ40)

7852 N
e.g.
Subarranged by Table P40 or P41

7852.A3 Nadīm, 'Abd Allāh, 1845-1896 (Table P-PZ40)

7854 O
Subarranged by Table P40 or P41

7856 P
Subarranged by Table P40 or P41

7858 Q
e.g.
Subarranged by Table P40 or P41

7858.A14 Qābādū, Abū al-Thanā 'Maḥmūd, d. 1871 (Table P-PZ40)

7858.A38 Qalfat, Nakhlah, 1851-1905 (Table P-PZ40)

7860 R
e.g.
Subarranged by Table P40 or P41

7860.A318 al-Rāfi'ī, 'Abd al-Ḥamīd, 1859-1932 (Table P-PZ40)

7862 S
e.g.
Subarranged by Table P40 or P41

7862.A274 Ṣabrī, Ismā'īl, 1854-1923 (Table P-PZ40)

7862.A275 Ṣabrī, Ismā'īl, 1886-1953 (Table P-PZ40)

7862.A519 Sa'īd, 'Alī Aḥmad (Table P-PZ40)

7862.A614 Sanūsī, Muḥammad ibn 'Uthmān, 1850?-1900 (Table P-PZ40)

7862.A777 Ṣarrūf, Ya'qūb, 1852-1927 (Table P-PZ40)

7862.A99 Sayyid Ḥāfiz (Table P-PZ40)

7862.H163 al-Shabībī, Muḥammad Jawād, 1864-1944 (Table P-PZ40)

7862.H3 Shawqī, Ahmad, 1868-1932 (Table P-PZ40)

7862.H48 Shidyāq, Aḥmad Fāris, 1804?-1887 (Table P-PZ40)

7862.H5 Shihāb al-Dīn Muḥammad ibn Ismā'īl, 1795 or 6-1857 or 8 (Table P-PZ40)

Shukrī, Muḥammad, 1935- , see PJ7818.H6

Arabic literature
Individual authors or works
Modern, 1801- -- Continued
7864 T
e.g.
Subarranged by Table P40 or P41
7864.A35 Ṭāhā Ḥusayn, 1889-1973 (Table P-PZ40)
7864.A365 al-Ṭahtawi, Rifa'ah Rafi, 1801-1873 (Table P-PZ40)
7864.A375 al-Tālaqānī, Mūsá, 1815-1881 (Table P-PZ40)
7864.U95 Ṭuwayr, 'Abd al-Laṭīf, d. 1785 (Table P-PZ40)
7866 U
e.g.
Subarranged by Table P40 or P41
Ūzūrīs, see PJ7862.A99
7868 V
Subarranged by Table P40 or P41
7870 W
Subarranged by Table P40 or P41
7872 X
Subarranged by Table P40 or P41
7874 Y
e.g.
Subarranged by Table P40 or P41
7874.A88 al-Yāzijī, Ibrāhīm, 1847-1906 (Table P-PZ40)
7874.A89 Yāzijī, Khalīl, 1856-1889 (Table P-PZ40)
7874.A9 al-Yāzijī, Nāṣīf, 1800-1871 (Table P-PZ40)
7876 Z
e.g.
Subarranged by Table P40 or P41
7876.A35 al-Zahāwī, Jamīl Ṣidqī, 1863?-1936 (Table P-PZ40)
7876.A647 Zangana, Haifa, 1950- (Table P-PZ40)
Zankanah, Hayfā', 1950, see PJ7876.A647
Zazaf, Muḥammad, see PJ7876.I4
7876.I4 Zifzāf, Muḥammad (Table P-PZ40)
By region or country
Arabian Peninsula
8000 General works (Table P-PZ25)
Special countries
For individual authors, see PJ7695.8+
8001 Bahrain (Table P-PZ25)
8002 Kuwait (Table P-PZ25)
8003 Oman (Table P-PZ25)
8004 Qatar (Table P-PZ25)
8005 Saudi Arabia (Table P-PZ25)
8006 United Arab Emirates (Table P-PZ25)
8007 Yemen (Yemen Arab Republic) (Table P-PZ25)
8008 Yemen (People's Dem. Rep.) (Table P-PZ25)
Arabic literature outside the Arabian Peninsula
8020 General
Special
For individual authors, see PJ7695.8+

Arabic literature
By region or country
Arabic literature outside the Arabian Peninsula
Special -- Continued
Asia
8025 General works
8030-8047 Iraq (Table P-PZ23 modified)
8050-8067 Jordan (Table P-PZ23 modified)
8070-8087 Lebanon (Table P-PZ23 modified)
8090-8107 Syria (Table P-PZ23 modified)
8110-8127 Iran (Table P-PZ23 modified)
8130-8147 Pakistan (Table P-PZ23 modified)
8150-8167 India (Table P-PZ23 modified)
8170-8187 Indonesia (Table P-PZ23 modified)
8190 Palestine. Israel (Table P-PZ25)
8192.A-Z Other, A-Z
Africa
8195 General works
8200-8217 Egypt (Table P-PZ23 modified)
8220-8237 Libya. Tripoli (Table P-PZ23 modified)
8240-8257 Tunis (Table P-PZ23 modified)
8260-8277 Algeria (Table P-PZ23 modified)
8280-8297 Morocco (Table P-PZ23 modified)
8300-8317 Sudan (Table P-PZ23 modified)
8360-8377 Zanzibar (Table P-PZ23 modified)
8390.A-Z Other, A-Z
Europe
8395 General works
8400-8417 Spain (Table P-PZ23 modified)
8420-8437 Sicily (Table P-PZ23 modified)
8440-8457 Malta (Table P-PZ23 modified)
8490.A-Z Other, A-Z
8500-8517 America (Table P-PZ23 modified)
Ethiopian languages
Class here works on the Semitic languages of Ethiopia
Cf. PJ2401+, Cushitic languages
8991-8999 General (Table P-PZ8a)
Special
Ethiopic (Geez)
Philology (Table P-PZ4)
9001 Periodicals. Societies. Serials
Collections
Texts. Sources, etc , see PJ9090+
Minor. Chrestomathies, see PJ9025
9003 Monographs. Studies
9007 History of philology
(9008) Bibliography
see Z
(9009) Biography
see PJ63-P64J, PJ3009
9011 Study and teaching
9014-9087 Language (Table P-PZ4)
9014 Treatises (General and General special)

Ethiopian languages
Special
Ethiopic (Geez)
Language -- Continued
9017 Script
Grammar
9019 Treatises in Ethiopic
Treatises in other languages. Compends (Advanced)
9020 Early to 1800
9021 1801-
9023 Elementary. Introductory
9025 Readers. Chrestomathies
Phonology
Cf. PJ9017, Script
9028 General works
9031 Pronunciation
9032 Accent
Morphology. Inflection. Accidence
9039 General works
9040 Word formation. Derivation. Suffixes, etc.
Noun. Verb, etc , see PJ9049+
9047 Tables. Paradigms
Parts of speech (Morphology and syntax)
9049 Miscellaneous
9051 Noun
9053 Adjective
9059 Pronoun
9061 Verb
9067 Particle. Adverb
9071 Syntax
9073 Grammatical usage of particular authors
9075 Style. Rhetoric
9081 Prosody. Metrics. Rhythmics
9083 Etymology
9087.A-Z Dictionaries. By author, A-Z
Literature
9090 History and criticism
9093 Special topics
Texts
9095 Inscriptions
9096 Collections (General and miscellaneous)
9097 Bible. Apocryphal books
Cf. BS115.A+, Early version
9098 Theological and ascetic literature
9099 Other
Including folk literature
9101.A-Z Translations of Ethiopic literature, A-Z (without original text)
9111 Tigrinya (Table P-PZ15a)
9131 Tigré (Table P-PZ15)
Amharic
9201-9250 Language (Table P-PZ5)

Ethiopian languages
Special
Amharic -- Continued
9260-9269 Literature (Table P-PZ24)
9269.A-Z Individual authors or works, A-Z
9269.A36 Afevork Ghevre Jesus, 1868-1947 (Table P-PZ24)
9269.G27 Gắbrắ-Egziabehér Gilay, ca. 1860-ca. 1914 (Table P-PZ24)
9280 Argobba (Table P-PZ15a)
9285 Gafat
9288 Gurage (Table P-PZ15a)
9293 Harari (Table P-PZ15)
(9500) Extinct languages of Western Asia of unknown or disputed relationship
see P901+

Indo-Iranian philology and literature
Indo-Iranian
General
Philology
1 Periodicals. Societies. Serials
Collections
Texts. Sources, see PK81
Monographs. Studies
2.A-Z3 Various authors. Series
2.Z5 Studies in honor of a particular person or institution, A-Z
3 Individual authors
5 Philosophy. Theory. Method. Relations
7 History of philology
Biography
9.A2 Collective
9.A3-Z Individual, A-Z
(10) Bibliography. Bio-bibliography
see Z7046+, Z7049.I6, Z7090, Z7101
Study and teaching
11 By region or country
13 By university, college, etc.
14 Encyclopedias. Dictionaries
15 Treatises (including history of Indo-Iranian languages)
For the languages here comprised, see PK101+
16 Compends
17 Criticism. Controversial discourses, reviews, etc.
18 Popular (Lectures, addresses, pamphlets, etc.)
19 Alphabet
Cf. PK119, Indo-Aryan
Cf. PK6102+, Iranian
Cf. PK6150, Middle Iranian
(20) Transliteration
see P226
Languages
21 Grammar
23 Phonology
27 Morphology. Inflection. Accidence
31 Word formation. Suffixes, etc.
Parts of speech (Morphology and syntax)
33 Noun. Adjective. Pronoun. Article. Numerals
35 Verb
41 Syntax
51 Style. Rhetoric
61 Prosody. Metrics. Rhythmics
65 Etymology. Semantics
Lexicography
71 Treatises
Dictionaries
75 General

Indo-Iranian
General
Languages
Lexicography
Dictionaries -- Continued
77 Special. Technical, etc.
79 Linguistic geography. Dialects
Literature
80 History and criticism
81 Collections
85 Translations
Indo-Aryan
101-118 Philology
Subdivide like PK1-PK18
119 Alphabet. Writing
Class here treatises restricted to the various types of writing used in the Indic languages, Kharosthi; Brahmi, and its derivatives, Gupta, Nagari, Devanagari, Bengali, Kaithi, etc.
Cf. P211+, Linguistics
Cf. PJ3019+, Semitic philology
Cf. PL1+
For the Tibeto-Burman and Tai scripts, see PL
119.5 Indus script
(120) Transliteration
see P226
121-185 Languages
Subdivide like PK21-PK85
Vedic
Philology
(201) Periodicals. Societies
see PK101
Collections
207 Serial
208 Studies in honor of a particular person or institution, A-Z
209 Individual authors
(211-220) Study and teaching. Encyclopedias, etc.
see PK111
Language (Table P-PZ3)
223 Treatises: History, relations, etc.
Cf. PK15, Indo-Iranian (General)
Cf. PK423, Sanskrit
Grammar
231 Comprehensive works. Compends (Advanced)
235 Elementary. Introductory
237 Readers. Chrestomathies
240 Phonology. Phonetics
243 Accentuation
245 Sandhi
259 Morphology. Inflection. Accidence
261 Word formation. Derivation. Suffixes
Parts of speech (Morphology and syntax)

Vedic
  Language
    Grammar
      Parts of speech (Morphology and syntax) -- Continued
270 Miscellaneous
271 Noun
273 Gender
274 Number
275 Case
276 Miscellaneous
277 Adjective
279 Numerals
281 Article
283 Pronoun
285 Verb
291 Mood
295 Tense
299 Miscellaneous
301 Particle
303 Adverb
305 Preposition
307 Conjunction
309 Interjection
313 Syntax
335 Style. Composition. Rhetoric
353 Prosody. Metrics. Rhythmics
361 Etymology
362 Names
363 Dictionaries (exclusively etymological)
364.A-Z Foreign elements, A-Z
365 Semantics
367 Synonyms. Homonyms
369 Particular words
Lexicography
373 Treatises
Dictionaries
375 Ancient
e. g.
375.N5 Nighantu
375.Y3 Yasha's Nirukta
379 Modern
Literature, see BL1112.2+
Sanskrit
Philology
401-418 Generalities: Periodicals. Societies, etc.
Divide like PK1-PK18
419 Alphabet
Cf. PK119, Indo-Aryan
420 Transliteration
Language
423 Treatises: History, relations, etc.
Study and teaching

	Sanskrit
	Language
	Study and teaching -- Continued
435	General
438.A-Z	By region or country, A-Z
439.A-Z	By school, university, etc., A-z
	Grammar (Vyākarana)
	Oriental authors
	Treatises in Sanskrit
475	Philosophy. Theory. Methodology
501	Collections and selections
505	Kātyāyana (3d or 2d cent. B.C.?). Vāttika
	Pṇini
	Aṣṭādhyāyī
511	Editions. By date
512	Translations and commentaries
	Eastern languages
513	Sanskrit. By author
515.A-Z	Other, A-Z
	Western languages
517.A-Z	Translations. By translator, A-Z
519	Works about Pāṇini and his grammar
521	Doubtful and spurious works
531	Pantañjali. Mahābhāṣya
531.A1	Editions. By date
531.A2-A6	Translations. By language
531.A7-Z	Criticism
541.A-Z	Other, A-Z
551	Minor (Specific treatises)
	e.g. Lingānuāsanas (on gender). Uṇādisūtras (derivation of nouns from verbs by means of suffixes)
(571)	Treatises in Prakrit
575	Treatises in modern Indo-Aryan languages
	Prefer the native languages for original texts
585.A-Z	Treatises in other Oriental languages, A-Z
	e. g.
585.J3	Japanese
653-669	Western authors (Table P-PZ2)
	Including works in English by Oriental authors
653	Theory. Methodology
654	Terminology. Nomenclature
655	History (of grammatical studies)
	Comprehensive works. Compends (Advanced)
663.A2	Early to 1875 (completion of Böthling's Dictionary)
663.A5-Z	Later, 1875-
(665)	Historical. Comparative
	see PK663
666	Introductory. Elementary
	Subdivide like PK663
669	Readers. Chrestomathies
673	Examinations, questions, etc.

Sanskrit
Language
Grammar (Vyākarana) -- Continued
676 Phonology
677 Phonetics
679 Pronunciation
681 Accent. Accentuation
682 Sandhi (Euphonic combinations of sounds in the sentence)
689 Alphabet
Cf. PK119, Indo-Aryan
691 Vowels. Diphthongs (Guṇa. Vṛddhi)
693 Consonants
694 Contraction (Hiatus, Elision)
695 Particular letters
e.g. Visarga; Anusvāra
701 Morphology. Inflection. Accidence
703 Word formation. Derivation. Suffixes, etc.
Noun, verb, etc , see PK721
711 Tables. Paradigms
Parts of speech (Morphology and syntax)
719 Miscellaneous
721 Noun
725 Gender
727 Number
729 Case
733 Adjective
735 Numerals
741 Pronouns
745 Verb
747 Person
749 Number
751 Voice
753 Mood
759 Tense
762 Infinitive. Participle
764 Participle, gerund, etc.
771 Particles
801 Syntax
811 Sentence
840 Style. Rhetoric
868 Translating
Prosody. Metrics. Rhythmics
871 History of the science
875 Treatises
885.A-Z Special. By form, A-Z
Etymology
901 Treatises
903 Names
905 Dictionaries (exclusively etymological)
906 List of roots
For works in Sanskrit, see PK925
907.A-Z Foreign elements, A-Z

Sanskrit
Language
Etymology -- Continued
910 Semantics
915 Synonyms. Homonyms
For works in Sanskrit, see PK925
919 Particular words
Lexicography
920 Collections
923 General works: History. Treatises
924 Criticism of particular dictionaries (By author or title of dictionary, A-Z)
Dictionaries
925 Sanskrit (only)
926 Polyglot
Class here equivalents in two or more languages arranged in columns, Sanskrit coming first
For others, see P361+
927.A-Z Sanskrit-Indo-Aryan, A-Z
e. g.
927.B4 Sanskrit-Bengali
Sanskrit-Indo-European
930 Polyglot
Prefer P765
931 Iranian (Avesta or Zend; Pahlavī; Persian)
Cf. PK6075, Iranian philology
European
933.A-Z English. By author, A-Z
935.A-Z Other Western European, A-Z
e. g.
935.G5 Sanskrit-German
935.L3 Sanskrit-Latin
937.A-Z Slavic, A-Z
e. g.
937.R8 Sanskrit-Russian
Sanskrit-Oriental
941.A-Z Dravidian. By language and author, A-Z
943.A-Z Malayan. By language and author, A-Z
945.A-Z Tibeto-Burman. By language and author, A-Z
946 Ural-Altaic
East Asian
947 Chinese
949 Korean
951 Japanese
Special
961 Particular authors
Prefer author or work in Sanskrit literature
963 Names
965 Terms and phrases, and other miscellaneous lists
969 Technical terms
Linguistic geography. Dialects, etc.

Sanskrit
Language
Linguistic geography.
Dialects, etc. -- Continued
974 General works
976.A-Z Local. by region, place, etc., A-Z
Literature, see PK2901+
Pali
Philology (Table P-PZ4)
1001 Periodicals. Societies. Yearbooks
Collections
Texts. Sources, etc , see PK4541+
Monographs. Studies
1002.A-Z3 Serial
1002.Z5A-Z Studies in honor of a particular person or institution, A-Z
1003 Individual authors
1004 Encyclopedias. Dictionaries
1006 Philosophy. Theory. Method
1007 History of philology
(1008) Bibliography. Bio-bibliography
see Z7090
1009 Biography. Memoirs. Correspondence
Study and teaching
1011 General works
1012 By country, university, etc.
1013 General works
Including treatises on the Pali language: History, relations, etc.
1015 Alphabet
Prefer PK119
(1016) Transliteration
see P226
Language
Treatises (General), see PK1013
Grammar
Eastern authors
1017 Treatises in Pali
e. g. Kaccāyana
1018.A-Z Treatises in other Oriental languages, A-Z
1020 Treatises in Western languages by Oriental authors
Western authors
Historical and comparative grammar, see PK1021
1021 Comprehensive works. Compends (Advanced)
1023 Elementary. Introductory
1025 Readers. Chrestomathies
1028 Phonology. Phonetics
1039 Morphology. Inflection. Accidence
1040 Word formation. Derivation. Suffixes, etc.
Cf. PK1049+, Parts of speech
Noun, verb, etc , see PK1049+
1047 Tables. Paradigms

Pali
Language
Grammar
Western authors -- Continued
Parts of speech (Morphology and syntax)
1049 Noun
1051 Adjective
1053 Adverb
1059 Pronoun
1061 Verb
1067 Particle
1071 Syntax
1073 Particular authors or works
1077 Style. Rhetoric
1081 Prosody. Metrics. Rhythmics
1083 Etymology
1084 Names
1085 Dictionaries (exclusively etymological)
Prefer PK1089 for works in Pali
1085.9 Lists of roots
1086 Synonyms. Homonyms
For works in Pali see PK1089
Lexicography
1087 Collections
1088 Treatises
Dictionaries
1089 Pali (only)
Including Moggallāna with interpretive works in other languages
1090.A-Z Pali-Eastern languages, A-Z
Pali-Western languages
1091 English
1093.A-Z Other, A-Z
1095 Special dictionaries
Literature, see PK4501+
Prakrit languages (Table P-PZ6)
1201 Periodicals. Societies. Collections
1203 General works. History of philology. Biography
(1203.9) Bibliography. Bio-bibliography
see Z7090
1204 Languages (History, relations, etc.)
1205 Study and teaching
Grammar
1206 Treatises in Eastern languages
1207 Treatises in Western languages
1208 Readers. Chrestomathies
1209 Phonology
(1211) Alphabet
see PK119
(1212) Transliteration
see P226
1213 Morphology. Inflection. Accidence
1214 Parts of speech (Morphology and syntax)

PK

Prakrit languages
Grammar -- Continued
1215 Syntax
1217 Style. Rhetoric
1219 Prosody. Metrics. Rhythmics
1221 Etymology
Lexicography
Dictionaries
1223 Prakrit and Eastern languages
1225 Prakrit and Western languages
1227 Provincialisms (Dēsya or Dēsī; Tatsamas; Tadbhavas)
Class here modern treatises and collections only
Cf. PK1221, Etymology
For the works by native scholars, see PK1206, PK1223
Special Prakrit languages
Subdivide each language by Table P-PZ8a omitting no. 8
1231-1239 Māhārāshtrī
1251-1259 Ardhamāgadhī
"Half-Māghadī," language of the canonical works of the Svētāmbara Jainas
Cf. PK5001+, Jaina literature
1271-1279 Jaina-Māhārāshtrī
Language of the non-canonical works of the Svētāmbara
1301-1309 Saurasēnī
1321-1329 Māgadhī
Cf. PK1480+, Asoka inscriptions
1341-1349 Dhakkī
1361-1369 Avantī
1401-1409 Pāiśacī
Cf. PK7001+, Dardic languages
Prakrit literature, see PK4990+
1421-1429 Apabhramsa (Table P-PZ8a)
1428 Literature (Table P-PZ15)
1428.9.A-Z Individual authors or works, A-Z (Table P-PZ40 or P-PZ43)
1428.9.A2 Abdularahamāna, 11th cent. (Table P-PZ40)
1428.9.D45 Dhāhila, 9th/10th cent. (Table P-PZ40)
1428.9.H27 Haribhadra Sūri, 12th cent. (Table P-PZ40)
1428.9.H4 Hemacandra, 1088-1172 (Table P-PZ40)
1428.9.N37 Narasenadeva (Table P-PZ40)
1428.9.P87 Puspadanta, 10th cent. (Table P-PZ40)
1428.9.R34 Raidhū, fl. 1383-1453 (Table P-PZ40)
1428.9.S15 Sādhāraṇa, 11th cent. (Table P-PZ40)
1428.9.S2 Sarahapāḍa, 8th cent. (Table P-PZ40)
1428.9.V5 Vibudha Śrīdhara, 12th cent. (Table P-PZ40)
1428.9.Y38 Yaśaḥkīrti, 13th cent. (Table P-PZ40)
1441-1449 Avahaṭṭha (Table P-PZ8a)
1448 Literature (Table P-PZ15)

Avahaṭṭha
Literature -- Continued
1448.9.A-Z Individual authors or works, A-Z
Subarrange individual authors by Table P-PZ40
Subarrange individual works by Table P-PZ43
1448.9.V53 Vidyāpati, Ṭhākura, 15th cent. (Table P-PZ40)
1469 Buddhist Hybrid Sanskrit
1470 Epigraphical Hybrid Sanskrit
Middle Indo-Aryan dialects
1471 General works
1472 Grammar
Asoka inscriptions
1480 Editions
Class here editions intended for linguistic study
For historical treatises, see DS451.5
1485 Translations
1488 Language
1490 Other
e. g. Cave inscriptions ("Lena" dialect)
Cf. R. Pischel, Grammatik der Prakritsprachen, Strassburg, 1900, p. 5
1501-2899 Modern Indo-Aryan languages (Table P-PZ5)
Class here works restricted to the modern Indo-Aryan languages, also works dealing with both Aryan and non-Aryan languages, unless decided preference is given to the latter, e. g. the "Linguistic survey of India" is classed here, with shelflist reference in PL and P381
For the Generalities: Periodicals. Societies, etc. (PK1501-1507), see PK101+, if not exclusively dealing with the modern Indo-Aryan languages
1501 Periodicals. Societies. Yearbooks
Collections
1502.A1 Texts. Sources, specimens, etc. By date of publication
Cf. PK1513, Readers
1502.A5-Z Monographs. Studies
(1503) Atlases. Maps. Charts
see PK1541.A1
1504 Philosophy. Theory. Method
1505 History of philology
(1506) Biography
see PK109
(1506.9) Bibliography. Bio-bibliography
see Z7049.I3
1507 Study and teaching
1508 General works
1509 History of languages
1510 Alphabet. Writing
Prefer P211; PK119
(1510.9) Transliteration
see P226
Grammar

PK

Modern Indo-Aryan languages
Grammar -- Continued
1511 Comprehensive works. Compends (Advanced)
1512 Elementary. Introductory
1513 Chrestomathies. Readers
1514 Terminology
1515 Phonology. Phonetics
1519 Morphology. Inflection. Accidence
1521 Parts of speech: Noun, verb, etc. (Morphology and syntax)
1523 Syntax
1527 Style. Rhetoric
1528 Translating
1529 Prosody. Metrics. Rhythmics
1531 Etymology
Lexicography
1535 Treatises
1537 Dictionaries
1539 Special. Technical, etc.
Linguistic geography
1541.A1 Atlases. Maps. Charts, etc. By date of publication
1541.A5-Z Treatises
1545 Dialects. Provincialisms, etc.
Particular languages and dialects, A-Z
Antarbēdī, see PK1941+
Asāmī, see PK1550+
Assamese
Language
1550.A1-A5 Periodicals. Societies. Collections
1550.A6-Z General works
1550.5 Alphabet. Transliteration
Cf. PK119, Indo-Aryan
Grammar
1551 Treatises
1552 General special
1553 Textbooks
Including exercises, phrase books, readers
1554 Style. Rhetoric
1555 Etymology
Dictionaries
1555.2 Assamese
1555.4 Polyglot
1556 English
1557.A-Z Other languages, A-Z
1559.A-Z Dialects, A-Z
1559.K36 Kāmrūpī
1559.M3 Mayāng (Bishnupuriyā)
1560-1569 Literature (Table P-PZ24)
1569.A-Z Individual authors or works, A-Z (Table P-PZ40, or P-PZ43)
e. g.

Modern Indo-Aryan languages
Particular languages and dialects, A-Z
Assamese
Literature
Individual authors or works, A-Z -- Continued

1569.A34 Āgarawālā, Ānandacandra, 1874-1940 (Table P-PZ40)
1569.A49 Ājāna Phakira, 17th cent. (Table P-PZ40)
1569.A52 Ananta Ācāryya, fl. 1714-1744 (Table P-PZ40)
1569.A53 Ananta Kandalī, 16th cent. (Table P-PZ40)
1569.B16 Baikuṇṭhanātha, Bhāgawata-Bhaṭṭācārya, ca. 1558-1638 (Table P-PZ40)
1569.B212 Baladewa Sūryakhari Daiwajña, 18th cent. (Table P-PZ40)
Barā, Mahima, 1926- , see PK1569.B623
Baragohāñi Nirupamā, 1932- , see PK1569.B266
1569.B266 Bargohain, Nirupama (Table P-PZ40)
1569.B29 Barua, Bireswar (Table P-PZ40)
1569.B3 Barua, Navakanta, 1926- (Table P-PZ40)
Baruwā, Bīreśwara, see PK1569.B29
1569.B3244 Baruwā, Hemacandra, 1835-1896 (Table P-PZ40)
Baruwā, Nawakānta, 1926- , see PK1569.B3
1569.B39 Bezbarua, Lakshminath, 1868-1938 (Table P-PZ40)
Bhūñā, Nakulacandra, 1895-1968, see PK1569.B5
1569.B5 Bhuyan, Nakul Chandra, 1895-1968 (Table P-PZ40)
1569.B623 Bora, Mahim, 1926- (Table P-PZ40)
Calihā, Saurabha Kumāra, 1933- , see PK1569.C55
1569.C55 Chaliha, Saurav Kumar (Table P-PZ40)
1569.C57 Choudhuri, Ramkanta, 1846-1889 (Table P-PZ40)
1569.D22 Das, Jogesh, 1927- (Table P-PZ40)
Dāsa, Yogeśa, 1927- , see PK1569.D22
1569.D229 Dāsā Bholānātha, 1858-1929 (Table P-PZ40)
1569.D76 Duara, Jatindranath, 1892-1964 (Table P-PZ40)
Duwarā, Yatīndranātha, see PK1569.D76
1569.F37 Farwell, Nidhi Levi, d. 1873 (Table P-PZ40)
1569.G53 Gagai, Ganesa, 1910-1938 (Table P-PZ40)
Gogoi, Ganeshchandra, 1910-1938, see PK1569.G53
1569.G565 Gopāla Miśra, 16th cent. (Table P-PZ40)
1569.G5695 Goswāmī, Hemacandra, 1872-1928 (Table P-PZ40)
1569.M25 Madhavadeva, 1489-1596 (Table P-PZ40)
Mādhawa Kandali, 14th cent , see PK1569.M26
1569.M26 Mādhawakandalī, 14th cent. (Table P-PZ40)
1569.M344 Mahanta, Ratneśwara, 1864-1893 (Table P-PZ40)
1569.M355 Majindāra Baruwā Durgaprasāda, 1870-1928 (Table P-PZ40)
1569.P528 Phukan, Anandaram Dhekial, 1829-1859 (Table P-PZ40)
Rājakhowā, Śailadhara, 1892-1968, see PK1569.R293
1569.R285 Rajkhowa, Benudhar, 1872-1955 (Table P-PZ40)
1569.R293 Rajkhowa, Sailadhar, 1892-1968 (Table P-PZ40)

PK

Modern Indo-Aryan languages
Particular languages and dialects, A-Z
Assamese
Literature
Individual authors or works, A-Z -- Continued
1569.R3 Ramarayachar, 17th cent. (Table P-PZ40)
1569.R34 Ramasaraswati, 16th cent. (Table P-PZ40)
Rāyacaudhurī, Ambikāgirī, 1885-1967, see PK1569.R6
1569.R6 Roychaudhari, Ambikagiri, 1885-1967 (Table P-PZ40)
1569.R83 Rudrasimha, King of Assam, 18th cent. (Table P-PZ40)
1569.S24 Saikia, Bhabendra Nath, 1932- (Table P-PZ40)
Ṣaikia, Chandraprasad, see PK1569.S25
Śaikīyā. Bhabendra Nātha, 1932- , see PK1569.S24
1569.S25 Śaīkiyā, Candraprasāda, 1928- (Table P-PZ40)
1569.S29 Sankaradeva, 1449-1569 (Table P-PZ40)
1569.S352 Ṣarma, Dinesh (Table P-PZ40)
1569.S445 Ṣarmā, Kailāsa, 1934- (Table P-PZ40)
Śarmmā, Dineśa, see PK1569.S352
Ṣharma, Kailash, 1934- , see PK1569.S445
1569.S67 Śrīdhara Kandali, 15th cent. (Table P-PZ40)
Awadhī, see PK1941+
Baghēlī, see PK1951+
Bāgrī, see PK2469.B3
Baiswārī, see PK1941+
Bangālī, see PK1651+
Bāgarū, see PK1960
Bastarī, see PK1914
Behar, see PK1801+
Bengali
Language (Table P-PZ5)
1651 Periodicals. Societies. Yearbooks
Collections
1652.A1 Texts. Sources. Specimens, etc. By date of publication
Cf. PK1665, Phonology
Cf. PK1713, Literature
1652.A5-Z Monographs. Studies
(1653) Atlases. Maps. Charts, etc.
see PK1691
1654 Philosophy. Theory. Method
1655 History of philology
(1656) Biography
see PK109
1657 Study and teaching (Courses of study, curricula, syllabi, etc.)
1658 General works
1659 History (of the language)

Modern Indo-Aryan language
Particular languages and dialects, A-Z
Bengali
Language -- Continued
1660 Alphabet
Cf. P211+, Linguistics
Cf. PK119, Indo-Aryan
(1660.9) Transliteration
see P226
Grammar
1661 Theory. Terminology
(1661.3) History
see PK1655
1661.5 Treatises in Oriental languages
1662 Comprehensive works. Compends (Advanced)
1663 Elementary. Introductory
1664 Chrestomathies. Readers
1665 Phonology. Phonetics
1667 Orthography and spelling
1669 Morphology. Inflection. Accidence
1671 Parts of speech (Morphology and syntax)
1673 Syntax
1677 Style. Rhetoric
1679 Prosody. Metrics. Rhythmics
1681 Etymology
Lexicography
1685 Treatises
1687 Dictionaries
1689 Special: Technical, etc.
Linguistic geography
1691.A1 Atlases, maps, charts, etc. By date of publication
1691.A5-Z Treatises
1695 Dialects. Provincialisms
Literature (Table P-PZ23)
History
1700 Periodicals. Societies. Collections
1701 General works. Compends
1703 Collections
1704 Biography (Collective)
Special periods
1706 Early to 1800
1708 19th-20th centuries
1710 Poetry
1711 Drama
1712 Other special forms
Collections
1712.5 Periodicals. Societies. Serials
1713 General
1714 Poetry
1715 Drama
1716 Other special forms
1717.A-Z Local, A-Z (Table P-PZ26)

Modern Indo-Aryan language
Particular languages and dialects, A-Z
Bengali
Literature -- Continued
Individual authors
Through 1960

1718.A-Z A - Tag
e. g.
1718.A14 Ābadula Hākima, fl. 1620-1690
1718.A145 Abdul Hye, Mirza, 1919-
1718.A238 Abul Hussain, 1897-1938
1718.A247 Ācārya, Haricorana, 1861-1941
1718.A254 Ācārya, Phaṇibhūshaṇa, 1931-
Acharya, Haricharan, 1861-1941, see PK1718.A247
Acharya Phanibhushan, 1931- , see PK1718.A254
1718.A3176 Āhchānaullā, Khānabāhādura, 1874-1965
Akabarauddīna, 1895-1978, see PK1718.A39
1718.A39 Akbaruddin, 1895-1978
1718.A4152 Ālāola, 1607?-1680?
1718.A422 Ālī, Mirjā Mohāmmada Iusapha, 1858-1920
Ālī, Śāheda, see PK1718.A44
Ālī, Śaokata, 1936- , see PK1718.A443
1718.A44 Ali, Shahed
1718.A443 Ali, Shaukat
1718.A64 Āphajala, Āli, ca. 1738- ca. 1811
Banaphula, 1899-1979, see PK1718.M794
Bandyopādhyāya, Bibhūtibhūshana, see PK1718.B298
1718.B2882 Bandyopādhyāya, Candraśekhara, fl. 1870-1885
1718.B294 Bandyopadhyaya, Sachindranath, 1920-
Bandyopādhyāya, Śacīdranātha, 1920- , see PK1718.B294
Bandyopādhyāya, Tārāśankara, 1898-1971, see PK1718.B2985
1718.B298 Banerjee, Bibhuti Bhusan, 1896?-1950
1718.B2985 Banerjee, Tarasankar, 1891-1971
1718.B2994 Banerji, Hemchandra, 1838-1903
1718.B32 Banerji, Rangalal, 1826-1887
1718.B34 Baṛāla Akshayakumāra, 1860-1919
1718.B353 Bāṛu Caṇḍīdāsā
1718.B3535 Bārui, Kailāsa, fl. 1880-1896
Basu, Amṛtalāla, see PK1718.B59
1718.B366 Basu, Candranātha, 1844-1910
1718.B3725 Basu, Jogendra Chandra, 1854-1907
1718.B3745 Basu, Manomohana, 1831-1912
1718.B378 Basu, Rāmarāma, ca. 1757-1813
Begama, Rokeýā, see PK1718.R55
Begum, Rokeya, see PK1718.R55

Modern Indo-Aryan language
Particular languages and dialects, A-Z
Bengali
Literature
Individual authors
Through 1960
A - Tag -- Continued

1718.B429	Bhabānīcaraṇa Bandyopādhyāya, 1787-1848
1718.B463	Bhāratacandra Rāya, 1712-1760
1718.B4672	Bhaṭṭācārya Kṛṣṇa Kamala
1718.B48	Bhattacharya, Mahashveta, 1926-
	Bhaṭṭācārya, Bijanabihārī, 1906- , see PK1718.B53
1718.B53	Bhattacharyya, Bijanbihari, 1906-
1718.B537	Bhuluya-Baba, Avadhut, 1862-1941
	Bidyābinoda, Kshīrodaprasāda, 1863-1927, see PK1729.V53
1718.B557	Bidyāratna, Ramakumāra, 1836?-1901
	Bidyāsāgara, Īśvaracandra, 1820-1891, see PK1729.V5
1718.B5614	Bijayagupta, 15th cent.
1718.B5617	Bipradāsa, 15th cent.
1718.B59	Bose, Amritlal, 1853-1929
1718.B66	Bose, Rajnarain, 1826-1899
1718.B77	Bṛndabanadāsa, fl. 1540
	Cakrabartī, Jagannāth, 1924- , see PK1718.C419
1718.C298	Caṇḍidāsa, 1417-1477
1718.C33	Carey, William, 1761-1834
	Caṭṭopādhyāya, Śaratcandra, see PK1718.C45
1718.C377	Caudhurānī, Phayajunnesā, 1834-1903
	Caudhurī, Munīra, 1925-1971, see PK1718.C597
1718.C4152	Chakravarty, Biharilal, 1835-1894
1718.C419	Chakravorty, Jagannath, 1914-
1718.C43	Chatterji, Bankim Chandra, 1838-1894
1718.C44	Chatterji, Sanjiv Chandra, 1834-18892
1718.C45	Chatterji, Saratchandra, 1876-1938
	Chaṭṭopādhyaya, Śaratcandra, 1876-1938, see PK1718.C45
1718.C597	Chowdhury, Munir, 1925-1971
1718.D2	Dāda Ālī, 1852-1936
1718.D2525	Das, Chitta Ranjan, 1870-1925
1718.D2676	Dāsa, Gobinda, 1855-1918
1718.D2683	Dāsa, Mukunda, 1821-1934
1718.D33	Datta, Akshayakumāra, 1820-1886
1718.D3385	Datta Kedāranātha, 1837-1911
1718.D374	Daulat Qazi, 1600-1638
1718.D66	Donāgājī, 17th cent.
1718.D74	Dutt, Michael Madhusudan, 1824-1873
1718.D75	Dutt, Romesh Chunder, 1848-1909

PK

Modern Indo-Aryan language
Particular languages and dialects, A-Z
Bengali
Literature
Individual authors
Through 1960
A - Tag -- Continued

1718.D88 Dvārikādāsa, 17th cent.
1718.F28 Fauzulla, Shekh
1718.G348 Ghanarāma Cakrabarttī, 18th cent.
1718.G465 Ghose, Amarendra, 1907-1962
1718.G4713 Ghose, Benoy, 1918-
1718.G4718 Ghose, Girishchandra, 1844-1912
1718.G474 Ghosh, Kumaresh, 1919-
Ghosh, Subodh, 1909- , see PK1718.G548
Ghosha, Amarendra, see PK1718.G465
Ghosha, Binaya, 1918- , see PK1718.G4713
1718.G498 Ghosha, Gopālacandra, 1863-1912
1718.G4989 Ghosha, Kālīprasanna, 1843-1910
Ghosha, Kumāreśa, 1919- , see PK1718.G474
1718.G548 Ghosha, Subodha, 1909-1980
1718.G66 Goswami, Vijaya Krishna
1718.G824 Gupta, Mahendra Nath, 1855-1932
Hai, Mirja Abadula, see PK1718.A145
1718.H25 Hai, Muhammad Abdul, 1919-1969
Hāi, Muhammada Ābadula, see PK1718.H25
Haricaraạ, Ācārya, 1861-1941, see PK1718.A247
Haricharan Acharya, 1861-1941, see PK1718.A247
Hossain, Rokeya Sakhawat, see PK1718.R55
1718.H845 Husain, Mir Musharraf, 1848-1911
Husayana, Rokeyā Sakhāoyāt, see PK1718.R55
Husena, Abula, 1897-1938, see PK1718.A238
1718.I74 Isalāmābādī, Mohāmmada Manirujjāmāna, 1875-1950
1718.I8 Islam, Kazi Nazrul, 1899-1976
1718.I93 Īśvaracandra Gupta, 1812-1859
1718.J26 Jagajjībana Ghoshāla, 17th cent.
1718.J278 Jamiruddīna, Munsi Sekha, 1870-1973
1718.J33 Jayānanda, 16th cent.
1718.J9 Jyotirmayi Devi, 1894-
Jyuotirmmayī Debī, 1894-1988, see PK1718.J9
1718.K254 Kādambarī Debī, 1859-1884
1718.K343 Karamullā, 18th cent.
1718.K346 Karim, Abdul, 1871-1953
1718.K363 Kāśīrāmadāsa, 17th cent.
1718.K43 Ketakādāsa Kshemānanda, ca. 17th cent.
1718.K66 Kṛshṇacaraṇa Dāsa, 18th cent.
1718.K68 Kṛshṇakamala Gosvāmī, 1811-1888
1718.K684 Kṛshṇakānta, 1819-1892

Modern Indo-Aryan language
Particular languages and dialects, A-Z
Bengali
Literature
Individual authors
Through 1960
A - Tag -- Continued

1718.K69 Kṛṣṇadāsa Kavirāja Gosvāmī, b. 1518
1718.K7 Kṛttibāsa
1718.L35 Lālan Fạkir, 1774-1890
Lālana Śāha, see PK1718.L35
Mahāśvetā Debī, 1926- , see PK1718.B48
1718.M224 Mahiuddin, 1906-1975
Mahiuddina, 1906-1975, see PK1718.M224
1718.M24247 Maitreya, Akshayakumāra, 1861-1930
1718.M24266 Majumadāra, Harinātha, 1833-1896
1718.M24272 Majumadāra, Kedaranātha, 1870-1926
1718.M24273 Majumadāra, Kṛshṇacandra, 1834-1907
1718.M247 Mālādhara Basu, 15th cent.
1718.M2476 Mallabarman, Adwaita
Mallabarmana, Advaita, 1914-1951, see PK1718.M2476
1718.M25215 Mānikadatta
1718.M2522 Mānikarāma Gānguli, 18th cent.
1718.M253 Manna, Gunamay, 1925-
Mānnā, Guṇamaya, 1925- , see PK1718.M253
Māśahādī, Reyāja Uddīna Āhamada, 1859-1919, see PK1718.M259
1718.M259 Mashhadi, Reaz-al-Din Ahmad, 1859-1919
1718.M27 Mayūrabhatta
1718.M484 Mitra, Dinabandhu, 1829-1874
1718.M539 Mitra, Umeśacandra
1718.M786 Mukharji, T.N.
1718.M79136 Mukherjee, Prabhatkumar, 1873-1932
1718.M79157 Mukherji, Bhudev, 1827-1894
1718.M794 Mukhopadhyay, Balai Chand, 1899-1979
1718.M79445 Mukhopadhyay, Nilkantha, 1842-1911
1718.M7994 Mukhopādhyāya, Bhūdeba, 1827-1894
1718.M88 Mukunda Rām, Cakravartī
1718.M883 Mullens, Hannah Catherine
1718.M93 Mustāfī, Ardhenduśekhara, 1850-1908
1718.N337 Nandi, Bipinabihārī, 1870-1937
1718.N356 Narahari Cakrabartī, 18th cent.
1718.N357 Naraharicakrabarttī, 17th cent.
1718.N358 Narottama Dasa, 16th cent.
1718.N359 Nasrullāha Khondakāra, ca. 1560-ca. 1625
Nazrul Islam Kazi, 1899-1976, see PK1718.I8
1718.N566 Nityānnanda Dāsa, b. 1537
Oduda, Kaji Abadula, 1896-1970, see PK1729.W27
1718.O97 Oyāliullāha, Mohāmmada, 1907-1978
1718.P2 Pagala Kanai, 1809-1889
1718.P73 Prasannamayī Debī, 1857-1939

Modern Indo-Aryan language
Particular languages and dialects, A-Z
Bengali
Literature
Individual authors
Through 1960
A - Tag -- Continued

1718.P75 Prithvichandra, Raja of Pakur, d. 1835
1718.Q7 al-Quraishi, Muḥammad Qasim, 1852-1951
1718.R184 Rādhākṛshṇa Dāsa Bairāgī, 19th cent.
1718.R185 Rādhāramaạ, 1834-1916
1718.R188 Raghunātha Bhāgavatācāryya
1718.R189 Raghunāthadāsa, 18th cent.
1718.R236 Rājā Hāsana, 1854-1922
1718.R242 Rāmacandra Dāsa, 17th cent.
1718.R243 Rāmacandra Gosvāmī, b. 1533 or 4
1718.R245 Rāmāipaṇḍita
1718.R248 Ramananda Yati, 18th cent.
1718.R25 Rāmaprasāda Rāẏa, 18th/19th cent.
1718.R2514 Rāmaprasāda Sena, 1718-1775
1718.R29 Ray, Dinendrakumar, 1869-1943
1718.R3145 Ray Choudhury, Upendra Kishore, 1863-1915
Raya, Dīnendrakumāra, 1869-1943, see PK1718.R29
Rāyā Sukumāra, see PK1718.R665
Rāyacaudhurī Sarojakumāra, 1902-1972, see PK1718.R68
1718.R3465 Rāyaśekhara, 16th cent.
1718.R55 Rokeya, Begum
Rokeyā Sakhāoyāt Husāyana, see PK1718.R55
Rokeya Sakhawat Hossain, see PK1718.R55
1718.R6 Roy, Dwijendra Lal, 1864-1913
1718.R665 Roy, Sukumar, 1887-1923
1718.R68 Roy Choudhury, Saroj Kumar, 1902-1972
1718.S249 Ṣāha Muhammada Sagīra, 14th/15th cent.
Śaikha, Āsakāra Ibane, see PK1718.S493
1718.S2714 Ṣaiyada Sulatāna, 1550-1648
Śāmasujjamāna, -Abula Phajala, 1927- , see PK1718.S275
1718.S275 Ṣamsuzzaman, 1927-
1718.S2753 Śankara Kabicandra
1718.S3133 Ṣarakāra, Akshayacandra, 1846-1917
1718.S3286 Śarkar, Jogindranath, 1866-1937
1718.S347 Ṣastri, Sibnath, 1847-1919
1718.S364 Śekha Cānda, 1560-1625
1718.S375 Sen, Atulprasad, 1871-1934
1718.S3823 Sen, Dineshchandra, 1866-1936
1718.S385 Sen, Nabin Chandra, 1847-1909
1718.S39 Sen, Rajanikanta, 1865-1910
1718.S42 Sen, Saurin
1718.S455 Sena, Caṇḍīcaraṇa, 1845-1906

Modern Indo-Aryan language
Particular languages and dialects, A-Z
Bengali
Literature
Individual authors
Through 1960
A - Tag -- Continued

1718.S4553	Sena, Debendranātha, 1858-1920
1718.S456	Sena, Jaladhara, 1860-1939
	Sena, Rajanikanta, see PK1718.S39
	Senagupta, Kiranaśankara, see PK1718.S48
1718.S48	Sengupta, Kiran Shankar, 1918-
1718.S493	Shaikh, Askar Ibne
1718.S5	Shastri, Hara Prasad, 1853-1931
1718.S574	Śīkadāra, Tārācaraṇa
1718.S5784	Siṃha, Kālīprasanna, 1840-1870
1718.S649	Sircar, Dineschandra
1718.S774	Śrīrāya Binoda, 16th cent.
1718.S78	Śrīśrīgauṛabhaktāmṛta laharī
1718.S794	Śukura Māhmuda, 1680-1750
1718.S88	Svarṇakumārī Debī
1718.T2	Tagore, Abanindranath, 1871-1951
1718.T223	Tagore, Balendranath, 1870-1899
1718.T226	Tagore, Devendranath, 1817-1905
	Tagore, Rabindranath, 1861-1941
	Collected works
1719	By date
1720	By editor
1721	Selections
	Translations (Collected works)
1722.A2A-Z	English. By translator, if given, or date
1722.A3-Z	Other. By language, subarranged by translator
1723	Separate works
1724	Apocryphal, spurious works, etc.
1725.A1-A19	Periodicals. Societies. Collections
1725.A2-A3	Dictionaries, indexes, etc.
1725.A4-A44	Autobiography, diaries, etc.
1725.A45	Letters. By date of imprint
1725.A46-A469	Letters to particular individuals. By correspondent (alphabetically)
1725.A5-Z	Biography and criticism
	Criticism
1726	General works
1727.A-Z	Special topics, A-Z
1727.A38	Aesthetics
1727.A53	Animals
1727.A55	Anniversaries
1727.B38	Bauls (Sect)
1727.B4	Beauty
1727.B8	Buddha and Buddhism
1727.C43	Characters

PK

Modern Indo-Aryan language
Particular languages and dialects, A-Z
Bengali
Literature
Individual authors
Through 1960
Tagore, Rabindranath, 1861-1941
Criticism
Special topics, A-Z -- Continued

1727.C45 China
1727.C64 Colors
1727.D34 Dance
Death, see PK1727.L5
1727.D7 Drama
1727.E38 Education
1727.E8 Essays
1727.F5 Fiction
1727.F53 Film and video adaptations
1727.F64 Folklore
1727.G6 Good
1727.H56 History
1727.H77 Human beings
1727.H78 Humanity
1727.H8 Humor
1727.I55 India
1727.I6 Indo-Aryan philology
1727.I63 Influence
1727.J8 Juvenile literature
1727.L35 Language
1727.L5 Life and death
1727.L55 Literature
1727.L6 Love
1727.M87 Music
1727.N38 Nature
1727.P45 Philosophy
1727.P6 Poetry
1727.P66 Political and social views
1727.R4 Religion
1727.R55 Rivers
1727.S3 Science
1727.S68 Soviet Union
1727.S8 Style
1727.S95 Symbolism
1727.V35 Vaishnavism
Video adaptations, see PK1727.F53
1727.W6 Women
1729 Tag - Z
e. g.
1729.T325 Tagore, Sourindro Mohun, Sir, 1840-1914
1729.T353 Tantrabibhụti, 17th cent.
1729.T356 Tāraka, Goṁsāi, 1845-1914
1729.T38 Ṭhakkura, Bhaktibinoda
1729.T386 Thakūra, Dvijendranātha, 1840-1926

Modern Indo-Aryan language
Particular languages and dialects, A-Z
Bengali
Literature
Individual authors
Through 1960
Tag-Z -- Continued

1729.T389 Thākura, Jyotirindranātha, 1849-1925
1729.T42 Ṭhākura, Satyendranātha, 1842-1923
1729.T7 Tribedī, Rāmendrasundara, 1864-1919
1729.V5 Vidyasagar, Iswar Chandra, 1820-1891
1729.V53 Vidyavinod, Kshirod Prasad, 1863-1927
1729.W27 Wadud, Kazi Abdul, 1896-1970
Waliullah Muhammad, see PK1718.O97

1961-
The author number is determined by the second letter of the name, unless otherwise specified
Subarrange each author by Table P-PZ40 unless otherwise indicated

1730.1 Anonymous works. By title, A-Z
1730.12 A (Table P-PZ40)
1730.12.H55 Ahmed, Momtazuddin (Table P-PZ40)
Ahameda, Humālyūna, see PK1730.23.U6
1730.12.H62 Ahmed Mir, 1925-1979 (Table P-PZ40)
Ājāda, Ābida, see PK1730.12.Z28
1730.12.Z28 Azad, Abid (Table P-PZ40)
1730.12.Z49 Azizul Haq (Table P-PZ40)
1730.13 Ba - Bg (Table P-PZ40)
1730.13.A73 Bashir, Murtaza (Table P-PZ40)
Basīra, Murtajā, see PK1730.13.A73
1730.14 Bh (Table P-PZ40)
The author number is determined by the third letter of the name
1730.15 Bi - Bz (Table P-PZ40)
1730.16 Ca - Cg (Table P-PZ40)
Caṭṭopādhyāẏa, Kāmākshīprasāda, 1917-1976, see PK1730.17.A64
Caṭṭopādhyāẏa, Sādhana, 1943, see PK1730.17.A58
1730.17 Ch (Table P-PZ40)
The author number is determined by the third letter of the name
1730.17.A58 Chattopadhyay, Sadhan, 1943- (Table P-PZ40)
1730.17.A64 Chattopadhyaya, Kamakshiprasad, 1917-1976 (Table P-PZ40)
1730.18 Ci - Cz (Table P-PZ40)
1730.19 D (Table P-PZ40)
1730.19.A86 Datta, Jyotiprakāśa (Table P-PZ40)
Dutta, Jyoti Prakash, 1939- , see PK1730.19.A86
1730.2 E (Table P-PZ40)

	Modern Indo-Aryan language
	Particular languages and dialects, A-Z
	Bengali
	Literature
	Individual authors
	1961- -- Continued
1730.21	F (Table P-PZ40)
1730.22	G (Table P-PZ40)
1730.22.U535	Guha, Śiśira, 1940- (Table P-PZ40)
1730.23	H (Table P-PZ40)
1730.23.A33	Haider, Rashid (Table P-PZ40)
	Haka, Ājījula, 1935- , see PK1730.12.Z49
	Haka, Sāmasula, see PK1730.23.A635
1730.23.A635	Haque, Samsul, 1937- (Table P-PZ40)
1730.23.A68	Hasan, Abul (Table P-PZ40)
	Hāsāna, Ābula, 1947-1975, see PK1730.23.A68
	Hāyadāra, Raśīda, 1942- , see PK1730.23.A33
	Hosena, Selinā, 1947- , see PK1730.36.L54
1730.23.U6	Humāyun, Ahmed, 1948- (Table P-PZ40)
1730.24	I
1730.24.D7	Idris, Kazi Mohammad (Table P-PZ40)
	Idrisa, Kājī Mohāmmada, 1906-1975, see PK1730.24.D7
1730.25	J (Table P-PZ40)
	Jayenauddīna, Saradāra, 1923-1986, see PK1730.36.R3
1730.26	K (Table P-PZ40)
1730.26.A16	Kabir, Shafiqul (Table P-PZ40)
	Kabira, Śaphikula, see PK1730.26.A16
	Kamāla, Suphiyā, see PK1730.39.U35
1730.27	L (Table P-PZ40)
1730.28	Ma (Table P-PZ40)
	The author number is determined by the third letter of the name
	Mamatāja Begama, 1932- , see PK1730.29.O46
	Manajura, Makabulā, 1939- , see PK1730.28.Q2
1730.28.Q2	Maqbula Manzur, 1939- (Table P-PZ40)
1730.29	Mb - Mz (Table P-PZ40)
	Mira, Ahamada, see PK1730.12.H62
1730.29.O46	Momataja Begama, 1932- (Table P-PZ40)
1730.29.U4555	Mukhopadhyay, Pavtra (Table P-PZ40)
	Mukhopādhyāya, Pabitra, 1940- , see PK1730.29.U4555
1730.3	N (Table P-PZ40)
1730.31	O (Table P-PZ40)
1730.32	P (Table P-PZ40)
1730.32.A75	Pathak, Ateendriya, 1939- (Table P-PZ40)
	Pathaka, Atindriya, 1939- , see PK1730.32.A75
1730.33	Q (Table P-PZ40)

Modern Indo-Aryan language
Particular languages and dialects, A-Z
Bengali
Literature
Individual authors
1961- -- Continued
1730.34 Ra (Table P-PZ40)
The author number is determined by the third letter of the name
1730.34.I34 Raihan, Zahir, 1934-1972 (Table P-PZ40)
Rāyahāna, Jahira, see PK1730.34.I34
1730.35 Rb - Rz (Table P-PZ40)
1730.36 Sa (Table P-PZ40)
The author number is determined by the third letter of the name
Ṣāhābuddīna, Phajala, see PK1730.38.A34
1730.36.H43 Śahidullā, Rudra Muhammada (Table P-PZ40)
Śahidullā, Rudra Muhammada, 1956-1991, see PK1730.36.H43
1730.36.L54 Ṣalina Husain (Table P-PZ40)
Śaphika, Māhamuda, see PK1730.38.A3
1730.36.R3 Sardar, Jainuddin, 1923-1986 (Table P-PZ40)
1730.37 Sb - Sg (Table P-PZ40)
1730.38 Sh (Table P-PZ40)
The author number is determined by the third letter of the name
1730.38.A3 Shafique, Mahmud (Table P-PZ40)
1730.38.A34 Shahabuddin, Fazal (Table P-PZ40)
1730.39 Si - Sz (Table P-PZ40)
1730.39.U35 Sufia Kamal (Table P-PZ40)
1730.4 T (Table P-PZ40)
Tālukadāra, Māhabuba, 1941- , see PK1730.4.A37
1730.4.A37 Talukdar, Mahboob (Table P-PZ40)
1730.41 U (Table P-PZ40)
1730.42 V (Table P-PZ40)
1730.43 W (Table P-PZ40)
1730.44 X (Table P-PZ40)
1730.45 Y (Table P-PZ40)
1730.46 Z (Table P-PZ40)
(1791-1799) Spoken (Colloquial) Bengali (Table P-PZ8)
For reference only; see PK1651+
Bhaṭēālī, see PK2649.B3
Bhaṭṭiānī, see PK2639.B3
1800 Bhīlī (Table P-PZ15a)
Cf. PK2225, Khāndhēsī
Bhojpurī, see PK1825+
1801-1831 Bihārī (Table P-PZ15a)
General (Table P-PZ8a)
Dialects
1810 Angika (Table P-PZ15a)
1811-1819 Maithilī (Tirhutia) (Table P-PZ8a)

PK

	Modern Indo-Aryan languages
	Particular languages and dialects, A-Z
	Bihārī
	Dialects
	Maithilī (Tirhutia) -- Continued
1818.9.A-Z	Individual authors or works, A-Z (Table P-PZ40, or P-PZ43)
	e. g.
1818.9.B5	Bhupatīndramalla, Maharaja, 1695-1722 (Table P-PZ40)
1818.9.C27	Caturbhuja, fl. 1493 (Table P-PZ40)
1818.9.G68	Govindādasa, fl. 1497-1535 (Table P-PZ40)
1818.9.H33	Harinandana Dāsa, 19th cent. (Table P-PZ40)
1818.9.J32	Jagajjyotir Malla, Raja of Bhaktapur, fl. 1613-1637 (Table P-PZ40)
1818.9.J34	Jagatprakāśamalla, King of Bhaktapur, fl. 1644-1673 (Table P-PZ40)
1818.9.J428	Jha, Badarinatha (Table P-PZ40)
1818.9.J43424	Jha, Candā, 1830-1909 (Table P-PZ40)
1818.9.J448	Jhā, Jīvana, 1848-1912 (Table P-PZ40)
1818.9.J4482	Jhā, Jīvanātha, fl. 1875 (Table P-PZ40)
1818.9.J465	Jhā, Muralīdhara, 1869-1929 (Table P-PZ40)
1818.9.J468	Jhā, Parameśvara, 1850-1925 (Table P-PZ40)
1818.9.J95	Jyotirīśvara, 14th cent. (Table P-PZ40)
1818.9.L28	Lakshmi Nath, 1778-1872 (Table P-PZ40)
1818.9.L29	Lāladāsa, 1856-1921 (Table P-PZ40)
1818.9.M279	Manabodha, 18th cent. (Table P-PZ40)
1818.9.M558	Miśra, Jibacha, 1863-1923 (Table P-PZ40)
1818.9.N3	Nandīpati (Table P-PZ40)
1818.9.S4	Ṣiddhinarasimha, Malla, (Table P-PZ40)
1818.9.S73	Śrīkānta Gaṇaka, 18th cent. (Table P-PZ40)
1818.9.U45	Umāpati Upādhyāya, fl. 1525-1600 (Table P-PZ40)
1818.9.V5	Vidyāpati Ṭhākura, 15th cent. (Table P-PZ40)
1818.97	Khotta (Table P-PZ15a)
1819	Kurmali (Table P-PZ15a)
1820	Tharu (Table P-PZ15a)
1821-1824	Magahī (Table P-PZ11)
1825-1828	Bhojpurī (Table P-PZ11)
1828.A-Z	Individual authors or works (Table P-PZ40, or P-PZ43)
	e. g.
1828.K86	Kumāra Virala, 1954- (Table P-PZ40)
1828.L35	Lakshmī Sakhī, 1841-1914 (Table P-PZ40)
1828.L65	Lorikāyana (Table P-PZ40)
	Pāṇḍeya, Babana, 1954- , see PK1828.K86
1830.A-Z	Subdialects, A-Z
(1830.N3)	Nagpuriā see PK1830.S23
1830.S23	Sadani. Sadan (Table P-PZ16)
1830.S8	Standard

Modern Indo-Aryan language
Particular languages and dialects, A-Z
Bihari
Dialects
Bhojpurī
Subdialects, A-Z -- Continued
1830.W4 Western (Pūrbī)
1831 Bajjika (Table P-PZ15a)
Bīkānērī, see PK2469.B5
Braj Bhākhā, see PK1961+
Bundēlī (Bundēlkhandī), see PK1968
1833 Chakma (Table P-PZ15a)
1833.9.A-Z Individual authors or works, A-Z (Table P-PZ40, or P-PZ42)
e. g.
1833.9.S5 Śibacraṇa (Table P-PZ40, or P-PZ42)
Chamĕāḷī, see PK2610.C4
Chhattīsharhī, see PK1959
1834 Danuwar Rai (Table P-PZ15a)
1835 Darai (Table P-PZ15a)
Ḍingaḷ, see PK2461+
1836 Divehi (Table P-PZ15a)
Ḍōgrā (or Ḍōgrī), see PK2645+
1837 Dumaki
Eastern Hindī, see PK1941+
Eastern Pahāṛī, see PK2595+
Elu
see PK2801+, PK2841+
Gādī, see PK2610.G3
Gaṛhwālī, see PK2605.G3
Gipsy (Gypsy), see PK2896+
Gorkhālī, see PK2595+
Gujarā, see PK1841+
Gujarati
1841-1849 Language (Table P-PZ8a, except no. 8))
1850-1859 Literature (Table P-PZ24)
1859.A-Z Individual authors, A-Z
e. g.
Subarrange each author by Table P-PZ40 unless otherwise specified
1859.A35 Akhā, 17th cent. (Table P-PZ40)
1859.A557 Amṛtakalaśa, 16th cent. (Table P-PZ40)
Anāmī, 1918- , see PK1859.P292
1859.A559 Ānandaghana, Maha Yogi, 18th cent. (Table P-PZ40)
1859.A64 Anubhavānanda, 17th cent. (Table P-PZ40)
1859.A755 Āśānanda Barahaṭhṭha, 1506-1603 (Table P-PZ40)
1859.B4 Bhālaṇa, 1426?-1500? (Table P-PZ40)
1859.B4647 Bhaṭṭa, Choṭālāla Narabherāma, 1850-1937 (Table P-PZ40)
1859.B4656 Bhaṭṭa, Keśavalāla Harirāma, 1851-1896 (Table P-PZ40)

PK

Modern Indo-Aryan language
Particular languages and dialects, A-Z
Gujarati
Literature
Individual authors, A-Z -- Continued

1859.B4657 Bhaṭṭa, Maṇisankara Ratanjī, 1867-1923 (Table P-PZ40)
1859.B497 Bhīma, fl. 1493 (Table P-PZ40)
1859.B498 Bhojo, 1785-1850 (Table P-PZ40)
1859.B645 Brahmananda, Swami, 1771-1831? (Table P-PZ40)
Brokara, Gulābadāsa, see PK1859.B76
1859.B76 Broker, Gulabdas Harjivandas, 1909- (Table P-PZ40)
1859.C26 Cārana, Isaradāsa, 1458-1565 or 6 (Table P-PZ40)
1859.C64 Choṭama (Table P-PZ40)
1859.D3 Dalal, Jayantilal Ghelabhai, 1909-1970 (Table P-PZ40)
Dalāla, Jayanti, see PK1859.D3
1859.D346 Dalapatarāma Ḍāhyābhāī, 1820-1898 (Table P-PZ40)
1859.D361457 Dāsī Jīvana, d. 1824 or 5 (Table P-PZ40)
1859.D367 Dayārāma, 1767-1852 (Table P-PZ40)
1859.D368 Desāī, Bālābhāī Vīracanda, 1908-1969 (Table P-PZ40)
1859.D48 Devānanda, Swami, 1803-1854 (Table P-PZ40)
1859.D525 Dhīro, 1753-1825 (Table P-PZ40)
1859.D57 Divatia, Narsinhrao Bholanath, 1859-1937 (Table P-PZ40)
1859.D85 Durasā Āṛhā, b. 1535 (Table P-PZ40)
1859.D87 Durlabha, 1696-1736 (Table P-PZ40)
1859.D88 Dvivedi, Manilal Nabhubhai (Table P-PZ40)
1859.G344 Gandhi, Mohandas Karamchand, 1869-1948 (Table P-PZ40)
1859.G39 Gangāsatī (Table P-PZ40)
1859.G85 Guṇavinaya, fl. 1584-1619 (Table P-PZ40)
Jayabhikkhu, 1908-1965, see PK1859.D368
1859.J38 Jayavantasūri, 17th cent. (Table P-PZ40)
1859.J4 Jebalia, Nanabhai H. (Table P-PZ40)
Jebaliyā, Nānābhāī Ha., 1938- , see PK1859.J4
1859.J48 Jhaveri, Dahyabhai Dholshaji, 1867-1902 (Table P-PZ40)
1859.J6 Joshi, Umashankar Jethalal, 1911- (Table P-PZ40)
Jośī, Umāśankara, 1911- , see PK1859.J6
1859.K19 Kadakia, Krishnakant O. (Table P-PZ40)
Kaḍakiyā, Kṛshṇakānta O , see PK1859.K19
Kalāpī, 1874-1900, see PK1859.S87
1859.K265 Kamalasekhara, 17th cent. (Table P-PZ40)
1859.K2718 Kanthāriyā Bālāśaṅkara VUāsarām 1859-1898 (Table P-PZ40)

Modern Indo-Aryan language
Particular languages and dialects, A-Z
Gujarati
Literature
Individual authors, A-Z -- Continued

1859.K284 Kāśīsuta, Śeghajī, ca. 1558-ca. 1603 (Table P-PZ40)
1859.K29 Kavi, Dalpatram Dahyabhai, 1820-1898 (Table P-PZ40)
1859.K45 Khabaradāra, Aradeśara Pharāmajī, 1881-1953 (Table P-PZ40)
Khabardar, Ardeshir Framji, see PK1859.K45
1859.K7 Kshamākalaśa, fl. 1494-1497 (Table P-PZ40)
1859.K84 Kusumakar, 1893-1962 (Table P-PZ40)
Kusumākara, 1893-1962, see PK1859.K84
1859.L8 Luhāra, Tribhuvanadāsa Purushottamadāsa, 1908- (Table P-PZ40)
1859.M2 Mādhava, fl. 1649 (Table P-PZ40)
Mahetā, Harakisana, 1928- , see PK1859.M4382
Mahetā, Īla Āraba, see PK1859.M4383
1859.M295 Mahetā, Nandaśankara Tulajāsankara, 1835-1905 (Table P-PZ40)
1859.M299 Mahetā, Rāyacandrabhāī Ravajībhāī, 1868-1901 (Table P-PZ40)
Mahetā, Tāraka, 1929- , see PK1859.M464
Mahetā, Yasodhara, 1909-1989, see PK1859.M47
1859.M317 Mahīrāja, 12th cent. (Table P-PZ40)
1859.M318 Mahīrāja, 16th cent. (Table P-PZ40)
1859.M326 Malaycandra (Table P-PZ40)
1859.M332 Māṇikyasundara Sūri, fl. 1422 (Table P-PZ40)
Māịkyasundarasūri, fl. 1422, see PK1859.M332
1859.M355 Marajhabāna, Jāṃhāngīra Beharāmajī, 1848-1920 (Table P-PZ40)
1859.M357 Mareez, 1917- (Table P-PZ40)
Marījha, 1917- , see PK1859.M357
1859.M368 Māya Ḍiyara Jayu (Table P-PZ40)
1859.M4382 Mehta, Harkisan, 1928- (Table P-PZ40)
1859.M4383 Mehta, Ila Arab, 1938- (Table P-PZ40)
1859.M445 Mehta, Mohanlal Tulsidas, 1910- (Table P-PZ40)
1859.M464 Mehta, Tarak, 1929- (Table P-PZ40)
1859.M47 Mehta, Yashodhar Narmadashanker, 1909- (Table P-PZ40)
1859.M478 Mekaṇa, 1666-1729 (Table P-PZ40)
1859.M58 Modi, Chinu (Table P-PZ40)
Modi, Cinu, see PK1859.M58
1859.M72 Muktānanda, Swami, 1756-1828 (Table P-PZ40)
1859.N24 Nākara, 1493?-1573? (Table P-PZ40)
1859.N25 Narahari, 1615-1643 (Table P-PZ40)
1859.N27 Narasiṃha Mehetā, 1414-1481 (Table P-PZ40)
1859.N3 Narmadāśankara Lālaśankara Dave, 1833-1886 (Table P-PZ40)
1859.N38 Nayasundara, 1542-1613 (Table P-PZ40)

Modern Indo-Aryan language
Particular languages and dialects, A-Z
Gujarati
Literature
Individual authors, A-Z -- Continued

1859.N48 Nīlakaṇṭha, Mahīpatarāma Ruparāma, 1829-1891 (Table P-PZ40)
1859.N5 Nilkanth, Ramanbhai Mahipatram, Sir, 1868-1928 (Table P-PZ40)
1859.N53 Nirānta, 1747-1825 (Table P-PZ40)
1859.N55 Nishkuḷānanda, Swami, 1765-1847 (Table P-PZ40)
1859.P18 Padmanābha, 15th cent. (Table P-PZ40)
1859.P235 Pandya, Natavarlal Kuberbhai, 1920- (Table P-PZ40)
1859.P236 Paṇḍyā, Navalarāma Lakshmīrāma, 1836-1888 (Table P-PZ40)
1859.P2672 Parikh, Priyakant, 1934- (Table P-PZ40)
Pārīkha, Priyaknta, 1934- , see PK1859.P2672
Patal, Dahyabhaī A. (Dahyabhai Ashabhai), see PK1859.P295
1859.P2776 Patel, Mohanlan, 1927- (Table P-PZ40)
1859.P285 Patel, Parajit, 1940- (Table P-PZ40)
1859.P292 Patel, Ranjit Mohanlal, 1918- (Table P-PZ40)
1859.P295 Patela, Dāhyābhāī Āsārāma, 1920- (Table P-PZ40)
Patela, Mohanalāla, 1927, see PK1859.P2776
Paṭela, Parājita, 1940- , see PK1859.P285
1859.P555 Pingaḷaśībhāī Pātābhāī, 1856-1939 (Table P-PZ40)
1859.P7 Premānanda, 1636-1734 (Table P-PZ40)
1859.P713 Premānanda, Swami, 1784-1855 (Table P-PZ40)
1859.P72 Prītamadāsa, 1717-1797 (Table P-PZ40)
Puvāra, Indu, 1940- , see PK1859.P9
1859.P9 Puwar, Indu, 1940- (Table P-PZ40)
1859.R22 Rāghavajī, 17th/18th cent. (Table P-PZ40)
1859.R248 Raj Chandra, 1868-1901 (Table P-PZ40)
1859.R252 Rāje, 18th cent. (Table P-PZ40)
1859.R265 Raṇachoda, fl. 1694-1804 (Table P-PZ40)
1859.R67 Ṛshabhadāsa, 1575-1635 (Table P-PZ40)
1859.R74 Rudradaman I. (Table P-PZ40)
Ṣāha, Rājendra, see PK1859.S483
1859.S236 Śamaḷabhaṭa, 18th cent. (Table P-PZ40)
1859.S237 Samayasundara, 17th cent. (Table P-PZ40)
1859.S238 Sāmyājī Jhūlā, 1575-1646 (Table P-PZ40)
1859.S483 Shah, Rājendra Keshavlal, 1913- (Table P-PZ40)
1859.S567 Śivalāla Dhaneśvara, 1850-1899 (Table P-PZ40)
Sopāna, 1910- , see PK1859.M445
Sudaram, 1908- , see PK1859.L8
Surati, Abida, 1935- , see PK1859.S88

Modern Indo-Aryan language
Particular languages and dialects, A-Z
Gujarati
Literature
Individual authors, A-Z -- Continued
1859.S87 Sursinghji Takatsinghji, Thakur of Lathi, 1874-1900 (Table P-PZ40)
1859.S88 Surti, Abid, 1935- (Table P-PZ40)
1859.T476 Ṭhākora Balavantarāya Kalyāṇarāya, 1869-1952 (Table P-PZ40)
1859.T5 Thakore, Balvantrai Kalianrai (Table P-PZ40)
1859.T67 Trīkamadāsa, 1734-1800 (Table P-PZ40)
1859.T75 Tripathi, Govardhanarāma Mādhavarāma, 1855-1907 (Table P-PZ40)
1859.U27 Udayabhanu, 16th cent. (Table P-PZ40)
1859.U273 Udayakalaśa, fl. 1552-1581 (Table P-PZ40)
Usanas, 1920- , see PK1859.P235
1859.V236 Vaitāla, b. 1677? (Table P-PZ40)
1859.V27 Varasaḍā, Māvala, b. 1797 (Table P-PZ40)
1859.V55 Vishṇudāsa, 1558-1628 (Table P-PZ40)
1859.V563 Viśvanātha Jānī, ca. 1508-ca. 1663 (Table P-PZ40)
1859.V565 Viśvavandya (Table P-PZ40)
1859.Y38 Yaśodhīra, 16th cent. (Table P-PZ40)
Dialects
1870 Saurashtri (Table P-PZ15a)
1911 Gujuri (Table P-PZ15a)
1914 Halbī (Table P-PZ15a)
1921-1924 Hāṛautī (Table P-PZ11)
Hariānī, see PK1960
Hindī, Urdū, Hindustānī languages
Hindī
General
Class here all works on the Hindī language except those dealing specifically with any one of the dialects of Hindī
1931-1939 Language (Table P-PZ8a, omitting no. 8)
Literature, see PK2030+
Special dialects, Eastern
Awadhī (Baiswārī and Eastern Hindī in general)
1941-1944 Language (Table P-PZ9, nos. 1-4)
1947 Literature (Table P-PZ25)
1947.9.A-Z Individual authors, A-Z
e. g.
Subarrange each author by Table P-PZ40 unless otherwise specified
1947.9.B3 Banādāsa, Mahatma, 1821 or 2-1892 or 3 (Table P-PZ40)
1947.9.D5 Dharmadāsa (Table P-PZ40)
1947.9.G57 Giridhara, 18th cent. (Table P-PZ40)
1947.9.K3 Kamalakumvari Devajū, Rani of Sarila (Table P-PZ40)

PK

Modern Indo-Aryan language
Particular languages and dialects, A-Z
Hindi, Urdu, Hindustani languages
Hindi
Special dialects, Eastern
Awadhi
Literature
Individual authors, A-Z -- Continued

1947.9.K58 Khvājā Ahamada (Table P-PZ40)
1947.9.L35 Lāladāsa, 18th cent. (Table P-PZ40)
1947.9.L67 Lorikāyana (Table P-PZ40)
1947.9.M3 Malik Muhammad Jayasi, fl. 1540 (Table P-PZ40)
1947.9.M316 Malūkadāsa, 1574?-1682? (Table P-PZ40)
1947.9.M58 Mītā, 1690-1768 (Table P-PZ40)
1947.9.N87 Nur Muhammad, fl. 1744 (Table P-PZ40)
1947.9.R28 Rāghunathadāsa Rāmasanehī, d. 1882 or 3 (Table P-PZ40)
1947.9.R37 Ravidāsa, 15th cent. (Table P-PZ40)
1947.9.S89 Sundaradāsa, 1596?-1689? (Table P-PZ40)
1947.9.T83 Tulasīdāsa, 1532-1623 (Table P-PZ40)
1951-1957 Baghēlī (Bāghēlkhandī) (Table P-PZ40)
1951-1954 Language (Table P-PZ9, nos. 1-4)
1957 Literature (Table P-PZ25)
1959 Chattisgarhi. Chhattisgarhi (Table P-PZ15a)

Special dialects, Western

1959.97 Badayuni (Table P-PZ16)
1960 Bāngarū (Table P-PZ15a)
1960.9.A-Z Individual authors or works, A-Z (Table P-PZ40, or P-PZ43)

e. g.

1960.9.A33 Ahamadabakhśa, Thānesarī, 19th cent. (Table P-PZ40)

Braj Bhākhā

1961-1964 Language (Table P-PZ9, nos. 1-4)
1967 Literature (Table P-PZ25)
1967.9.A-Z Individual authors, A-Z

e. g.

Subarrange each author by Table P-PZ40 unless otherwise specified

1967.9.A23 'Abdur Rahim Khan, Khan Khanan, 1556-1627 (Table P-PZ40)
1967.9.A4 'Alam, Shaikh, fl. 1583 (Table P-PZ40)

Ālama, fl. 1583, see PK1967.9.A4

1967.9.A5 Ānandaghana, fl. 1719-1739 (Table P-PZ40)
1967.9.A55 Antarajānī (Table P-PZ40)
1967.9.A84 Ātmārāma, 18th cent. (Table P-PZ40)
1967.9.B27 Bakhatāvara, d. 1805? (Table P-PZ40)
1967.9.B3 Bakhśī Hamsarāja, 18th cent. (Table P-PZ40)
1967.9.B35 Balabhadra Miśra, b. 1543? (Table P-PZ40)

Modern Indo-Aryan language
Particular languages and dialects, A-Z
Hindi, Urdu, Hindustani languages
Hindi
Special dialects, Western
BrajBhakha
Literature
Individual authors, A-Z -- Continued

1967.9.B37 Banārasīdāsa, 1586-1641? (Table P-PZ40)
1967.9.B42 Bhagavat Mudita (Table P-PZ40)
1967.9.B43 Bhaṭṭadevācārya, fl. 1423-1428 (Table P-PZ40)
1967.9.B47 Bhikhāridāsa, fl. 1734-1750 (Table P-PZ40)
1967.9.B49 Bhūdaradāsa, 1699 or 1700-1765 or 6 (Table P-PZ40)
1967.9.B5 Bhūshaṇa, 1613?-1715? (Table P-PZ40)
1967.9.B54 Bihārī Lāla, Jānī Paṇḍita, b. 1838 or 9 (Table P-PZ40)
1967.9.B6 Bodhā, 18th cent. (Table P-PZ40)
1967.9.B74 Ḅrjarāja, 1846-1919 (Table P-PZ40)
1967.9.B76 Ḅrndāvanadāsa, 18th cent. (Table P-PZ40)
1967.9.C25 Caraṇadāsa, 1703-1782 (Table P-PZ40)
1967.9.C265 Caturbhuja Dāsa, Swami, 17th cent. (Table P-PZ40)
1967.9.C275 Caturbhujamiśra (Table P-PZ40)
1967.9.C47 Chaitanya, 1486-1534 (Table P-PZ40)
1967.9.D25 Dāmodaradāsa, fl. 1520-1553 (Table P-PZ40)
1967.9.D3 Das, Jagannath, 1866-1932 (Table P-PZ40)
1967.9.D33 Daulatarāma Kāsalīvāla (Table P-PZ40)
1967.9.D35 Dayārāma, 1767-1852 (Table P-PZ40)
1967.9.D4 Deva, 1673-1745? (Table P-PZ40)
1967.9.D44 Dhruvadāsa, 17th cent. (Table P-PZ40)
1967.9.G26 Gadādhara Bhaṭṭa, 16th cent. (Table P-PZ40)
1967.9.G34 Gangādhara, 1842-1915 (Table P-PZ40)
1967.9.G66 Govindaśaraṇa Devācārya (Table P-PZ40)
1967.9.G86 Gurdas Guni (Table P-PZ40)
1967.9.H36 Haricaraṇadāsa, 1708-1787 (Table P-PZ40)
1967.9.H376 Harirāya (Table P-PZ40)
1967.9.H56 Hita Harivaṃśa Gosvami, 1502-1552 (Table P-PZ40)
1967.9.K22 Kabir, 15th cent. (Table P-PZ40)
1967.9.K27 Kālidāsa Trivedī, fl. 1692-1718 (Table P-PZ40)
1967.9.K37 Kesa (Table P-PZ40)
1967.9.K4 Keśavadāsa, 1555?-1617? (Table P-PZ40)
1967.9.K747 Kṛshṇa Kavi (Table P-PZ40)

PK

Modern Indo-Aryan language
Particular languages and dialects, A-Z
Hindi, Urdu, Hindustani languages
Hindi
Special dialects, Western
BrajBhakha
Literature
Individual authors, A-Z -- Continued

1967.9.K75	Kṛshṇakavi, fl. 1687-1691 (Table P-PZ40)	
1967.9.K82	Kumbhakarṇa, 17th cent. (Table P-PZ40)	
1967.9.K84	Kum̐varaskanda Girī (Table P-PZ40)	
1967.9.L3	Lāla Balavīra (Table P-PZ40)	
1967.9.M3	Mādhavarāma, 1683?-1770? (Table P-PZ40)	
1967.9.M33	Mānasiṃha, Maharaja of Ayodhya, 1820-1870 (Table P-PZ40)	
1967.9.M34	Manoharadāsa (Table P-PZ40)	
1967.9.M36	Matirāma, 17th cent. (Table P-PZ40)	
1967.9.M48	Mirzā Abdurrahamāna (Table P-PZ40)	
1967.9.M483	Miśra, Bhāskara Cūrāmaṇi Gopāladāsa, fl. 1633 (Table P-PZ40)	
1967.9.M65	Mohanalāla Miśra, fl. 1550-1560 (Table P-PZ40)	
1967.9.M67	Molārāma, 1743-1833 (Table P-PZ40)	
1967.9.M86	Muralīdhara, b. 1683 or 4 (Table P-PZ40)	
1967.9.N2	Nābhādāsa, fl. 1585 (Table P-PZ40)	
1967.9.N25	Nāgarīdāsa, 1699-1764 (Table P-PZ40)	
1967.9.N28	Nārāyaṇa, Swami, 1828?-1900? (Table P-PZ40)	
1967.9.N3	Narottama Dāsa, 16th cent. (Table P-PZ40)	
1967.9.N35	Navaranga, Swami, 1648-1718 (Table P-PZ40)	
1967.9.N48	Nevāja (Table P-PZ40)	
1967.9.P3	Padmākara, 1753-1833 (Table P-PZ40)	
1967.9.P33	Padumanadāsa (Table P-PZ40)	
1967.9.R2	Rāghavadāsa, fl. 1660 (Table P-PZ40)	
1967.9.R24	Raghuraj Singh, Maharaja of Rewa, d. 1880 (Table P-PZ40)	
1967.9.R26	Rājadhara, 18th cent. (Table P-PZ40)	
1967.9.R265	Rāma, fl. 1676-1698 (Table P-PZ40)	
1967.9.R274	Rāmanātha Jyotishī, 1874-1953 (Table P-PZ40)	
1967.9.R278	Rasakhāna, 16th/17th cent. (Table P-PZ40)	
1967.9.R28	Rasalīna, Gulāmanabī, b. 1699 (Table P-PZ40)	
1967.9.R287	Rasika Govinda, fl. 1793-1833 (Table P-PZ40)	
1967.9.R29	Rasikadeva, Swami, b. 1635 (Table P-PZ40)	
	Ratnkara, Jagannāthadāsa, 1866-1932, see PK1967.9.D3	

Modern Indo-Aryan language
Particular languages and dialects, A-Z
Hindi, Urdu, Hindustani languages
Hindi
Special dialects, Western
BrajBhakha
Literature
Individual authors, A-Z -- Continued

1967.9.R32 Ratnāvalī, 1520 or 1-1594 or 5 (Table P-PZ40)
1967.9.S14 Ṣadhāru, 14th cent. (Table P-PZ40)
1967.9.S16 Śāhajī, King of Tanjore, fl. 1684-1712 (Table P-PZ40)
1967.9.S17 Sāhibasiṃha Mṛgendra, 19th cent. (Table P-PZ40)
1967.9.S4 Senāpati, ca. 1589-ca. 1669 (Table P-PZ40)
1967.9.S64 Ṣomanātha, fl. 1737-1750 (Table P-PZ40)
1967.9.S7 Śrīkṛṣṇabhaṭṭa, 18th cent. (Table P-PZ40)
1967.9.S88 Sundarakum̐varī, b. 1734 (Table P-PZ40)
1967.9.S9 Sūradāsa, 1483?-1563? (Table P-PZ40)
1967.9.T5 Thākura Dāsa, 1766-ca. 1823 (Table P-PZ40)
1967.9.T64 Ṭoḍaramala, 1740-1766 (Table P-PZ40)
1967.9.T8 Tulasīdāsa, 1532-1623 (Table P-PZ40)
1967.9.V43 Vidagdhamādhavāvārttā (Table P-PZ40)
1967.9.V47 Vihārī Lāla, Kavi (Table P-PZ40)
1967.9.V48 Vihārīdāsa (Table P-PZ40)
1967.9.V5 Vishṇudāsa (Table P-PZ40)
1967.9.V7 Vṛnda, 1643-1723 (Table P-PZ40)
1967.9.V73 Vṛndāvanadāsa (Table P-PZ40)
1968 Bundēlī (Table P-PZ15a)
1968.9.A-Z Individual authors or works, A-Z (Table P-PZ40, or P-PZ43)
e. g.
1968.9.B35 Bakhśī Hamsarāja, 18th cent. (Table P-PZ40)
1968.9.H37 Harisevaka Miśra, 17th cent. (Table P-PZ40)
1968.9.I88 Īsurī, 1824-1909 (Table P-PZ40)
1968.9.J33 Jaganika, fl. 1170 (Table P-PZ40)
1968.9.J53 Jñānī, fl. 1714-1744 (Table P-PZ40)
1969.1 Kanaujī (Table P-PZ16)
1969.3 Khari Boli (Table P-PZ16)
1970.A-Z Other dialects, A-Z
1970.M37 Marari
1970.P68 Powari
1970.5 Dakhini. Dakhini Hindustani. Dakhini Urdu (Table P-PZ16)
1970.59.A-Z Individual authors or works, A-Z (Table P-PZ40, or P-PZ43)
1970.59.G55 Ghavvāsī, 17th cent. (Table P-PZ40)

PK

Modern Indo-Aryan language
Particular languages and dialects, A-Z
Hindi, Urdu, Hindustani languages -- Continued
Urdū
1971-1979 Language (Table P-PZ8a, omitting no. 8)
Literature, see PK2151+
Hindustānī
1981-1989 Language (Table P-PZ8a, omitting no. 8)
2000.A-Z Dialects, A-Z
Class here dialects considered generally Hindustānī for which no clear distinction is made between Hindū and Urdū
(2000.D3) Dakhini Hindustani
see PK1970.5-59
2000.F54 Fini Hindi (Table P-PZ16)
Use only .x-.x4
2000.S8 Surinam Hindustānī (Table P-PZ16)
Use only .x-.x4
Literature
see PK2030+, PK2151+
Hindī, Urdū, Hindustānī literatures
Hindī, Hindustānī literature
Literary text may be written in devanāgarī script, urdū (Persian-Arabic) script, or the Latin alphabet
History (Table P-PZ23)
2030 Periodicals. Societies. Serials
2031 General works
2032 General special
2033 Collected essays
2034 Biography (Collective)
2035 Origins to 1500
2036 1500-1800
2037 19th century
2038 20th century
Poetry
2040 General works
By period
2040.2 To 1500
2040.3 1500-1800
2040.4 19th century
2040.5 20th century
2041 Drama
2042 Other
Local, see PK2101+
Collections
2046 Periodicals. Societies. Serials
2047 General and miscellaneous
2049 Selections. Anthologies
By period
2050 Medieval
2051 16th-18th centuries

Modern Indo-Aryan language
Particular languages and dialects, A-Z
Hindi, Urdu, Hindustani literatures
Hindi, Hindustani literature
Collections
By period -- Continued
2052 19th century
2053 20th century
Poetry
2057 General
2058 Selections. Anthologies
2059 Women poets
By period
2062 Medieval
2063 16th-18th centuries
2064 19th century
2065 20th century
2069.A-Z Special forms or subject,s A-Z
2069.C45 Children's poetry
2069.C68 Couplets
2069.E64 Epic poetry
2069.N87 Nursery rhymes
2069.R44 Religion
2069.R48 Revolutionary poetry
2069.V47 Verse satire
2069.W6 Women
2071 Drama
2075 Prose
2077 Fiction
2078.A-Z Other prose forms, A-Z
2078.E8 Essays
2078.L4 Letters
2078.W5 Wit and humor
Local, see PK2101+
Folk literature
(2081) History
see subclass GR
Texts
2085 Folk songs
(2089) Tales, etc.
see subclass GR
(2091) Translations
see subclass GR
Individual authors and works, A-Z
2095.A-Z Through 1550/1660
2095.A63 Amīr Khusraw Dihlavī, ca. 1253-1325
2095.A65 Ananta-das, 15th cent.
2095.D28 Dādūdayāla, 1544-1603
2095.D294 Dāmodarapaṇḍita, d. 1317?
2095.D3 Dāūda, 14th cent.
2095.D5 Dharamadāsa, 15th cent.
2095.G6 Gorakhanātha
2095.K3 Kabir, 15th cent.

PK

Modern Indo-Aryan language
Particular languages and dialects, A-Z
Hindi, Urdu, Hindustani literatures
Hindi, Hindustani literature
Individual authors and works, A-Z
Through 1550/1600 -- Continued

2095.K69 Kṛpārāma, b. 1513
2095.L67 Lorikayana (Table P-PZ43)
2095.M3 Malik Muḥammad Jayasi, fl. 1540
2095.M35 Manjhan, fl. 1545
2095.M5 Mīrabāī, fl. 1516-1546
2095.N2 Nābhādāsa, fl. 1585
2095.P34 Paraśurāmadeva, ca. 1393-ca. 1538
2095.R4 Ravidāsa, 15th cent.
2095.R6 Roḍa, 11th cent.
2095.S23 Sabhācanda, Muni, 16th cent.
2095.S47 Shrī Candra, 1492?-1643?
2095.S8 Sūradāsa, 1483?-1563?
2095.V55 Vishṇūdāsa
2096 1550/1600-1800
2096.A45 Akhā, 17th cent.
2096.A68 Amṛtarāya, poet
2096.A7 Ānåndaghana, fl. 1719-1739
2096.B33 Banārasīdāsa, 1586-1641?
2096.B5 Bhikhārīdāsa, fl. 1734-1750
2096.B63 Bodhā, 18th cent.
2096.C24 Candadāsa, 17th cent.
2096.C3 Caraṇa Dāsa, 1703-1782
Caraṇadāsa, Swami, 1703-1782, see PK2096.C3
2096.D35 Dariyā Sāhaba, 1674-1777 or 8
2096.G5 Gharībadāsa, 1717-1782?
2096.G52 Ghulām Nabī Rasalīn, b. 1699
2096.G54 Giridhara Purohita, 17th cent.
2096.G78 Gulābasiṃha, 18th cent.
2096.H34 Haricaraṇadāsa, 1708-1787
2096.J32 Jaitarāma, 18th cent.
2096.J34 Jana Jasavanta, d. 1618
2096.J37 Jayamalla, 1708-1796
2096.J38 Jayarāmadāsa, 18th cent.
2096.J6 Jodharāja, fl. 1728
2096.J83 Jugatānanda, fl. 1743-1814
2096.K35 Kāsimaśāha, fl.1721
2096.K4 Keśavadāsa, 1555?-1617?
2096.L32 Lakhapatisiṃha, King of Cutch, 1710-1761
2096.L335 Lāla, Kavi
2096.M25 Mādhavarāma, 1683?-1770?
2096.M294 Maṇḍana, 17th cent.
2096.M35 Māvajī, 18th cent.
2096.N34 Nandadāsa, fl. 1568
2096.N36 Naraharadāsa Bārahaṭa
2096.N39 Nazīr Akbarābādī, Valī Muḥammad, 1725?-1825?
2096.N56 Nipaṭa Nirañjana, 1623-1698

Modern Indo-Aryan language
Particular languages and dialects, A-Z
Hindi, Urdu, Hindustani literatures
Hindi, Hindustani literature
Individual authors and works, A-Z
1550/1600-1800 -- Continued

2096.N58 Nitānanda, d. ca. 1799
2096.P34 Pāạnātha, 1618-1694
2096.P7 Prāṇanātha, 1618-1694
2096.R25 Rādhāramaṇadāsa
2096.R32 Rāmadāsa, b. 1608
2096.R34 Rasakhāna, 16/17th cent.
2096.R4 Reṇa, 1741-1871
2096.R64 Rohala, d. 1782
2096.R83 Rūpasāhi, 18th cent.
2096.S3 Sahajo Bāī, fl. 1743
2096.S33 Santadāsa "Vairāgī," 1642-1739
2096.S48 Sevādāsa Nirañjanī, 1641-1741
2096.S77 Sukhadeva, Miśra, 17th cent.
2096.S8 Sundaradāsa, 1596?-1689?
2096.S85 Sūrati Miśra, fl. 1709-1737
2096.T75 Tulasī Sāhaba, 1763-1843
2096.T85 Turasīdasa, Saint
2096.U7 Usman, fl. 1613
2097 1800-1899
2097.A54 Amīradāsa, Sadhu, 1783?-1865?
2097.A72 Āśārāma, 1865?-1920?
2097.B27 Banādāsa, Mahatma, 1821-1892 or 3
2097.B29 Banga Mahilā, 1882-1949
2097.B53 Bharatiyā, Śivacandra
2097.B54 Bhaṭṭa, Bālakṛshṇa, 1844-1914
2097.B74 Bṛjarāja, 1846-1919
2097.C26 Candraśekhara, 1798-1875
2097.C28 Candūlāla, 1862 or 3-1919
2097.C57 Chidakashi, Hemraj, 1851-1903
2097.D3 Das, Srinivas, 1851-1887?
2097.D33 Datta Dvijendra, 1871-1909
2097.D37 Daulatarāma, 1798 or 99-1866
2097.D39 Dayārāma, 1776-1852
2097.D85 Dwivedi, Mahavir Prasad
2097.G27 Gaṇeśasiṃha
2097.G28 Gaṇgā Rāma, 1853?-1902?
2097.G29 Gangādāsa, 1823-1913
2097.G55 Giridhara Dasa, 1833-1860
2097.G66 Gopālarāma, 1866-1946
2097.G8 Gupta, Balmukund, 1865-1907
Gvāla, 1791-1867 or 8, see PK2097.G9
2097.G9 Gvali, b. 1791
Hariścandra, Bhāratendu, 1850-1885, see PK2097.H3
2097.H3 Harishchandra, Bhartendu, 1850-1885
2097.H33 Harisiṃha, 19th cent.
2097.H87 Huzur, Maharaj, 1829-1898

PK

Modern Indo-Aryan language
Particular languages and dialects, A-Z
Hindi, Urdu, Hindustani literatures
Hindi, Hindustani literature
Individual authors and works, A-Z
1800-1899 -- Continued

2097.K45 Khattri, Deoki Nandan, 1861-1913
2097.L33 Lachirāma, 1841-1904
2097.M4 Mehta, Lajjaram Sharma, 1863-1931
2097.M48 Mīra, Murāda, 1823-1895
2097.M49 Miśra, Govindanārāyaṇa, 1859-1923
2097.M5 Miśra, Pratāpanārāyaṇa, 1856-1894
2097.M74 Mṛgendra, 1826-1902
2097.N55 Nirmaḷadāsa, 1765 or 6-1878
2097.P25 Palatū Sāhiba, fl. 1800
2097.P3 Pāṭhaka, Śrīdhara, 1858-1928
2097.P8 Purushottama Kavi, 1863-1938
2097.R313 Rājakumāra Maherāmaṇajī, fl. 1782-1867
2097.R32 Ram, Sardha, fl. 1866
2097.R325 Rāma Dāsa, Miśra, 1821-1892
2097.R347 Rasika Bihārī, b. 1844
2097.R354 Rasika Sundara, 19th cent.
2097.R37 Rāva Gulābasiṃha, 1830-1901
2097.S24 Śambhū, 1854-1908
2097.S27 Śarmā, Nāthūrāmaśankara, 1859-1932
2097.S55 Siṃha, Umarāvaji
2097.S84 Svāmī, Kevalarāma
2097.T53 Ṭhākura Ātmāhamsa, 1834-1896
2097.V57 Visvanath Singh, Marharaja of Rewa, 1789-1854
2097.V92 Vyāsa, Ambikādatta

2098 1900-1960

Avatare, Śhankaradeva, 1926, see PK2098.A89
2098.A89 Avtare, Shanker Dev, 1926-
Candrakāra, see PK2098.S5353
Caturasena, Acharya, 1891-1960, see PK2098.C525
Caturvedī, Bhagavata Śaraṇa, see PK2098.C26
2098.C26 Caturvedī, Bhagavataśaraṇa
2098.C525 Chatursen, 1891-1960
2098.C555 Chiranjit, 1919-
Cirañjita, 1919- , see PK2098.C555
Ḍālamiyā Dineśanandini, 1915- , see PK2098.D27
2098.D27 Dalmia, Dinesh Nandini, 1915-
2098.D275 Damodara Sadana, 1929-
2098.D3273 Dāsa, Rādhākrshṇa, 1865-1907
2098.D383 Deen, Sitaram
Dīna, Sītārāma, 1929-1989, see PK2098.D383
Dvivedī, Sohanalāla, see PK2098.D96
2098.D96 Dwivedi, Sohan Lal
2098.G25 Gangadhar, Madhukar

Modern Indo-Aryan languages
Particular languages and dialects, A-Z
Hindi, Urdu, Hindustani literatures
Hindi, Hindustani literature
Individual authors and works, A-Z
1900-1960 -- Continued

	Gangādhara, Madhukara, 1934- , see PK2098.G25
2098.G27	Garg, Prabhulal, 1906-
2098.G734	Gupta, Bālamukunda, 1865-1907
	Kākā Hātharasi, 1906- , see PK2098.G27
2098.M264	Maheshwari, Dwarika Prasad, 1916-
	Māheśvarī, Dvārikāprasāda, 1916- , see PK2098.M264
2098.M3	Mahto, Mohanlal, 1902-
2098.M35	Mathur, Girja Kumar, 1919-
	Māthura, Girijā Kumāra, 1919- , see PK2098.M35
2098.M455	Mishra, Kanhaiya Lal, 1906-
2098.M457	Mishra, Shiv Sagar, 1927-
2098.M46	Mishra, Vaidyanath, 1911-
2098.M475	Miśra, Mādhava Prasāda, 1871-1907
	Nāgārjuna, 1911- , see PK2098.M46
2098.N333	Nārāyaṇaprasāda Betāba, 1872-1945
2098.P28	Pāṇḍe, Vinodacandra, 1932-
	Paṇḍeya, Vinoda, Candra, 1932- , see PK2098.P28
2098.P3185	Pant, Gaura, 1923-
2098.P32918	Pareek, Surya Karan, 1902-1939
	Pārīka, Sūryakaraṇa, see PK2098.P32918
	Prabhākara, Kanhaiyālāla Miśra, see PK2098.M455
	Premacanda, see PK2098.S7
	Premchand, see PK2098.S7
	Rākeśa, Mohana, see PK2098.R36
2098.R36	Rakesh, Mohan, 1925-1972
	Rāmavṛksha Benīpurī, 1899-1968, see PK2098.S482
2098.R3757	Rao, Balkrishna, 1913-
2098.R377	Rastogi, Vinod, 1923-
	Rastogī, Vinoda, 1923- , see PK2098.R377
	Rāva Bālakṛshṇa, 1913- , see PK2098.R3757
	Sadana, Dāmodara, 1929- , see PK2098.D275
2098.S2314	Sahay, Raghuvir, 1929-
2098.S2316	Sahāya, Brajanandana
	Sahāya, Raghuvīra, 1929- , see PK2098.S2314
2098.S2754	Sapre, Mādhavarāva, 1871-1931
2098.S2775	Saral, Shri Krishna, 1919-
	Sarala Śrīkṛṣṇa, 1919- , see PK2098.S2775
	Śarmā, Rājendra, 1923- , see PK2098.S473
	Śarma, Rāmagopāla, see PK2098.S4786
2098.S294	Śarmā, Revatī Sarana, 1924-

PK

Modern Indo-Aryan languages
Particular languages and dialects, A-Z
Hindi, Urdu, Hindustani literatures
Hindi, Hindustani literature
Individual authors and works, A-Z
1900-1960 -- Continued

	Sastri, Jānakivallabha, see PK2098.S523
2098.S473	Sharma, Rajendra, 1923-
2098.S4786	Sharma, Ram Gopal, 1929-
2098.S482	Sharma, Rambriksha, 1901-1968
	Sharma, Reoti Sharan, 1924- , see PK2098.S294
2098.S523	Shastri, Janaki Vallabha, 1916-
2098.S5353	Shukla, Puttu Lal
2098.S5356	Shukla, Rameshwar, 1915-
	Śivanī, 1923- , see PK2098.P3185
2098.S7	Srivastava, Dhanpat Rai, 1881-1936
	Śukla, Rāmeśvara, 1915- , see PK2098.S5356
2098.U7	Upādhyāya, Ayodhyāsibmha, 1865-1947
	Vājapeyī, Bhagavatīprasāda, 1899- , see PK2098.V25
2098.V25	Vajpeyi, Bhagwati Prasad, 1899-1973
	Varmā, Vṛndāvanalāla, 1890-1969, see PK2098.V4
2098.V4	Verma, Brindavan Lal, 1890?-
	Viyogī, Mohanalāla Mahato, 1899-1990, see PK2098.M3
2098.1-46	1961-
	The author number is determined by the second letter of the name, unless otherwise specified
	Subarrange each author by Table P-PZ40 unless otherwise indicated
2098.1	Anonymous works. By title, A-Z
2098.12	A
2098.13	Ba - Bg
2098.14	Bh
	The author number is determined by the third letter of the name
2098.15	Bi - Bz
2098.16	Ca - Cg
2098.17	Ch
	The author number is determined by the third letter of the name
2098.17.I5	Chintamunnee, Moonishwurlall
2098.18	Ci - Cz
	Cintāmaṇi, Muniśvaralāla, see PK2098.17.I5
2098.19	D
2098.2	E
2098.21	F
2098.22	G
2098.23	H
2098.24	I

Modern Indo-Aryan language
Particular languages and dialects, A-Z
Hindi, Urdu, Hindustani literatures
Hindi, Hindustani literature
Individual authors and works, A-Z
1961- -- Continued

2098.25 J
2098.26 K
Kṛshṇa Kumāra, 1951- , see PK2098.26.R75
2098.26.R75 Kṛshṇakumāra, 1951-
2098.27 L
2098.28 Ma
The author number is determined by the third letter of the name
2098.29 Mb - Mz
2098.29.I712 Mishra, Bhagawati Sharan, 1939-
Miśra, Ghagavatīśarana, 1939- , see PK2098.29.I712
2098.3 N
2098.3.E3 Neeraj, Jai Singh, 1929-
Nīraja, Jayasiṃha, 1929- , see PK2098.3.E3
2098.31 O
2098.32 P
Pālīvāla, Kṛshạdatta, see PK2098.32.A44
2098.32.A44 Paliwal, Krishna Dutt
2098.32.A574 Pant, Pradeep, 1941-
Panta, Pradīpa, 1941- , see PK2098.32.A574
2098.33 Q
2098.34 Ra
The author number is determined by the third letter of the name
2098.35 Rb - Rz
2098.36 Sa
The author number is determined by the third letter of the name
Śailajā, Santosha, 1937- , see PK2098.36.N75
Sakuna Satya, 1946- , see PK2098.36.T86
2098.36.N75 Ṣantosha Ṣailajā, 1937-
Ṣarata Kumāra, see PK2098.38.A63
Śastrī, Gaẹśa Muni, 1931- , see PK2098.38.A758
Śastrī, Umeśa, see PK2098.38.A79
2098.36.T86 Satya Śakuna, 1946-
2098.37 Sb - Sg
Śesha, Śankara, see PK2098.38.E54
2098.38 Sh
The author number is determined by the third letter of the name
2098.38.A63 Sharat, 1937-
2098.38.A758 Shastri, Ganeshmuni, 1931-
2098.38.A79 Shastri, Umesh

PK

Modern Indo-Aryan language
Particular languages and dialects, A-Z
Hindi, Urdu, Hindustani literatures
Hindi, Hindustani literature
Individual authors and works, A-Z
1961-
Sh -- Continued
2098.38.E54 Shesh, Shanker, 1933-1981
2098.38.U47 Shukla, Amar Nath, 1938-
2098.39 Si - Sz
Siṃha, Brajanārāyana, 1929- , see PK2098.39.I49475
Siṃha, Dūdhanātha, 1936- , see PK2098.39.I495
2098.39.I49475 Singh, Braj Narain, 1929-
2098.39.I495 Singh, Doodhnath, 1936-
Śukla, Amaranātha, see PK2098.38.U47
2098.4 T
2098.41 U
2098.42 V
2098.43 W
2098.44 X
2098.45 Y
2098.46 Z
Local
India (including Sri Lanka)
History
2101 General
2102 Special
Collections
2103 General
2104 Special
Outside of India
2105 Asia (Persia, Farther India, East Indies, etc.)
Africa
2111 History
2112 Collections
2114.A-Z By country, A-Z (Table P-PZ26)
2115.A-Z Individual authors and works, A-Z
Subarrange each author by Table P-PZ40 unless otherwise specified
America
United States and Canada
History
2120 General
2121 By state, region, etc.
2122 Collections
2124.A-Z Individual authors, A-Z
2126-2130 Spanish American and Brazil
Divide like PK2120-PK2124
Translations
2141-2142 From Hindī into other languages (Table P-PZ30)

Modern Indo-Aryan language
Particular languages and dialects, A-Z
Hindi, Urdu, Hindustani literatures -- Continued
2151-2200 Urdū literature (Table P-PZ22)
Individual authors, A-Z
2198.A-Z Early to 1857
Subarrange each author by Table P-PZ40 unless otherwise specified
2198.A24 Ābrū, d. 1733 (Table P-PZ40)
2198.A32 Āfrīdī, Qāsim 'Alī Khān, ca. 1769-1810 (Table P-PZ40)
2198.A323 Afsos, Sher Alī Ja'farī, 1735-1809 (Table P-PZ40)
2198.A33 Afzal, Muḥammad Afzal, d. 1625 (Table P-PZ40)
2198.A34 Afẕal, Sayyid Faẓal 'Alī, 1664-1734 (Table P-PZ40)
2198.A35 Aḥmad Junaidī, 17th cent. (Table P-PZ40)
2198.A36 Aḥmad Sharīf Gujarātī, d. 1656 (Table P-PZ40)
2198.A38 'Ajiz (Table P-PZ40)
'Alī Akbar, 17th cent , see PK2198.A35
2198.A42 'Alī Naẓar (Table P-PZ40)
2198.A425 Amānat, 1816-1858 (Table P-PZ40)
2198.A433 Amīnuddin 'Alī A'lā, Sayyid Shāh, 1599-1675 (Table P-PZ40)
2198.A44 Amīr Khusrau Dihlavī, ca. 1253-1325 (Table P-PZ40)
2198.A48 Anis, Mir Babbar Ali, 1802-1874 (Table P-PZ40)
2198.A74 Asar Dihlavī, Khvājah Muḥammad Mīr, 1735-1794 (Table P-PZ40)
2198.A75 Ashraf Biyābānī, Shāh Ashrafuddīn, 1460-1529 (Table P-PZ40)
2198.A77 Asir, 1800-1883 (Table P-PZ40)
2198.A8 Ātish Lakhnavī, Khvājah Ḥaidar 'Alī, 1778-1846 (Table P-PZ40)
2198.A95 Āzurdah, Ṣadruddīn, 1789-1868 (Table P-PZ40)
2198.B327 Bandaḥ Navāz, 1321-1422 (Table P-PZ40)
2198.B336 Bāqir Āgāh Velūrī, 1745-1806 (Table P-PZ40)
2198.B34 Barq, Mīrzā Muḥammad Razā Khān, 1790?-1857 (Table P-PZ40)
2198.B43 Be Ṣabr, Bālmukand, 1812-1885 (Table P-PZ40)
2198.B47 Benī Narā'in Dihlavī, 1776?-1838? (Table P-PZ40)
2198.B87 Burhānuddīn Jānam, Shāh, 1543-1582 (Table P-PZ40)
2198.D33 Dabīr, Mirza, 1803-1875 (Table P-PZ40)
2198.D48 Dil, Muhammad 'Ābid (Table P-PZ40)

Modern Indo-Aryan language
Particular languages and dialects, A-Z
Hindi, Urdu, Hindustani literatures
Urdu literature
Individual authors, A-Z
Early to 1857 -- Continued

2198.F27 Faiz, Mīr Shamsuddīn, 1780 or 81-1866 or 67 (Table P-PZ40)
2198.F37 Faqīr Muḥammad Khān Goyā, d. 1850 (Table P-PZ40)
2198.F39 Falī, Fazl 'Alī, fl. 1733 (Table P-PZ40)
2198.G4 Ghalib, Mirza Asadullah Khan, 1797-1869 (Table P-PZ40)
(2198.G46) Ghavvāṣī
see PK1970.59.G55
2198.G48 Ghazanfar Husain (Table P-PZ40)
2198.G487 Ghulam Qadir Shah, d. 1762 (Table P-PZ40)
2198.G54 Gīlanī, Shamsuddīn, fl. 1854-1867 (Table P-PZ40)
2198.H26 Ḥafīz, 1862-1924 (Table P-PZ40)
2198.H3 Hasan, Mīr, fl. 1786 (Table P-PZ40)
2198.H314 Hāshmī Bījāpūrī, d. 1697 (Table P-PZ40)
2198.H317 Ḥasrat 'Aẓīmābādī, 1728 or 9-1795 or 6 (Table P-PZ40)
2198.H33 Ḥātim, Ẓuhūruddīn, b. 1699 (Table P-PZ40)
2198.H85 Hunar, Sayyid Aḥmad, 18th cent. (Table P-PZ40)
2198.H89 Ḥuzūr 'Aẓīmābādī, Shaikh Ghulām Yaḥyā, 19th cent. (Table P-PZ40)
2198.I2 Ibrahim 'Adil Shah II, Sultan of Bijapur, 1580-1627 (Table P-PZ40)
2198.I43 Imān, Sher Muḥammad Khān, d. 1806 (Table P-PZ40)
2198.I5 Inshā', Inshā'allāh Khān, 1756-1817 (Table P-PZ40)
2198.I84 Ishq, Mīr (Table P-PZ40)
2198.I85 'Ishrat Barelvī, Mīr Ghulām 'Alī, 1770-1820 (Table P-PZ40)
2198.J26 Ja'far 'Alī Khān Zakī, d. 1778 (Table P-PZ40)
2198.J28 Jahān, Bīnī Narā'in (Table P-PZ40)
2198.J37 Jauhar, Mādhūrām, 1810-1880 (Table P-PZ40)
2198.J8 Jur'at, Qalandar Bakhsh, d. 1810 (Table P-PZ40)
2198.K3 Karīmuddīn, 1821-1879 (Table P-PZ40)
2198.K43 Khvājah Mīr, 1719?-1785? (Table P-PZ40)
2198.K85 Kunvar, Apūrbo Krishnā, 1815-1867 (Table P-PZ40)
2198.M23 Mahar, Ḥātim 'Alī, 1815-1879 (Table P-PZ40)
2198.M27 Malik Khushnūd, 17th cent. (Table P-PZ40)

Modern Indo-Aryan language
Particular languages and dialects, A-Z
Hindi, Urdu, Hindustani literatures
Urdu literature
Individual authors, A-Z
Early to 1857 -- Continued

2198.M28 Mamnun Dihlavī, Mīr Nizāmuddīn, d. 1844 (Table P-PZ40)
2198.M34 Maẓhar Jān Jānān, Habīb Ullah, 1699-1780 (Table P-PZ40)
2198.M49 Mīr, Mīr Taqī, d. 1810 (Table P-PZ40)
2198.M52 Mīr Amman Dihlavī, fl. 1801-1806 (Table P-PZ40)
2198.M56 Mir Hasan Shah Haqiqat Barelvi, 1772 or 3-1833 (Table P-PZ40)
2198.M6 Momin, Khan, 1800-1851? (Table P-PZ40)
2198.M75 Muḥabbat Khān, 1750-1808 (Table P-PZ40)
2198.M78 Muḥammad Bahadur Shah II, King of Delhi, 1775-1862 (Table P-PZ40)
2198.M79 Muḥammad Quli Qutb Shah, Sultan of Golkunda, 1565-1612 (Table P-PZ40)
2198.M8 Muḥammad Rafī , ca. 1713-1781 (Table P-PZ40)
2198.M86 Mukhliṣ Murshidābādī, Mīr Bāqir, 18th cent. (Table P-PZ40)
2198.M87 Munīr Shikohābādī, 1814-1880 (Table P-PZ40)
2198.M874 Muntaẓar Lakhnavī, Nūrulislām, 1769?-1806? (Table P-PZ40)
2198.M877 Muqīmī, b. 1554? (Table P-PZ40)
2198.M88 Muṣḥafī, Ghulām Hamdānī, 1750-1824 (Table P-PZ40)
2198.N26 Nādir, Mirzā Kalb-i Husain Khān, 1812-1878 (Table P-PZ40)
2198.N28 Nain Sukh, fl. 1759-1806 (Table P-PZ40)
2198.N32 Nāmī, Ḥisāmuddīn Ḥaider Khān, d. 1846 (Table P-PZ40)
2198.N327 Nāsikh Imām Bakhsh, 1771 or 2-1838 (Table P-PZ40)
2198.N33 Nasīm, Asghar 'Alī Khān, 1799?-1866? (Table P-PZ40)
2198.N34 Naṣīm, Daya Shankar Kaul, 1811-1843 (Table P-PZ40)
2198.N36 Naṣīr, Shāh (Table P-PZ40)
2198.N363 Naṣīruddīn Ḥaidar, Nawab of Oudh, d. 1837 (Table P-PZ40)
2198.N37 Nassākh, 'Abdulghafūr Khān (Table P-PZ40)
2198.N38 Naẓīr Akbarābādī, 1740-1830 (Table P-PZ40)
2198.N39 Naẓīrī, d. 1613 (Table P-PZ40)
2198.N47 Nihāl Cand Lāhaurī (Table P-PZ40)
2198.N49 Niẓām, 1819?-1872 (Table P-PZ40)
2198.N5 Niẓāmī, Fakhr Dīn (Table P-PZ40)

Modern Indo-Aryan language
Particular languages and dialects, A-Z
Hindi, Urdu, Hindustani literatures
Urdu literature
Individual authors, A-Z
Early to 1857 -- Continued

2198.N8 Nuṣratī, d. 1673 (Table P-PZ40)
2198.Q28 Qādrī, Ḥifiẓullāh (Table P-PZ40)
2198.Q3 Qā'im, Muḥammad Qiyāmuddīn, 1726?-1795? (Table P-PZ40)
2198.Q36 Qalaq, d. 1879 (Table P-PZ40)
2198.R26 Rāghib, Muḥammad Ja'far Khān, d. 1800 (Table P-PZ40)
2198.R3 Rajab 'Ali Beg Surūr, ca. 1787-1867 (Table P-PZ40)
2198.R37 Rashk, Mīr 'Alī Ausat, 19th cent. (Table P-PZ40)
2198.R38 Raushan 'Alī, 17th cent. (Table P-PZ40)
2198.R55 Rind, Sayyid Muḥammad Khān, d. 1851 or 2 (Table P-PZ40)
2198.S13 Saadat Ali Khan, Nawab Wazir of Oudh, d. 1814 (Table P-PZ40)
2198.S14 Sa'ādat Yār Khān, d. 1835 (Table P-PZ40)
2198.S16 Ṣafīr Bilgirāmī, 1834-1890 (Table P-PZ40)
2198.S19 Sahbā'ī, Imām Bakhsh, 1802 or 3-1857 (Table P-PZ40)
2198.S26 Sarmad, Muḥammad Sa'īd, 1618-1660 or 61 (Table P-PZ40)
2198.S29 Sayyid 'Abbas 'Alī, 18th cent. (Table P-PZ40)
2198.S55 al-Shāhid, Muḥammad ibn Ismā'īl, d. 1831 (Table P-PZ40)
2198.S554 Shaiftah, Muṣṭafā Khān, fl. 1833-1866 (Table P-PZ40)
2198.S57 Shauq, Mirzā (Table P-PZ40)
2198.S583 Shauqi, Hasan, 16th cent. (Table P-PZ40)
2198.S586 Shīv Lāl, 17th cent. (Table P-PZ40)
2198.S59 Shu'ūr Bilgrāmī, d. 1860 (Table P-PZ40)
2198.S6 Sirāj Aurangābādī, 1712-1763 (Table P-PZ40)
2198.S65 Soz, Mīr, d. 1798 (Table P-PZ40)
2198.S86 Suharvardī, Shāh Niyāz Aḥmad Qādirī Cishtī, d. 1834 (Table P-PZ40)
2198.S93 Sulaimān Shikoh, Mirzā, d. 1838 (Table P-PZ40)
2198.T33 Taḥsīn al-Dīn (Table P-PZ40)
2198.T337 Tālib 'Ali Khan 'Aishī, 1783-1824 (Table P-PZ40)
2198.T36 Taslīm, Mahdī Bakhsh, 19th cent. (Table P-PZ40)
2198.T87 Turāb, Turāb 'Alī, 18th cent. (Table P-PZ40)
2198.V3 Vajhī, 17th cent. (Table P-PZ40)

Modern Indo-Aryan language
Particular languages and dialects, A-Z
Hindi, Urdu, Hindustani literatures
Urdu literature
Individual authors, A-Z
Early to 1857 -- Continued
2198.V33 Valā, Maẓhar 'Ali Khān, fl. 1805 (Table P-PZ40)
Valī, 17th/8th cent , see PK2198.V34
2198.V34 Valī, Shamsuddin, 1668?-1742? (Table P-PZ40)
2198.V37 Vāstī, Fazl-i Rasūl, 1813-1879 (Table P-PZ40)
2198.V39 Vazīr, Khvājah, d. 1854 (Table P-PZ40)
2198.W35 Wajid 'Ali Shah, King of Oudh, 1821-1896 (Table P-PZ40)
2198.Y36 Yaqīn, In'āmullāh Khān (Table P-PZ40)
2198.Z3 Zauq, Shaikh Muḥammad Ibrāhīm, 1789-1854 (Table P-PZ40)
2199 1857-1946 (Table P-PZ40, or P-PZ43)
e. g.
'Abdulaq, 1869-1961, see PK2199.H3
2199.A39 Ahmad, Ghulam, Hazrat Mirza, 1839?-1908 (Table P-PZ40)
2199.A423 Ahmad Razā Khān (Table P-PZ40)
2199.A5 Akbar Allabhābādī, 1846-1921 (Table P-PZ40)
2199.A52 Akbar Dānāpūrī, Shāh, 1843- 1909 (Table P-PZ40)
2199.A535 Akhtar, Jān Nisār, 1914-1976 (Table P-PZ40)
2199.A73 Amīr Mīnāī, Amīr Aḥmad, 1828-1900 (Table P-PZ40)
2199.A7565 Ārzū Lakhnavī, Sayyid Anvar Ḥusain, 1873-1951 (Table P-PZ40)
2199.A77 Asar Lakhnavī, Mirzā Ja'far 'Alī Khan, 1885-1967 (Table P-PZ40)
2199.A797 'Askarī, Mirzā Muḥammad, b. 1869 (Table P-PZ40)
2199.A84 Auj Lakhnavī, Mirzā Muḥammad Ja'far, 1853-1917 (Table P-PZ40)
2199.A9 Āzād, Muḥammad, 1846-1916 (Table P-PZ40)
2199.A914 Āzād, Muḥammad Ḥusain, ca. 1834-1910 (Table P-PZ40)
2199.A96 'Azmi Dihlavī, 1867-1934 (Table P-PZ40)
2199.B345 Bayān Muḥammad Murtaẓā, 1850-1900 (Table P-PZ40)
2199.B37 Bedam Shāh Vārsī, 1882?-1936 (Table P-PZ40)
2199.B442 Bekal Utsahi, Mohammad Shafi Khan Lodi, 1928- (Table P-PZ40)
2199.B495 Bilgrāmī, 'Abdullāh Ḥusain (Table P-PZ40)
2199.D24 Dāgh Dihlavī, 1831-1905 (Table P-PZ40)
2199.D3 Dar, Ratan Nath, 1846-1902 (Table P-PZ40)

Modern Indo-Aryan language
Particular languages and dialects, A-Z
Hindi, Urdu, Hindustani literatures
Urdu literature
Individual authors, A-Z
1857-1946 -- Continued

2199.D53 Dil Shāhjahānpūrī, 1875-1959 (Table P-PZ40)
2199.F255 Faiz, Faiz Ahmad, 1911- (Table P-PZ40)
2199.F284 Fakhruddīn Khayālī, Sayyid, 1841-1908 (Table P-PZ40)
2199.F3 Fānī Badāyūnī, 1870-1942 (Table P-PZ40)
2199.F37 al-Fayyāẓ, Sayyid Abūlfaẓl, 19th cent. (Table P-PZ40)
2199.F55 Firāq Gorakhpūrī, 1896-1982 (Table P-PZ40)
2199.H25 Ḥāfiẓ. Vilāyatullāh, 1873-1949 (Table P-PZ40)
2199.H278 Ḥairat, Sayyid 'Ināyat Aḥmad Naqvī Qubā'ī, 1862-1939 (Table P-PZ40)
2199.H297 Ḥālī, Khvājah Altāf Ḥusain, 1837-1914 (Table P-PZ40)
2199.H3 Haq, Abdul, 1869-1961 (Table P-PZ40)
2199.H338 Hasan, Saadat, 1912-1955 (Table P-PZ40)
Ḥasrat Mūhānī, 1875-1951, see PK2199.H37
2199.H37 Hasrat Mūhānī, Fazalulhasan, 1875-1951 (Table P-PZ40)
2199.H86 Hussain, Mohammad, ca. 1834-1910 (Table P-PZ40)
2199.H87 Hussain, Syed Anwar, 1873-1951 (Table P-PZ40)
2199.I65 Iqbal, Muhammad, Sir, 1877-1938 (Table P-PZ40)
2199.I83 Ismā'īl Merathī, 1844-1917 (Table P-PZ40)
2199.J25 Ja'farī, Sayyid Ṣafdar Ḥusain (Table P-PZ40)
2199.J337 Jalāl, Ẓāmin 'Alī, 1834-1909 (Table P-PZ40)
2199.J338 Jalīl Mānakpūrī, 1864-1946 (Table P-PZ40)
2199.J38 Jāved Lakhnavī, Bandah Kāẓim, 1864?-1921 (Table P-PZ40)
2199.J46 Jigar Bisvani, 1871-1958 (Table P-PZ40)
2199.J6 Josh Malihabadi, Shabbir Hasan Khan (Table P-PZ40)
Josh Molīḥabādī, 1896- , see PK2199.J6
2199.K415 Khān, 'Abdulghaffār, 1864-1933 (Table P-PZ40)
2199.M3 Mahdī Ifādī, 1870?-1921 (Table P-PZ40)
2199.M3183 Mahr, Ghulām Rasūl, 1895-1971 (Table P-PZ40)
2199.M319 Mā'il Dihlavī, Mumtāzuddīn Aḥmad Khān, 1866-1894 (Table P-PZ40)
Manṭo, Sa'ādat, Ḥasan, see PK2199.H338
2199.M47 Mīrājī, 1912-1949 (Table P-PZ40)

Modern Indo-Aryan language
Particular languages and dialects, A-Z
Hindi, Urdu, Hindustani literatures
Urdu literature
Individual authors, A-Z
1857-1946 -- Continued

2199.M49 Mirzā, Muḥammad 'Azīz, 1865-1912 (Table P-PZ40)
2199.M5 Mirza Khan, 1831-1905 (Table P-PZ40)
2199.N22 Nādir Kakorvī, Nādir 'Alīkhān, 1857-1912 (Table P-PZ40)
2199.N333 Nāṣir 'Alī, Mīr, 1827-1933 (Table P-PZ40)
2199.N34 Naẓar, Naubat Rā'e, 1866-1923 (Table P-PZ40)
2199.N35 Nazīr Aḥmad, 1836-1912 (Table P-PZ40)
2199.N4 Nazm Tabātabā'i, 1852-1933 (Table P-PZ40)
2199.N55 Nisār Qaraulvī, Sayyid Nisār Ḥusain, 1861?-1946 (Table P-PZ40)
2199.N62 Naẓāmī Badāyūnī, 1872-1947 (Table P-PZ40)
2199.P25 Paramananda, Swami, fl. 19th cent. (Table P-PZ40)
2199.P33 Patras, Ahmad Shah Bukhārī, 1898-1958 (Table P-PZ40)
2199.Q277 Qaiṣer Vārsī Murādābādī, Sayyid Abdulghanī Shāh, 1887- (Table P-PZ40)
2199.R365 Rāshidulkhairī, 1868-1936 (Table P-PZ40)

Riyāẓ Khairābādī, 1853-1935, see PK2199.R5

2199.R5 Riyāẓ Khairābādī, Riyāẓ Aḥmad, 1853-1935 (Table P-PZ40)

Rizavi, Masud Hasan, see PK2199.R52

2199.R52 Rizvī, Sayyid Mas'ud Ḥasan, 1893-1975 (Table P-PZ40)
2199.R8 Ruswa, Mirza Mohammad Hadi, 1857-1931 (Table P-PZ40)

Ṣafī Aurangābādī, 1893-1954, see PK2199.S16

2199.S16 Ṣafī Aurangābādī, Bahbūd 'Alī, 1893-1954 (Table P-PZ40)
2199.S164 Ṣafī Lakhnavī, 1862-1950 (Table P-PZ40)
2199.S2 Sajjād Ḥusain, 1856-1915 (Table P-PZ40)
2199.S227437 Sagar, Ramanand, 1917- (Table P-PZ40)
2199.S3 Salīm, Vaḥīduddīn, d. 1928 (Table P-PZ40)

Sarshār, Ratan Nāth, see PK2199.D3

2199.S4187 Shad Arifi, Ahmad Ali Khan Laddan, 1903?- (Table P-PZ40)
2199.S46 Shād 'Azīmābādī, 1846-1927 (Table P-PZ40)
2199.S4626 Shahbāz, 'Abdulghafūr, d. 1908 (Table P-PZ40)
2199.S463 Shāhid Aḥmad Dihlavī, 1906-1967 (Table P-PZ40)

Modern Indo-Aryan language
Particular languages and dialects, A-Z
Hindi, Urdu, Hindustani literatures
Urdu literature
Individual authors, A-Z
1857-1946 -- Continued

2199.S47 Sharar, 'Abdulḥalīm, 1860-1926 (Table P-PZ40)
2199.S474 Sharf, Āghā Ḥajjū, fl. 1828-1875 (Table P-PZ40)
2199.S477 Shauq Nīmvī, 1861-1904 (Table P-PZ40)
2199.S5 Shibli Numani, Muḥammad, 1857-1914 (Table P-PZ40)
2199.S563 Sīmāb Amrohvī, 1850-1928 (Table P-PZ40)
2199.S76 Ṣūfī, Sayyid Shāh Farzand Alī, 1838-1900 (Table P-PZ40)
2199.S78 Sukhan Dihlavī, Khvājah Sayyid Fakhruddīn Ḥusain, 1839-1900 (Table P-PZ40)
2199.S8 Surur Jahānābādī, Durgā Sahā'e, 1873-1910 (Table P-PZ40)
2199.T22 Ta'assuff, Ḥusain 'Alī (Table P-PZ40)
2199.T363 Taslīm, Amīrullāh, 1820-1911 (Table P-PZ40)
2199.U4 'Umar, Muhammad, 1904-1963 (Table P-PZ40)
2199.U7 'Urūj, Dūlhā Sāhib, b. 1865 (Table P-PZ40)
2199.Z28 Ẓafar 'Alī Khān, 1873-1956 (Table P-PZ40)
2199.Z37 Ẓarīf Lakhnavī, 1870-1937 (Table P-PZ40)
2200 1947- (Table P-PZ40, or P-PZ43)
Anand, Satyapal, 1931- , see PK2200.A48
2200.A48 Ānand Satyah Pāl (Table P-PZ40)
Bekal Utsāhī, 1928- , see PK2200.B442
2200.B442 Bekal Utsāhī, Mohammad Shafi Khan Lodi, 1928 (Table P-PZ40)
Muṣlihuddīn, Sayyi, see PK2200.S4355
Shād, 'Ārifī, 1900-1964, see PK2200.S4187
2200.S4187 Shad Arifi, Ahmad Ali Khan Laddan, 1903?- (Table P-PZ40)
Shaukat, Thānuī, 1904- , see PK2200.U4
2200.S4355 Shaz Tamkanat (Table P-PZ40)
2200.U4 'Umar, Muhammad, 1904- (Table P-PZ40)
Translations (Table P-PZ30)
2211-2212 From Urdū into other languages
Hindko, see PK2269.H5
2215-2218 Jaipurī (Table P-PZ11)
Jangalī, see PK2639.M3
Jatkī, see PK2639.M3
Jaṭu, see PK1960
Jaunsārī, see PK2610.J3
Jullundur Dōābī, see PK2639.J8
Kachchhī, see PK2790.K3
Kanaujī, see PK1969.1
Kaṇḍiālī, see PK2649.K3

Modern Indo-Aryan languages
Particular languages and dialects, A-Z -- Continued
Kangri dialect, see PK2649.K4
Kāshmīrī, see PK7021+
2225 Khāndhēsī
Khas-kurā, see PK2595+
Kiūṭhalī, see PK2610.K5
2231-2239 Kōnkaṇī (Table P-PZ8a)
Kōnkaṇī (Dialect of Bhīlī), see PK1800
Kuḷui, see PK2610.K8
Kumaunī, see PK2605.K8
2251 Lambadi
A mixed form of speech with some western form of Rājasthānī as its basis
Cf. PK2701+
Lahnda
2261-2267 Language (Table P-PZ8a, no. 1-7)
2268 Other special
Including etymology
2269.A-Z Dialects, A-Z
2269.H5 Hindko
(2269.S35) Sirāikī
see PK2892.95.S55
2270 Literature (Table P-PZ25)
Lāṛī, see PK2790.L2, PK2790.L3
Ludhiānī, see PK2639.L8
(2291-2294) Magahī
see PK1821+
(2311-2319) Maithilī
see PK1811+
Mājhī, see PK2631+
2331-2339 Mālvī (Ujainī) (Table P-PZ8a)
A dialect of Rājathānī
Cf. PK2701+, Rājasthānī
Mālwāī, see PK2639.M3
Marāṭhī
A dialect of Rājasthānī
Cf. PK2701+, Rājasthānī
Language (Table P-PZ6)
2351 Periodicals. Societies. Collections
2353 General treatises
2355 Study and teaching
Grammar
2356 Treatises in Oriental languages
Prefer classification with language
2357 Treatises in Western languages
2358 Exercises. Chrestomathies. Phrase books, etc.
2359 Phonology. Phonetics
2361 Alphabet
(2362) Transliteration
see P226
2363 Morphology. Inflection. Accidence

PK

Modern Indo-Aryan language
Particular languages and dialects, A-Z
Marathi
Language
Grammar
Treatises in
Western languages -- Continued
2365 Syntax
2369 Prosody. Metrics. Rhythmics
2371 Etymology
Lexicography
Dictionaries
2373 Equivalents in Eastern languages
2375 Equivalents in Western languages
Dialects. Provincialisms, etc.
2377 General works
2378.A-Z Special. by name or place, A-Z
2378.A73 Are
2378.K67 Koshti
2378.N34 Nāpuri
2378.V37 Varhadi-Nagpuri (Table P-PZ16)
2400-2418 Literature (Table P-PZ23)
2418.A-Z Individual authors or works, A-Z (Table P-PZ40, or P-PZ43)
2418.A335 Ādinātha Bhairava, fl. 1834-1845 (Table P-PZ40)
2418.A58 Apte, Hari Narayan, 1864-1919 (Table P-PZ40)
2418.B3 Bahiṇī, ca. 1628-ca. 1700 (Table P-PZ40)
Bālakavī, 1890-1918, see PK2418.T48
Bee, 1892-1947, see PK2418.G797
2418.B38 Bhide, Vidyadhar Vaman (Table P-PZ40)
2418.C294 Candrakīrti, fl. 1825 (Table P-PZ40)
2418.C52 Cipaḷūṇakara, Vishṇu Kṛshṇa, 1850-1882 (Table P-PZ40)
2418.C6 Cokhāmeḷā, d. 1318 (Table P-PZ40)
2418.D25 Dāmale, Kṛshṇājī Keśava, 1866-1905 (Table P-PZ40)
2418.D256 Dāmodarapaṇḍita, d. 1317? (Table P-PZ40)
2418.D277 Darekara, Govinda Tryambaka, 1874-1926 (Table P-PZ40)
2418.D278 Dāsagaṇu, Maharaja, 1868-1962 (Table P-PZ40)
2418.D3 Dāsopanta, 1551-1615 (Table P-PZ40)
Desāi, Raṇajita, 1928-1992, see PK2418.D38
2418.D38 Desai, Ranjit, 1928-1992 (Table P-PZ40)
Deśapāṇḍe, Nirmalā,1929- , see PK2418.D4185
2418.D4185 Deshpande, Nirmala, 1929- (Table P-PZ40)
2418.D45 Deval, G.B., 1855-1916 (Table P-PZ40)
2418.E4 Ekanātha, ca. 1548-ca. 1609 (Table P-PZ40)
2418.E43 Elhaṇa (Table P-PZ40)
2418.F8 Fule, Joti Govindrao, 1827-1890 (Table P-PZ40)
2418.G3283 Gaṇeśanạtha, 17th cent. (Table P-PZ40)
2418.G3286 Gangādhara, 19th cent. (Table P-PZ40)

Modern Indo-Aryan language
Particular languages and dialects, A-Z
Marathi
Literature
Individual authors or works, A-Z -- Continued

2418.G67 Gorhe, Candraśekhara Śivārama, 1871-1937 (Table P-PZ40)
2418.G797 Gupte, Narayan Murlidhar, 1872-1947 (Table P-PZ40)
2418.G895 Gurudāsa, 17th cent. (Table P-PZ40)
2418.H387 Hayagrīvācārya, ca. 1265-ca. 1324 (Table P-PZ40)
2418.H65 Honājībālā, fl. 1784-1792 (Table P-PZ40)
2418.J35 Janābāī (Table P-PZ40)
2418.J48 Jñānadeva, fl. 1290 (Table P-PZ40)
2418.J586 Joshi, Mrinalini Madhusudan, 1927- (Table P-PZ40)
Jośī, Mṛṇālinī, 1927- , see PK2418.J586
2418.K286 Kanekar, Anant, 1904- (Table P-PZ40)
Kāṇekara, Ananta, 1904- , see PK2418.K286
2418.K298 Kāniṭakara, Kāśībāī, 1861-1948 (Table P-PZ40)
2418.K323 Karkhanis, Trimbak Sitaram, 1874-1956 (Table P-PZ40)
2418.K414 Kelkar, Narsinha Chintaman, 1872-1947 (Table P-PZ40)
2418.K424 Ketkar, Shridhar Venkatesh, 1884-1937 (Table P-PZ40)
2418.K427 Khāḍilakara, Kṛrshṇājī Prabhākara, 1872-1948 (Table P-PZ40)
2418.K58 Kirloskar, B.P., 1843-1885 (Table P-PZ40)
2418.K63 Kolhaṭakara, Śrīpāda Kṛshṇa, 1871-1934 (Table P-PZ40)
2418.K668 Kṛshṇadāsa, Muni, fl. 1652 (Table P-PZ40)
2418.K6682 Kṛshṇadāsa Śāmā, 15th cent. (Table P-PZ40)
2418.K6694 Kṛshṇadāva Kadama, 1840-1912 (Table P-PZ40)
Mādhava Jūliyana, see PK2418.P319
2418.M283 Mādhavānuja, 1872-1916 (Table P-PZ40)
2418.M284 Mādhavasvāmī, ca. 1668-ca. 1758 (Table P-PZ40)
2418.M2977 Mahammadabābā Śrīgondekara, 17th cent. (Table P-PZ40)
2418.M3 Mahipatī, 1715-1790 (Table P-PZ40)
2418.M68 Moropanta, 1729-1794 (Table P-PZ40)
2418.M78 Mukteśvara, 1608-1660 (Table P-PZ40)
2418.M82 Mukundarāja, 13th cent. (Table P-PZ40)
2418.M828 Murārimalla, 17th cent. (Table P-PZ40)
2418.N22 Nāgadevācārya, 13th cent. (Table P-PZ40)
2418.N2247 Nāgeśa cent. (Table P-PZ40)
2418.N23 Nāmadeva, 1270-1350 (Table P-PZ40)
2418.N246 Naraharī Sonāra, 14th cent. (Table P-PZ40)
2418.N2618 Nārāyaṇa, 1793-1868 (Table P-PZ40)

Modern Indo-Aryan language
Particular languages and dialects, A-Z
Marathi
Literature
Individual authors or works, A-Z -- Continued

2418.N2645 Narīndrabāsa, 13th cent. (Table P-PZ40)
2418.N29 Navarasanārāyana, fl. 1693-1745 (Table P-PZ40)
2418.P236 Padmanji, Baba, 1831-1906 (Table P-PZ40)
2418.P2598 Panduranga Govinda Sastri Parakhi (Table P-PZ40)
2418.P26 Panvalkar, S.D. (Table P-PZ40)
Pāṇavalakara, Śrī Da, see PK2418.P26
2418.P31395 Pāṭīla, B.B. (Table P-PZ40)
Pāṭīla, Bā. Bha (Bābāsāheba Bharamagauḍā), 1939-1961, see PK2418.P31395
Paṭvardhana, Mādhavarāva, see PK2418.P319
2418.P319 Patwardhan, M.T., 1894-1939 (Table P-PZ40)
Pedaṇekara, Nārāyaa Rā, 1936- , see PK2418.P374
2418.P374 Pednekar, Narayan Ramchandra, 1936- (Table P-PZ40)
2418.P574 Phule, Sāvitrībāī, 1831-1897 (Table P-PZ40)
2418.P757 Pradhāna, Bajābā Rāmācandra, 1838-1886 (Table P-PZ40)
2418.R26 Rāmadaśa, b. 1608 (Table P-PZ40)
2418.R272 Rāmānanda, Swami (Table P-PZ40)
2418.R276 Rāmapaṇḍita, 18th cent. (Table P-PZ40)
2418.R287 Rāne, Bābājīrāva, 1874-1913 (Table P-PZ40)
Rāṅgaṇekara, Mo. Ga, 1907- , see PK2418.R3
2418.R3 Rangnekar, Motiram Gajanan (Table P-PZ40)
2418.R365 Ravalobāsa, 1352?-1372? (Table P-PZ40)
2418.R47 Reṇukādāsa, 18th cent. (Table P-PZ40)
2418.S234 Śāhajī, King of Tanjore, fl. 1684-1712 (Table P-PZ40)
2418.S237 Śahāmunī (Table P-PZ40)
2418.S2537 Saldanha, Antonio de, 1598-1663 (Table P-PZ40)
2418.S256 Samarthaśishya (Table P-PZ40)
2418.S2775 Sarasvatī Gangādhara, 15th cent. (Table P-PZ40)
2418.S427 Serfoji II, Raja of Tanjore, fl. 1798-1832 (Table P-PZ40)
Śevaḍe, Indumatī, 1917- , see PK2418.S473
2418.S473 Sheorey, Indumati, 1917- (Table P-PZ40)
2418.S48 Shirwadkar, Vishnu Vaman, 1912- (Table P-PZ40)
Śiravāḍakara, Vi. Vā., 1912- , see PK2418.S48
2418.S554 Sivadīna Kesarīnātha, 1698-1774 (Table P-PZ40)
2418.S6312 Śrīdharasvāmī Nājharekara (Table P-PZ40)
2418.S64 Śrīpatinātha, fl. 1879-1883 (Table P-PZ40)
2418.S7 Stephens, Thomas, 1549-1619 (Table P-PZ40)

Modern Indo-Aryan language
Particular languages and dialects, A-Z
Marathi
Literature
Individual authors or works, A-Z -- Continued
2418.S93 Syāmarāja, 18th cent. (Table P-PZ40)
2418.T315 Tambe, Bhaskar Ramchandra, 1874-1941 (Table P-PZ40)
2418.T48 Ṭhomare, Tryambaka Bāpūjī, 1890-1918 (Table P-PZ40)
2418.T53 Tilak, Lakshmibai (Gokhale), 1873-1936 (Table P-PZ40)
2418.T54 Tilak, Narayan Vaman, 1862?-1919 (Table P-PZ40)
2418.T8 Tukārāma, ca. 1608-ca. 1649 (Table P-PZ40)
2418.V33 Vāmana, Paḍṇḍita, 17th cent. (Table P-PZ40)
2418.V57 Vipraviśvanātha, fl. 1647 (Table P-PZ40)
2418.V62 Vishṇudāsa, 1844-1917 (Table P-PZ40)
Mārwāṛī (Ḍingaḷ)
Cf. PK2701+, Rājasthānī
2461-2469 Language (Table P-PZ8a, omitting no. 8)
2469.A-Z Dialects. Provincialisms, etc. (Table P-PZ8a, omitting no. 8)
2469.B3 Bāgrī (Table P-PZ8a)
2469.B5 Bīkānērī (Table P-PZ16)
2469.M4 Mēwāṛī (Mērwāṛī) (Table P-PZ8a)
2469.S4 Shekhawati (Table P-PZ8a)
2469.T3 Thaḷī (Table P-PZ8a)
2469.W34 Wagdi (Table P-PZ16)
2470-2479 Literature (Table P-PZ24)
2479.A-Z Individual authors or works, A-Z (Table P-PZ40, or P-PZ43)
e. g.
2479.K5 Khiḍiyā Jagā, fl. 1658 (Table P-PZ40)
2479.L3 Lacchīrāma Kucāmaṇī (Table P-PZ40)
2479.L35 Lāngīdāsa Maheḍu, 18th cent. (Table P-PZ40)
2479.M34 Māna, fl. 1660 (Table P-PZ40)
2479.M35 Mañcha, Manasārāma, 1770-1841 (Table P-PZ40)
2479.N3 Narapati Nālha, 12th cent. (Table P-PZ40)
2479.R353 Rājiyā Rāvanā, b. 1769 (Table P-PZ40)
2479.S27 Śaṅkaradāna Samaura, 1828-1878 (Table P-PZ40)
2479.S9 Sūryamalla, 1815-1868 (Table P-PZ40)
Sūryamalla Miśraa, 1815-1868, see PK2479.S9
Mayāng, see PK1559.M3
Mērwārī, see PK2469.M4
Mēwāṛī, see PK2469.M4
2511 Mēwātī (Table P-PZ15)
Cf. PK2701+, Rājasthānī
Nāgpuri, see PK2378.N34
Nagpuriā, see PK1830.N3
Nepalī, see PK2595+
2521 Nimadi (Table P-PZ15a)
Oṛiyā (Uriyā)

PK

Modern Indo-Aryan language
Particular languages and dialects, A-Z
Oṛiyā (Uriyā) -- Continued
2561-2569 Language (Table P-PZ8a, omitting no. 8)
2570-2579 Literature (Table P-PZ24)
2579.A-Z Individual authors or works, A-Z
e. g.
2579.A2 Abhimanyu Sāmanta Siṃhāra, 1757-1806 (Table P-PZ40)
2579.A33 Acyutānanda Dāsa, b. 1482 (Table P-PZ40)
2579.A53 Ananta Dāsa (Table P-PZ40)
2579.A73 Arakshita, Dāsa, 17th cent. (Table P-PZ40)
2579.A75 Arjuna Dāsa, fl. 1520-1530 (Table P-PZ40)
2579.A77 Ārttatrāṇa Dāsa, 18th cent. (Table P-PZ40)
Bāhāliā, Bishnuprasāda, 1932- , see PK2579.B25
2579.B25 Bahalia, Vishnu Prasad, 1932- (Table P-PZ40)
2579.B254 Bajari Dāsa, 17th cent. (Table P-PZ40)
2579.B256 Bal, Nandakishore, 1875-1928 (Table P-PZ40)
Baḷa, Nadakiśora, 1875-1928, see PK2579.B256
2579.B258 Baḷadeba Ratha, 1789-1845 (Table P-PZ40)
2579.B259 Baḷārama Dāsa, 15th cent. (Table P-PZ40)
2579.B2595 Bāḷigaṁ Dāsa, 18th cent. (Table P-PZ40)
2579.B263 Bānamāḷī, 18th cent. (Table P-PZ40)
2579.B264 Banaṃāḷī Dāsa, 16th cent. (Table P-PZ40)
2579.B284 Bāranga, Siddha, 16th cent. (Table P-PZ40)
2579.B482 Bhaktacaraṇa Dāsa, 1729-1813 (Table P-PZ40)
2579.B4833 Bhima Bhoi, 1852-1895 (Table P-PZ40)
2579.B4834 Bhīmā Dhībara, 17th cent. (Table P-PZ40)
2579.B532 Bishnu Dāsa, fl. 1590-1600 (Table P-PZ40)
2579.B567 Biśvambhara (Table P-PZ40)
Biśvarañjana, 1947- , see PK2579.B58
2579.B58 Biswaranjan, 1947- (Table P-PZ40)
2579.B73 Brajanātha Baḍajenā, 1730-1795? (Table P-PZ40)
Caini, Ratnākara, 1945- , see PK2579.C47
2579.C26 Caitanya Dāsa, 15th cent. (Table P-PZ40)
2579.C47 Chaini, Ratnakar, 1945- (Table P-PZ40)
2579.D257 Das, Bijoyini, 1946- (Table P-PZ40)
2579.D327 Das, Hemant Kumar, 1939- (Table P-PZ40)
Dāsa, Bijayinī, 1946- , see PK2579.D257
Dāsa, Hemanta Kumāra, 1939- , see PK2579.D327
2579.D384 Dāsa, Satyabādī, 1838-1958 (Table P-PZ40)
2579.D392 Dāśarathịdāsa, fl. 1720-1731 (Table P-PZ40)
2579.D414 Deba, Jalandhara, 1872-1952 (Table P-PZ40)
2579.D54 Dhanañjaya Bhañja, 1611-1701 (Table P-PZ40)
2579.D548 Dibākara Dāsa, 17th cent. (Table P-PZ40)
2579.D55 Dīnakṛshṇa Dāsa, d. ca. 1715 (Table P-PZ40)
2579.G39 Gauracaraṇa Adhikārī, 1814-1890 (Table P-PZ40)
2579.G57 Gopālakṛshna Paṭṭanāyaka, 1784-1862 (Table P-PZ40)
2579.H2 Hāḍịdāsa, fl. 1772-1837 (Table P-PZ40)

Modern Indo-Aryan language
Particular languages and dialects, A-Z
Oriya (Uriya)
Literature
Individual authors or works, A-Z -- Continued

2579.I85 Iśvara Dāsa, 15th cent. (Table P-PZ40)
2579.J28 Jagannātha Dāsa, 1487-1547 (Table P-PZ40)
Jenāmani Narendra Kumāra, 1934- , see PK2579.R58
2579.K33 Kahnāi Campatirāya, 17th cent. (Table P-PZ40)
2579.K3314 Kahnāi Khuṇṭiā, fl. 1497-1509 (Table P-PZ40)
2579.K332 Kaiḷāsa (Table P-PZ40)
2579.K3543 Kanishka (Table P-PZ40)
2579.K43 Keśabarāja Haricandana, fl. 1697-1715 (Table P-PZ40)
2579.L63 Lokanātha Bidyādhara, 1657- (Table P-PZ40)
2579.M217 Madhusūdana, 19th cent. (Table P-PZ40)
2579.M235 Mahādeba Dāsa, 16th cent. (Table P-PZ40)
Mahānti, Cintm̐aṇi, 1867-1943, see PK2579.M2877
2579.M2877 Mahanty, Chintamaṇi, 1867-1943 (Table P-PZ40)
Mahāpātra, Godābarīśa, 1898-1965, see PK2579.M323
2579.M323 Mahapatra, Godavaris (Table P-PZ40)
2579.M3339 Mahāranā, Candramohana, 1870-1929 (Table P-PZ40)
2579.M33795 Mānagobinda Otā, 19th cent. (Table P-PZ40)
2579.M4 Mehera, Gangadhara, 1862-1924 (Table P-PZ40)
Nanda, Praharāja Satyanārāẏaṇa, 1943- , see PK2579.N19
2579.N19 Nanda, Satyanārāẏaṇa (Table P-PZ40)
2579.N222 Narasiṃha Seṇa, fl. 1530-1540 (Table P-PZ40)
2579.N226 Nārāyanadeva, Gajapati, ca. 1718-1767 (Table P-PZ40)
2579.N23 Nārāyanānanda Abadhūta, Swami (Table P-PZ40)
2579.N25 Ṇayak, Binod Chandra, 1919- (Table P-PZ40)
Ṅayaka, Bindoda, 1919- , see PK2579.N25
2579.P26816 Pāṇi, Jagannātha, 1836-1897 (Table P-PZ40)
Panigarhi, Ramesh Prasad, 1943- , see PK2579.P26854
2579.P26854 Pāṇigrāhī, Rameśa Prasāda, 1943- (Table P-PZ40)
2579.P2894 Patnaik, Guru Charan, 1918- (Table P-PZ40)
2579.P298 Pattanaik, Bhanja Kishore, 1922- (Table P-PZ40)
2579.P3 Pattanaik, Bibhuti Bhushan, 1936- (Table P-PZ40)
2579.P315 Pattanaik, Rabi, 1935- (Table P-PZ40)
Paṭṭanāyaka Bhañjakiśora, 1922, see PK2579.P298
Paṭṭanāyaka, Bibhūti, 1936- , see PK2579.P3

Modern Indo-Aryan languages
Particular languages and dialects, A-Z
Oriya (Uriya)
Literature
Individual authors or works, A-Z -- Continued

	Paṭṭanāyaka, Gurucaraṇa, 1918- , see PK2579.P2894
	Pattanayaka, Rabi, 1935- , see PK2579.P315
2579.P56	Pītambara Dāsa, 18th cent. (Table P-PZ40)
2579.P84	Purushottama Anangabhīma Deba, King of Orissa, fl. 1607-1622 (Table P-PZ40)
2579.P85	Purushottama Dāsa, 16th cent. (Table P-PZ40)
2579.R224	Rāmadāsa, fl. 1770 (Table P-PZ40)
2579.R2243	Rāmakṛshṇa Choṭarāya, Raja, 1779-1816 (Table P-PZ40)
	Rāo, Bhānujī, 1926- , see PK2579.R233
2579.R23	Rao, Madhusudan, 1853-1912 (Table P-PZ40)
2579.R233	Rao, Vanuji (Table P-PZ40)
	Ratha, Praphulla, 1936- , see PK2579.R254
2579.R254	Ratha, Praphullakumāra (Table P-PZ40)
2579.R25433	Ratna Dāsa, Kabi, fl. 1740-1800 (Table P-PZ40)
2579.R2544	Raut, Benudhar, 1925- (Table P-PZ40)
	Rāuta, Benudhara, 1925- , see PK2579.R2544
	Rāutarāya, Bindoda, 1930- , see PK2579.R258
2579.R258	Rautray, Binode, 1930- (Table P-PZ40)
2579.R27	Ray, Rajkishore, 1914- (Table P-PZ40)
	Rāya, Rājakiśora, 1914- , see PK2579.R27
2579.R338	Rāya, Rāmānanda, 15th cent. (Table P-PZ40)
2579.R34	Rāya, Rāmaśankara, 1857-1931 (Table P-PZ40)
2579.R58	Roy, Jenamani Narendra Kumar, 1934- (Table P-PZ40)
2579.R6	Roy, Radhanath, 1848-1908 (Table P-PZ40)
2579.S152	Sadānanda Kabisūryya Brahmā, b. 1738 (Table P-PZ40)
2579.S239	Sālabega, 17th cent. (Table P-PZ40)
2579.S25	Samal, Baishnab Charan, 1939- (Table P-PZ40)
	Samala, Baishnaba Carana, 1939- , see PK2579.S25
2579.S294	Sāralādāsa (Table P-PZ40)
2579.S365	Satyabādī Sāmantarāya, 19th cent. (Table P-PZ40)
2579.S4	Ṣenapati, Fakir Mohan, 1843-1918 (Table P-PZ40)
2579.S443	Śibadāsa (Table P-PZ40)
2579.S445	Siddheśvara Dāsa, 15th cent. (Table P-PZ40)
	Siṃ, Rabi, 1932- , see PK2579.S5
2579.S474	Siṃha Deo, Brajarāja, 1851-1907 (Table P-PZ40)
2579.S48	Siṃhadeba, Bīrabikrama, 1874 or 75-1911 (Table P-PZ40)
2579.S5	Ṣingh, Rabindranath, 1932- (Table P-PZ40)
2579.S54	Śiśuśankara Dāsa, 16th cent. (Table P-PZ40)
2579.S95	Sūryyamaṇi Cyau Pattanāyāka, 1773-1838? (Table P-PZ40)

Modern Indo-Aryan language
Particular languages and dialects, A-Z
Oriya (Uriya)
Literature
Individual authors or works, A-Z -- Continued
2579.S987 Śyāmasundara Deba, 19th cent. (Table P-PZ40)
2579.U6 Upendra Bhañja, 1670-1720 (Table P-PZ40)
2579.Y3 Yadumaṇi Mahāpātra, 1781-1866 (Table P-PZ40)
2579.Y35 Yaśobanta Dāsa, b. 1487 (Table P-PZ40)
2579.Y63 Yogī Mahāpātra, fl. 1152-1167 (Table P-PZ40)
2579.5.A-Z Dialects, A-Z
2579.5.A35 Adiwasi Oriya
(2579.5.K68) Kotia
see PK2579.5.A35
2579.5.S35 Sambalpuri
Pahāṛī
2591-2594 General (Table P-PZ11)
Cf. PK2701+, Rājasthānī
2595-2598 Eastern Pahāṛī (Nepāli, Parbate, Parbatiyā, Gorkhālī, Khas-kurā) (Table P-PZ11)
2598.A3-Z5 Individual authors or works, A-Z (Table P-PZ40, or P-PZ43)
e. g.
2598.B43 Bhānubhakta, 1812-1868 (Table P-PZ40)
2598.B48 Bhaṭṭa, Motīrāma, 1866-1896 (Table P-PZ40)
Kāñculī, Mañju, see PK2598.T6
2598.K75 Kshatrī, Pahalamāna Siṃha Svāra, 1878-1934 (Table P-PZ40)
2598.M53 Mishra, Yuddha Prasad, 1908- (Table P-PZ40)
Miśra, Yuddha Prasāda, 1908- , see PK2598.M53
Nandan, Premavinoda, 1935- , see PK2598.P77
2598.N417 Nepāla, Vaiyyākaraṇa, 1855-1924 (Table P-PZ40)
Pahalamāna Siṃha Svāra, see PK2598.K75
2598.P77 Premavinoda (Table P-PZ40)
2598.S3178 Śarmā, Bhavānī Prasāda, 1873-1930 (Table P-PZ40)
Sāyami, Dhūsvāṃ, 1931- , see PK2598.S39
2598.S39 Saymi, Dhooswan, 1931- (Table P-PZ40)
2598.S56 Shrestha, Siddhi Charan, 1912- (Table P-PZ40)
Śreshṭha, Siddhicaraṇa, 1912- , see PK2598.S56
2598.T6 Tivārī, Mañju (Table P-PZ40)
2599.A-Z Dialects, A-Z
2599.B67 Bote-Majhi (Table P-PZ16)
2599.K85 Kumali
2599.P37 Parvati
2601-2604 Central Pahāṛī (Table P-PZ11)
2605.A-Z Dialects, A-Z
2605.G3 Gaṛhwālī (Table P-PZ16)
2605.K8 Kumaunī (Table P-PZ16)
2606-2609 Western Pahāṛī (Himachali) (Table P-PZ11)

PK

Modern Indo-Aryan language
Particular languages and dialects, A-Z
Pahari
Western Pahāṛī (Himachali) -- Continued
2609.A-Z Individual authors or works, A-Z (Table P-PZ40, or P-PZ43)
e. g.
2609.L34 Lārvī, Bābājī, ca. 1865-1927 (Table P-PZ40, or P-PZ43)
2610.A-Z Dialects, A-Z
2610.B3 Baghātī
2610.B48 Bhalesi
2610.C4 Chamĕālī
2610.G3 Gadi (Table P-PZ16)
2610.J3 Jaunsārī
2610.K5 Kiūṭhalī
2610.K8 Kuluī (Table P-PZ16)
2610.M35 Mandeali (Table P-PZ16)
2610.S3 Satlaj
2610.S5 Sirmaurī (Table P-PZ16)
Pañjābī
Two dialects "Standard" (Mājhī) and Ḍōgrā
2631-2637 Language (Table P-PZ8a)
Dialects
2638 General works
2639.A-Z Subdialects, provincialisms, etc., A-Z
2639.B3 Bhṭṭiānī
2639.J8 Jullundur Dōābī
2639.L8 Ludhiānī
2639.M3 Mālwāī (Jangalī, Jaṭkī)
2639.P6 Pōwādhī
2639.R3 Rāṭhī
2645-2648 Ḍōgrā dialect (Ḍōgrī) (Table P-PZ11)
2648.A3-Z5 Individual authors or works, A-Z (Table P-PZ40, or P-PZ43)
e. g.
2648.J3 Jamvāla, Narasiṃha Deva, 1931- (Table P-PZ40)
Jamwal, Narsingh Dev, 1931- , see PK2648.J3
Khajuria, Narendar, see PK2648.K47
2648.K47 Khajūriyā, Narendra, 1933-1970 (Table P-PZ40)
2649.A-Z Subdialects, provincialisms, etc., A-Z
2649.B3 Bhaṭĕālī
2649.K3 Kaṇḍiālī
2649.K4 Kangri (Table P-PZ16)
2650-2659 Literature (Table P-PZ24)
2659.A-Z Individual authors or works, A-Z (Table P-PZ40 or P-PZ43)
e. g.
2659.A26 Addahamāṇa (Table P-PZ40)
2659.A3 Afẓal Aḥsan, Randhāvā (Table P-PZ40)
2659.A33 Ahimadayāra, 1768-1850 (Table P-PZ40)

Modern Indo-Aryan language
Particular languages and dialects, A-Z
Panjabi
Literature
Individual authors or works, A-Z -- Continued

2659.A335 Ahmad Yār, 1768-1845 (Table P-PZ40)
2659.A3854 Alī Haidara, 1690-1785 (Table P-PZ40)
Añcala, Sādhū, 1937- , see PK2659.S648
2659.A689 Ārifa, Kishana Singha, 1836-1900 (Table P-PZ40)
2659.A695 Arjun, 5th guru of the Sikhs, 1563-1606 (Table P-PZ40)
2659.A84 Atam Hamrahi, 1936- (Table P-PZ40)
2659.A866 Aṭawāla Kasūlapuru i, 1941- (Table P-PZ40)
Bachint Kaur, see PK2659.B24
2659.B24 Bacinta Kaura (Table P-PZ40)
Balabīra Singha, 1896-1974, see PK2659.B288
2659.B288 Balbir Singh, 1896-1974 (Table P-PZ40)
Bhallā Sarūpa Dāsa, see PK2659.S3646
2659.B45 Bhogal, Piara Singh, 1931- (Table P-PZ40)
Bhogala, Piār Siṅgha, 1931- , see PK2659.B45
2659.B5 Bir Singh, Bhai (Table P-PZ40)
2659.B8 Bullhe Shāh, 1680?-1785 (Table P-PZ40)
2659.B84 Būṭā Gujarātī, Muhammada, 1851-1930 (Table P-PZ40)
Candana, Amarajīta, 1946- , see PK2659.C484
2659.C346 Carana Singha, 1853-1908 (Table P-PZ40)
2659.C484 Chandan, Amarjeet, 1946- (Table P-PZ40)
2659.C5 Cheema, Niranjan Singh, 1937- (Table P-PZ40)
Cīmā, Nirañjana Siṅgha, 1937- , see PK2659.C5
2659.C56 Cirāgh A'vān, 1679-1732 (Table P-PZ40)
2659.D23 Damodara, 1486-1568 (Table P-PZ40)
2659.D34 Daulata Rāma, 1864-1934 (Table P-PZ40)
2659.D4619 Dhand, Raghubir, 1932- (Table P-PZ40)
Ḍhaṇḍa, Rahubīra, 1932- , see PK2659.D4619
Dila, Balabīra Singha, 1926- , see PK2659.S442
2659.D495 Dilashāda, Rāmalubhāiā Ānanda, 1868-1946 (Table P-PZ40)
Dīwāna Singha, 1921- , see PK2659.S4549
2659.F3 Farid-uddin, Shaikh, 1175?-1265 (Table P-PZ40)
2659.F383 Fazala Shāha, 1827 or 28-1890 (Table P-PZ40)
2659.G26 Gāragī, Balawanta, 1916- (Table P-PZ40)
Gāragī, Paritosha, 1923- , see PK2659.G3
Gargi, Balwant, see PK2659.G26
2659.G3 Gargi, Paritosh, 1923- (Table P-PZ40)
2659.G47 Ghulām Farīduddīn, Khvājah, 1845?-1901 (Table P-PZ40)
2659.G48 Ghulāma Rasūla, 1849-1892 (Table P-PZ40)
2659.G516 Giāna Singha, 1822-1921 (Table P-PZ40)
2659.G523 Gill, Darshan (Table P-PZ40)
Gilla, Darashana, see PK2659.G523
Gobind Singh, Guru, 1666-1708, see PK2659.G6

PK

Modern Indo-Aryan language
Particular languages and dialects, A-Z
Panjabi
Literature
Individual authors or works, A-Z -- Continued

2659.G6 Govinda Siṃha, 10th guru of the Sikhs, 1666-1708 (Table P-PZ40)
2659.G83 Gurādasa, Bhai, ca. 1555-1629 (Table P-PZ40)
2659.G848 Guramukha Singha, 1849-1898 (Table P-PZ40)
2659.H2 Hāfiza Barakhuradāra, 17th cent. (Table P-PZ40)
2659.H232 Haidar, Miyan Ali, 1690-1785 (Table P-PZ40)
Hamarāhī, Atama, 1936- , see PK2659.A84
2659.H326 Harnek Komal, 1943- (Table P-PZ40)
Hāsham Shāh, 1752?-1821?, see PK2659.H356
2659.H356 Hāshama Shāha, 1752?-1821? (Table P-PZ40)
2659.I22 Ibare, 1857?-1934 (Table P-PZ40)
2659.I44 Imam Bakhsh, 1806-1863 (Table P-PZ40)
2659.I84 Īsharadāsa (Table P-PZ40)
Jagarāoṃ, Kulawanta, 1939- , see PK2659.J27
2659.J27 Jagraon, Kulwant, 1939- (Table P-PZ40)
Jasawanta Siṅgha, 1941- , see PK2659.A866
2659.J315 Jaḻḻana, 1586-1644 (Table P-PZ40)
Jasūjā, Guracarana Singha, 1925- , see PK2659.J35
2659.J35 Jasuja, Gurcharan Singh, 1925- (Table P-PZ40)
2659.K2557 Kālidāsa, 1865-1944 (Table P-PZ40)
2659.K2743 Kanha Singha, 1861-1936 (Table P-PZ40)
2659.K2754 Kankaṇa (Table P-PZ40)
2659.K283 Karam Amritsari, 1853-1959 (Table P-PZ40)
Komala, Haraneka, Singha, 1943- , see PK2659.H326
2659.M24 Mahindara, 1931- (Table P-PZ40)
2659.M332 Māni Singha, 18th cent. (Table P-PZ40)
2659.M345 Māṛū Dāsa, Baba, d. 1852 (Table P-PZ40)
2659.M47 Mihr ʻAlī Shāh, Pīr, 1859-1937 (Table P-PZ40)
2659.M8 Muḥammad Bakhsh, 1830-1906? (Table P-PZ40)
2659.M813 Muḥammaduddīn Rājorvī, 1884-1980 (Table P-PZ40)
2659.M822 Mukabala (Table P-PZ40)
2659.M83 Musāfara, Guramukha Singha, 1899-1976 (Table P-PZ40)
Musafir, Gurmukh Singh, 1899-1976, see PK2659.M83
Mushatāka, Hazārā Siṅgha, 1917-1981, see PK2659.S484
2659.N25 Najābata (Table P-PZ40)
2659.N27 Nānak, 1st guru of the Sikhs, 1469-1538 (Table P-PZ40)
Nauranga Singha, d. 1963, see PK2659.S642
Pāndhī Nanakāạwī, 1929- , see PK2659.S37

Modern Indo-Aryan language
Particular languages and dialects, A-Z
Panjabi
Literature
Individual authors or works, A-Z -- Continued

2659.P46 Philaurī, Sharadhā Rāma, 1837-1881 (Table P-PZ40)
2659.P53 Pīlū, 16th cent. (Table P-PZ40)
2659.P55 Pīr Muḥammad, 18th cent. (Table P-PZ40)
2659.P56 Pīr Muḥammad Kāsbī, 17th cent. (Table P-PZ40)
2659.Q3 Qadir Yar, 1802-1891 (Table P-PZ40)
2659.R323 Rāma Dāsa, Baba, 18th cent. (Table P-PZ40)
Randhava, Afzal Ahsan, 1937- , see PK2659.A3
2659.R388 Ravidāsa, 15th cent. (Table P-PZ40)
2659.S22 Sachal, d. 1829 (Table P-PZ40)
2659.S23 Sadā Rāma, 1861-1933 (Table P-PZ40)
2659.S2326 Sādhūjana, 17th cent. (Table P-PZ40)
2659.S279 Sa'īn, Aḥmad 'Alī, 1859?-1937 (Table P-PZ40)
2659.S36315 Santareṇa, 1741-1871 (Table P-PZ40)
2659.S3633 Santokh Singh, 1788-1843 (Table P-PZ40)
Santokhasibmha, 1788-1843, see PK2659.S36315
2659.S3646 Sarūpa Dāsa, Bhallā (Table P-PZ40)
2659.S369 Saundhā, b. 1750 (Table P-PZ40)
2659.S37 Sawhney, Manohar Singh, 1929- (Table P-PZ40)
2659.S4138 Shāh, Sayyid Mubhammad, d. 1884 (Table P-PZ40)
2659.S414 Shah Husain, 1539-1599 (Table P-PZ40)
2659.S4144 Shah Muḥammad, 19th cent. (Table P-PZ40)
Shāha Muhammada, 19th cent , see PK2659.S4144
2659.S442 Singh, Balbir, 1926- (Table P-PZ40)
2659.S4549 Singh, Dewan, 1921- (Table P-PZ40)
2659.S456 Singh, Ditt, b. 1850? (Table P-PZ40)
2659.S47 Singh, Har Bhajan, 1911- (Table P-PZ40)
2659.S484 Singh, Hazara (Table P-PZ40)
Singh, Kahan, 1861-1936, see PK2659.K2743
2659.S642 Singha, Nauranga, d. 1963 (Table P-PZ40)
2659.S648 Singha, Sādhū (Table P-PZ40)
2659.S694 Soḍhi Miharawāna, 1581-1640 (Table P-PZ40)
2659.S789 Sukhabāsī Rāma Bedī, 1758-1848 (Table P-PZ40)
Sukhabīra, 1926- , see PK2659.S8
2659.S8 Sukhbir, 1926- (Table P-PZ40)
2659.S82 Sulṭān Bāhū, 1630-1691 (Table P-PZ40)
2659.S824 Sumer, 1910- (Table P-PZ40)
Sumera, Karatāra, Siṅgha, 1910-1992, see PK2659.S824
Tarana Tarana, Harabhajana Singha, 1911- , see PK2659.S47
2659.V37 Vāris, Shāh, fl. 1766 (Table P-PZ40)
Wīra Singha Bhāī, see PK2659.B5
2659.W45 Wīra Singha Bala, fl. 1812-1851 (Table P-PZ40)
2659.689 Arjun, 5th guru or the Sikhs, 1563-1606 (Table P-PZ40)

Modern Indo-Aryan languages
Particular languages and dialects, A-Z -- Continued
Pañjābī, Western, see PK2261+
Parbate (Parbatiyā), see PK2595+
2675 Parya (Table P-PZ15a)
Pōwādhī, see PK2639.P6
Pūrbī, see PK1830.W4
2701-2709 Rājasthānī (Table P-PZ8a)
2708.9.A-Z Individual authors or works, A-Z (Table P-PZ40, or P-PZ43)
e. g.
2708.9.B27 Bāhādara Ḍhaḍhī, 15th cent. (Table P-PZ40)
2708.9.B35 Bāṅkīdāsa, 1771-1833 (Table P-PZ40)
2708.9.B36 Barahaṭha, Kesarīsiṃha, 1872-1941 (Table P-PZ40)
2708.9.B576 Birajūkā, Rāmapratāpa, 19th cent. (Table P-PZ40)
2708.9.B58 Bīṭhū Sūjā, fl. 1534-1541 (Table P-PZ40)
2708.9.C25 Cailadāna Khiḍiyā, 19th cent. (Table P-PZ40)
2708.9.C33 Canda Baradāī, 1126-1192 (Table P-PZ40)
2708.9.D22 Dadhivāṛiyā, Kāyamadāna, d. 1870 (Table P-PZ40)
Daiyā, Sāṃvara, 1948- , see PK2708.9.D25
2708.9.D25 Daiya, Sanwar, 1948- (Table P-PZ40)
2708.9.D376 Devacandropādhyāya, 1689 or 90-1755 or 6 (Table P-PZ40)
2708.9.D86 Ḍungarasī Ratanū, fl. 1543-1593 (Table P-PZ40)
2708.9.D88 Durasā Āṛhā, 17th cent. (Table P-PZ40)
2708.9.G85 Gumānasiṃha, 1841-1914 (Table P-PZ40)
2708.9.H37 Harirāmadāsa, fl. 1743-1779 (Table P-PZ40)
2708.9.H4 Hemaratana, fl. 1588 (Table P-PZ40)
2708.9.I83 Īśaradāsa Bārahaṭha, 1539-1618 (Table P-PZ40)
2708.9.J23 Jāḍā Mehaṛū, 16th cent. (Table P-PZ40)
2708.9.J28 Jāyācārya, 1803-1881 (Table P-PZ40)
2708.9.J5 Jhūlā, Sāṃyāji, 1575-1646 (Table P-PZ40)
Karaṇīdāna Kaviyā, fl. 1730, see PK2708.9.K3
2708.9.K3 Karnidanji, fl. 1730 (Table P-PZ40)
Kesavadāsa Gāḍaṇa, ca. 1553-ca. 1630, see PK2708.9.K4
2708.9.K4 Kesodāsa Gāḍaṇa, ca. 1553-ca. 1630 (Table P-PZ40)
2708.9.K56 Khaṭakā Rājasthānī (Table P-PZ40)
2708.9.K57 Kisanā Āṛhā, fl. 1818-1838 (Table P-PZ40)
2708.9.K86 Kṛshṇadāsa, 1818-1900 or 1901 (Table P-PZ40)
2708.9.K87 Kuśalalābha, fl. 1559-1591 (Table P-PZ40)
2708.9.M3 Maharshi, Sitaram, 1932- (Table P-PZ40)
Maharshi, Sītārām, 1932- , see PK2708.9.M3
2708.9.M314 Mahśa, Kavi (Table P-PZ40)
2708.9.M34 Mānasāgara, fl. 1667-1690 (Table P-PZ40)
2708.9.M47 Mīrābāī, fl. 1516-1546 (Table P-PZ40)
2708.9.M53 Mithulala (Table P-PZ40)

Modern Indo-Aryan languages
Particular languages and dialects, A-Z
Rajasthani
Individual authors or works, A-Z -- Continued
Pārīka, Lakshimī Nārāyana, 1928- , see PK2708.9.P33
2708.9.P32 Pārīka, Sūrya Karana, 1902-1939 (Table P-PZ40)
2708.9.P33 Pārīkha, Śiva, 1928- (Table P-PZ40)
2708.9.P34 Pārśvadāsa (Table P-PZ40)
2708.9.P54 Pīradāna Lālasa, 1703-1736 (Table P-PZ40)
2708.9.P7 Pṛthvīrāja Rāṭhauṛa, 1549-1600 (Table P-PZ40)
2708.9.R267 Rāmadeva, 1406-1458 (Table P-PZ40)
2708.9.S3 Samayasundara, 17th cent. (Table P-PZ40)
Sāmyājī Jhūlā, 1575-1646, see PK2708.9.J5
2708.9.S316 Sankara Rāva, fl. 1837-1904 (Table P-PZ40)
2708.9.S317 Saradārasimha, King of Banera, 1723 or 4-1759 (Table P-PZ40)
2708.9.S35 Ṣevagarāma, fl. 1804-1850 (Table P-PZ40)
2708.9.S55 Śivadāsa (Table P-PZ40)
2708.9.S637 Srīdhara Vyāsa, 15th cent. (Table P-PZ40)
2708.9.S89 Surajana, 1583-1691 (Table P-PZ40)
2708.9.S9 Sūryamalla, 1815-1868 (Table P-PZ40)
Ṣūryamalla Miśraṇa, 1815-1868, see PK2708.9.S9
2708.9.U5 Ūmaradāna, 1851-1903 (Table P-PZ40)
2708.9.U59 Umārāma, Swami, d. 1896 (Table P-PZ40)
2708.9.V57 Vīrabhāṇṇa Ratanū, b. 1688 or 9 (Table P-PZ40)
2708.9.V9 Vyāsa, Śrīmanta Kumāra (Table P-PZ40)
Vyāsa, Śrīmantakumāra, 1927- , see PK2708.9.V9
Rāṭhī, see PK2639.R3
Romany, see PK2896+
Satlaj, see PK2610.A+
2781-2789 Sindhī (Table P-PZ8a)
The language of Sindh, closely related to Lahndā
Cf. PK2261+
2788.9.A-Z Individual authors or works, A-Z (Table P-PZ40, or P-PZ43)
e. g.
2788.9.A2 'Abd al-Laṭīf, Shah, ca. 1689-ca. 1752
2788.9.A54 'Alvī, Muḥammadu 'Alī Navāzu, 1854-1920
2788.9.A72 Aṣqharu, Sayyidu 'Alī Gauharu Shāhu, 1816-1845
2788.9.H28 Hammalu Faqīru Laqhārī, 1809-1880
2788.9.M535 Miṣrī Shāhu, 1828-1906
2788.9.Q32 Qalīc Beg, Mīrzā, 1853-1929
2788.9.R29 Rājaru, Maniṭhāru Faqīru, 1865-1938
2788.9.R65 Rohala, d. 1782
2788.9.S15 Saccal Sarmast, 1739-1829
2788.9.S23 Sāmī, 1730-1850
2788.9.S25 Sāngī, 'Abd al-Ḥusayn Khān, ca. 1851-1924
2788.9.S36 Shah Abdul Karim, 1536-1624

PK

Modern Indo-Aryan language
Particular languages and dialects, A-Z
Sīndhī
Individual authors or works, A-Z -- Continued
2788.9.S382 Shāhu Muḥammadu Dedaṛu, 1830-1892
2788.9.S563 Ṣiddīqu, Muḥammadu, 1756-1849
2788.9.T38 Tattawī, Muḥammad Hāshim ibn 'Abd al-Ghafur, 1692-1760
2788.9.Z37 Zamān, Khvājah, Muḥammadu, 1713-1774
2790.A-Z Dialects, A-Z
2790.K3 Kachchhi (Table P-PZ16)
2790.L2 Lārī (Table P-PZ16)
2790.L3 Lāsī (Table P-PZ16)
(2790.S5) Siraiki Sindhi
See PK2892.95.S56
2790.V5 Vichōlī (Table P-PZ16)
Sinhalese (Singhalese)
Language
2801 Periodicals. Societies. Yearbooks
Collections
2802.A1 Texts. Sources. Specimens, etc. By date of publication
2802.A5-Z Monographs. Studies
2805 History of philology
(2806) Biography
see PK109
(2806.9) Bibliography. Bio-bibliography
see Z7049.I3
2807 Study and teaching
2808 General works
2809 History (and relations of language)
2810 Alphabet. Writing
(2810.9) Transliteration
see P226
Grammar
2811 Treatises in Oriental languages
Western treatises
2812 Comprehensive works. Compends (Advanced)
2813 Elementary. Introductory
2814 Chrestomathies. Readers
2815 Phonology. Phonetics
2819 Morphology. Inflection. Accidence
2821 Parts of speech (Morphology and syntax)
2823 Syntax
2828 Translating
2829 Prosody. Metrics. Rhythmics
2831 Etymology
Lexicography
2835 Treatises
2837 Dictionaries
2839 Linguistic geography
Dialects. Provincialisms
2840 General

Modern Indo-Aryan language
Particular languages and dialects, A-Z
Sinhalese (Singhalese)
Language
Dialects. Provincialisms -- Continued
Particular dialects

2841-2844 Elu (Table P-PZ11)
Language of the earlier period preserved in the inscriptions and literary work, used for poetry to this day.
Cf. W. Geiger, Litteratur und sprache der Singhalesen, Strassburg, 1900

2845.A-Z Other, A-Z
2845.M3 Maldivian
2845.R6 Rodiyah
2845.V4 Veddah

2850-2859 Literature (Table P-PZ24)
2859.A-Z Individual authors or works, A-Z (Table P-PZ40, or P-PZ43)
e. g.
2859.A33 Alagiyavanna Mukaveṭi, 16th cent. (Table P-PZ40)
2859.C26 Calister Perera, B.P.A., 1948- (Table P-PZ40)
2859.C57 Colombage, Asoka, 1940- (Table P-PZ40)
Da Măl, Lāl Prēmanāt, 1929- , see PK2859.D39
Da Silvā, Sugatapāla, 1928- , see PK2859.D418
2859.D39 De Mal, Lal Premanath, 1929- (Table P-PZ40)
2859.D417 De Silva, John (Table P-PZ40)
2859.D418 De Silva, Sugathapala, 1928- (Table P-PZ40)
2859.D455 Dharmakīrti, Ēkanāyaka (Table P-PZ40)
Gajaman, Nōnā, 1758-1814, see PK2859.P452
Guṇavardhana, Dayananda, 1934- , see PK2859.G85
2859.G85 Gunawardena, Dayānanda, 1934- (Table P-PZ40)
Jayavardhana Guṇasiri, see PK2859.J328
2859.J328 Jayawardena Gunasiri, 1935- (Table P-PZ40)
Kalistar Perērā, Bī.Pī.Ē., 1948- , see PK2859.C26
2859.K32 Kankanamge, Leeleratna, 1938- (Table P-PZ40)
Kankānamge, Līlāratna, 1938- , see PK2859.K32
2859.K327 Kannangara, J.C., 1872-1966 (Table P-PZ40)
2859.K365 Kaviśvara, 14th cent. (Table P-PZ40)
2859.M53 Mītnvala, Kiyindu (Table P-PZ40)
Nandimitra, Ărăvvala, 1939- , see PK2859.N325
2859.N325 Nandimitra, Arawwala, 1939- (Table P-PZ40)
2859.P3 Parakramababu II, King of Ceylon, 13th cent. (Table P-PZ40)
2859.P356 Pattāyamē Lēkam, fl. 1768 (Table P-PZ40)

PK

Modern Indo-Aryan language
Particular languages and dialects, A-Z
Sinhalese (Singhalese)
Literature
Individual authors or works, A-Z -- Continued
2859.P452 Perumāl, Isabelā Kornēliyā, 1746?-1814 (Table P-PZ40)
2859.R22 Rāhula, Toṭagauvē (Table P-PZ40)
2859.V39 Vattavē, Hāmuduruvan (Table P-PZ40)
2859.V42 Vaturegama, Vimalēndra, 1914- (Table P-PZ40)
2859.V45 Vīdāgama Maitreya, 15th cent. (Table P-PZ40)
2891 Inscriptions
2892 Siraiki (Table P-PZ15a)
2892.9.A-Z Individual authors or works, A-Z (Table P-PZ40, or P-PZ43)
2892.9.A92 Āzād, Muḥammad Ḥusain, ca. 1834-1901 (Table P-PZ40)
2892.9.C57 Cirāqh A'vān, 1679-1732 (Table P-PZ40)
2892.9.F37 Farīd, Khvājah Ghulām, 1845?-1901 (Table P-PZ40)
2892.9.S23 Saccal Sarmast, 1739-1829 (Table P-PZ40)
2892.94 Dialects
2892.95.A-Z Special. By name or place, A-Z
2892.95.S55 Siraiki Hindki
2892.95.S56 Siraiki Sindhi
Sirmaurī, see PK2610.S5
Standard Bhojpurī, see PK1830.S8
Thalī (Mārwāṛī), see PK2469.T3
Tirhutia, see PK1811+
Ujainī, see PK2331+
Urdū
see PK1971+, PK2151+
Uriyā, see PK2561+
2893 Vaagri Boli (Table P-PZ15)
Veddah, see PK2845.V4
Vichōlī, see PK2790.V5
Western Bhojpurī, see PK1830.W4
Western Hindī, see PK1959.97+
Western Pañjābī, see PK2261+
2896-2899 Romany (Gipsy, Gypsy) (Table P-PZ11)
Indo-Aryan literature
History and criticism
(2901) Periodicals, societies, etc.
see PK1+, PK101+
2902 Encyclopedias. Dictionaries
Biography of scholars, teachers, etc.
2902.2 Collective
2902.3.A-Z Individual, A-Z
Treatises

Indo-Aryan literature
History and criticism
Treatises -- Continued
2903 General
1 *Comprehensive works dealing with the literature of India in general, i.e. old and modern; Aryan and non-Aryan*
2 *Works confined to the older literature (Vedic and Sanskrit, or comprising Vedic, Sanskrit, Prakrit and Pali literature)*
2905 General special
e.g. Sanskrit literature and the West
2907.A-Z Special topics, A-Z
2907.A35 Aesthetics
2907.A44 Allegory
2907.A58 Anthocephalus cadamba
2907.B53 Bhakti
2907.B62 Birds
2907.C5 Civilization
2907.C67 Coronations
2907.C74 Crime
2907.D48 Devotion
2907.D53 Dice
2907.D72 Draupadi (Hindu mythology)
2907.D74 Dreams
2907.E25 Ecology
2907.E5 Emotions
2907.E7 Erotic literature
2907.F55 Figures of speech
2907.F57 Fishes
2907.F6 Forests
2907.G4 Geography
2907.G63 Gods
2907.H36 Hanumān (Hindu deity)
2907.H55 Hinduism
2907.H86 Humanism
2907.I53 India
2907.I74 Irony
2907.K37 Kārttikeya (Hindu deity)
2907.K7 Krishna (Hindu deity)
2907.L47 Lenses
2907.L7 Love
2907.M28 Manasā (Hindu deity)
2907.M3 Marriage customs and rites
2907.M94 Mythology, Indic
2907.N35 Names, Personal
2907.N37 Nationalism
2907.N44 Nehru, Jawaharlal, 1889-1964
2907.P37 Patriotism
2907.P56 Pilgrims and pilgrimages
2907.P59 Plants

Indo-Aryan literature
History and criticism
Treatises
Special topics, A-Z -- Continued
2907.P65 Politics
2907.P85 Puns and punning
2907.R2 Rādhā (Hindu deity)
2907.R25 Rama (Hindu deity)
2907.S32 Seasons
2907.S45 Shivaji, Raja, 1627-1680
2907.S5 Simile
2907.S56 Sita (Hindu deity)
2907.S59 Siva (Hindu deity)
2907.S64 Society
2907.S88 Style, Literary
2907.S95 Symbolism of numbers
2907.T55 Time
2907.U56 Untouchables
2907.W6 Women
2908 Biography (Collective)
(2909) Bibliography
see Z6605.S3, Z7090
By period
2911 Vedic period
Classical Sanskrit, see PK2903
2915 Post-classical Sanskrit
Cf. PK1450, Prakrit literature; PK4501+, Pali literature; PK5001, Jaina literature
For works dealing with the vernacular literatures of Aryan India in general, see PK5401+, for those confined to the literature of a particular language, see that language PK1501+
Special forms
2916 Poetry
Epic
2917 General
2918 Special classes of epics
e.g. Itihasa or Purana; Kavya
2919 Special topics (not A-Z)
2927-2929 Lyric
Divide like PK2917-PK2919
2931-2933 Drama
Divide like PK2917-PK2919
2935-2937 Fables. Ethico-didactic literature
Divide like PK2917-PK2919
2941-2943 Narratives
Divide like PK2917-PK2919
2945-2947 Wit and humor. Satire
Divide like PK2917-PK2919
Collections
2971 General
2975 Selections. Anthologies

Indo-Aryan literature
Collections -- Continued
2976 Inscriptions
Translations. By language, A-Z
2977 Comprehensive
2978 Anthologies
2979 Inscriptions
(3000-3581) Vedic literature
Since May, 1981, the Library of Congress has classed Vedic literature in BL1112+
see BL1112+
Sanskrit (Post-Vedic) literature
General
History and criticism, see PK2903
3591 Collections
3595 Selections, anthologies, etc.
Poetry
Including epic, narrative, etc.
For religious, scientific texts, etc., see PK3901+
(3600) History and criticism
see PK2916+
3601 Collections
3605 Selections
3611 Itihāsas
(3621) Purāạs
see BL1140.2+
(3631-3649) Mahābhārata
see BL1138.2+
(3650) Pāñcarātra
see BL1141.7+
(3651-3669) Rāmāyana (By Vālmīki)
see BL1139.2+
3671 Kāvyas (Court epics)
3672 Mahākāvyas
3673.A-Z Other, A-Z
Lyrical poetry
3701 Collections
3703 Selections
Dramatic poetry
3721 Collections
3723 Selections
3741 Ethico-didactic poetry
Fables, tales, etc. Niti-Ṣastra
Hitopadeṣa
3741.H5 Texts
3741.H6 Translations. By language, A-Z
3741.H7 Criticism
Pañchatantra
3741.P2 Texts
3741.P3 Translations. By language, A-Z
3741.P4 Criticism
Slokāntara
3741.S55 Texts

PK

	Sanskrit (Post-Vedic) literature
	Poetry
	Ethico-didactic poetry
	Slokāntara -- Continued
3741.S56.A-Z	Translations, A-Z
3741.S57	Criticism
	Somadeva Bhaṭṭa
3741.S6	Texts
3741.S7	Translations. By language, A-Z
3741.S8	Criticism
	Ṣukasaptati
3741.S85	Texts
3741.S86	Translations. By language, A-Z
3741.S87	Criticism
3745	Drama
	Cf. PK3721+, Dramatic poetry
	Prose. Fiction
3750	General works
	By form
3758	Fiction
3760	Essay
3763	Letters
	Miscellaneous
3771	Gnomic-erotic literature
3781	Adages, proverbs, etc.
	Class here Sanskrit texts only
	For translations, see PN6418.5.S3
	Individual authors or works, through 1800
3791.A-Z	A - Bid (Table P-PZ40, or P-PZ43)
3791.A18	Abdur Rahim Khan, Khan Khanam, 1556-1627 (Table P-PZ40)
3791.A193	Abhayadeva, 13th cent. (Table P-PZ40)
3791.A194	Abhinanda, 9th cent. (Table P-PZ40)
3791.A195	Abhinavagupta, Rājānaka (Table P-PZ40)
3791.A3	Adbhutarāmāyaṇa (Table P-PZ40)
3791.A33	Ādirāmāyaṇa (Table P-PZ40)
3791.A35	Agastyapaṇḍita, 14th cent. (Table P-PZ40)
3791.A36	Ahobala, 14th cent. (Table P-PZ40)
3791.A37	Ajitasāgarasūri (Table P-PZ40)
3791.A38	Akbar Shah (Table P-PZ40)
3791.A42	Amaracandrasūri, 13th cent. (Table P-PZ40)
3791.A435	Amitagati, fl. 994-1017 (Table P-PZ40)
3791.A45	Amoghavarṣa, 814-880 (Table P-PZ40)
3791.A47	Anādimiśra, 18th cent. (Table P-PZ40)
3791.A48	Ānaṇdarāmāyaṇa (Table P-PZ40)
3791.A5	Ānandarāyamakhī, 18th cent. (Table P-PZ40)
3791.A53	Anangaharṣa, Mātrarāja (Table P-PZ40)
3791.A535	Anantācārya (Table P-PZ40)
3791.A536	Anantakavi (Table P-PZ40)
3791.A538	Anantapaṇḍita, 17th cent. (Table P-PZ40)
3791.A54	Andrapūrna (Table P-PZ40)
3791.A55	Anuruddha (Table P-PZ40)
3791.A6	Appayya Dīkṣita (Table P-PZ40)

Sanskrit (Post-Vedic) literature
Individual authors or works, through 1800
A - Bid -- Continued
3791.A624 Appayyadīkṣita III, 17th cent. (Table P-PZ40)
3791.A64 Arhaddāsa, 13th cent. (Table P-PZ40)
3791.A67 Aṣaga (Table P-PZ40)
3791.A7 Aśvaghoṣa (Table P-PZ40)
For Buddhist canonical literature by Áśvaghoṣa (Buddhacarita, Vajrasūcī, etc.), see BQ1280+
For his Saundarananda, see BQ905.N2A7
3791.A74 Atulakavi (Table P-PZ40)
3791.A82 Avadhūtasiddha (Table P-PZ40)
3791.B185 Baladeva Vidyābhūṣaṇa, 1720-1790 (Table P-PZ40)
3791.B186 Ballāla, of Benares, fl. 1600 (Table P-PZ40)
3791.B188 Bāṇa (Table P-PZ40)
3791.B189 Bāṇopādhyāya, 15th cent. (Table P-PZ40)
3791.B19 Basavaraja, King of Keladi, ca. 1684-ca. 1745 (Table P-PZ40)
3791.B1924 Bhagavantarāyamakhi, 17th/18th cent. (Table P-PZ40)
3791.B193 Bhallata, 9th cent. (Table P-PZ40)
3791.B2 Bharatakadvātriṃṣikā (Table P-PZ40)
3791.B252 Bhāravi (Table P-PZ40)
3791.B28 Bhartṛhari (Table P-PZ40)
3791.B4 Bhāsa (Table P-PZ40)
3791.B53 Bhāskarakavi (Table P-PZ40)
3791.B54 Bhāskarāya, fl. 1675-1751 (Table P-PZ40)
3791.B562 Bhaṭṭi (Table P-PZ40)
3791.B58 Bhavabhūti, 8th cent. (Table P-PZ40)
3791.B595 Bhīṣmamiśra, 18th cent. (Table P-PZ40)
3791.B6 Bhojaraja, King of Dhara (Table P-PZ40)
3791.B622 Bholānātha, 18th cent. (Table P-PZ40)
3791.B66 Bhūminātha (Table P-PZ40)
3792 Bidpai or Pilpai. Fables (Table P-PZ43)
3793 History of translations
e.g. North's English translation (1570), PR2326.N6; Early Spanish, Calila y Dimna, PQ6321.C16
Cf. PJ7741.A+, Arabic version. Kalilah wa-Dimnah
Cf. PK3741, Pañchatantra and Hitopadesa
Cf. PK6451, Persian version. Anvar i Suhaili
For popular collections, see PN989.I5
For early European texts, see PQ-PT
3794 Bid - Kal (Table P-PZ40)
3794.B62 Bilhana, 11th cent. (Table P-PZ40)
3794.B64 Bodhāyanakavi (Table P-PZ40)
3794.B7 Brahmatravaidyanātha (Table P-PZ40)
3794.B762 Buddhivijaya (Table P-PZ40)
3794.B8 Budhakauśika (Table P-PZ40)
3794.B84 Budhasvāmin (Table P-PZ40)

Sanskrit (Post-Vedic) literature
Individual authors or works, through 1800
Bid - Kal -- Continued

3794.C352 Candragomin (Table P-PZ40)
3794.C354 Candraśekhara, 16th cent. (Table P-PZ40)
3794.C355 Candraśekhara, Rājaguru, 18th cent. (Table P-PZ40)
3794.C375 Caturbhāṇī (Table P-PZ40)
3794.C382 Caturbhuja, fl. 1493 (Table P-PZ40)
3794.C39 Caturbhujamiśra (Table P-PZ40)
3794.C64 Cokkanāthamakhi, fl. 1684-1711 (Table P-PZ40)
3794.D24 Dāmodaragupta, fl. 779-813 (Table P-PZ40)
3794.D4 Daṇḍin, 7th cent. (Table P-PZ40)
3794.D555 Deva Prabha Sūrī (Table P-PZ40)
3794.D5562 Devarajāśarmā (Table P-PZ40)
3794.D5572 Devīdatta, 18th cent. (Table P-PZ40)
3794.D5576 Dhanadeśvara, 16th cent. (Table P-PZ40)
3794.D558 Dhanañjaya, 8th cent. (Table P-PZ40)
3794.D559 Dhanapāla, 10th cent. (Table P-PZ40)
3794.D5593 Dhanapala, fl. 1205 (Table P-PZ40)
3794.D5614 Dharmagupta, 14th cent. (Table P-PZ40)
3794.D562 Dharmasūri, 15th cent. (Table P-PZ40)
3794.D5652 Dhoyī, 12th cent. (Table P-PZ40)
3794.D5654 Ḍhuṇḍivyāsa, fl. 1684-1710 (Table P-PZ40)
3794.D57 Dinnāga (Table P-PZ40)
3794.D87 Durvāsas (Table P-PZ40)
3794.E3 Ekalingamāhātmya (Table P-PZ40)
3794.G33 Gangādevi, 14th cent. (Table P-PZ40)
3794.G34 Gangadhāra, 15th cent. (Table P-PZ40)
3794.G35 Gargasamhitā (Table P-PZ40)
3794.G37 Garuḍavāhanapaṇḍita (Table P-PZ40)
3794.G52 Ghanaśyāma (Table P-PZ40)
3794.G54 Ghaṭakarparakāvya (Table P-PZ40)
3794.G58 Gokulanātha (Table P-PZ40)
3794.G587 Gopadatta (Table P-PZ40)
3794.G59 Gopālakṛṣṇakavi, 17th cent. (Table P-PZ40)
3794.G62 Govardhana (Table P-PZ40)
3794.G63 Govindaṇātha, 17th cent. (Table P-PZ40)
3794.G86 Guṇasamudrasūri, fl. 1416 (Table P-PZ40)
3794.H154 Haṃsasandeśa (Table P-PZ40)
3794.H1552 Hanuman (Table P-PZ40)
3794.H157 Haradattasūri (Table P-PZ40)
3794.H15922 Haricandra (Table P-PZ40)
3794.H159232 Haridevamiśra, 16th cent. (Table P-PZ40)
3794.H15924 Harihara (Table P-PZ40)
3794.H15925 Harihara, 13th cent. (Table P-PZ40)
3794.H15927 Harijīvana Miśra, 17th cent. (Table P-PZ40)
3794.H3 Harsavardhana, King of Thānesar and Kanauj, fl. 606-647 (Table P-PZ40)
3794.H45 Hastimalla, fl. 1290 (Table P-PZ40)
3794.H46 Hemacandra, 1088-1172 (Table P-PZ40)
3794.H472 Hemavijaya, 1565-1631 (Table P-PZ40)
Hemavijayagani, 1565-1631, see PK3794.H472

Sanskrit (Post-Vedic) literature
Individual authors or works, through 1800
Bid - Kal -- Continued

3794.H5	Hita Harivaṃśa Gosvāmī, 1502-1552 (Table P-PZ40)
3794.I483	Immaḍi Gurusiddha Śivayogī (Table P-PZ40)
3794.I82	Īsvaraśarma, fl. 1750 (Table P-PZ40)
3794.J252	Jagadīśvara Bhattācārya (Table P-PZ40)
3794.J2525	Jagannātha, of Kāvalavaṃśa, 18th cent. (Table P-PZ40)
3794.J253	Jagannātha Dāsa, 1487-1547 (Table P-PZ40)
3794.J254	Jagannātha Paṇḍitarāja (Table P-PZ40)
3794.J255	Jambumuni (Table P-PZ40)
3794.J256	Jānakīprasādabhaṭṭa, b. 1665 or 6 (Table P-PZ40)
3794.J258	Janārdana, 17th cent. (Table P-PZ40)
3794.J26	Jaṭāsiṃhanandi, 7th cent. (Table P-PZ40)
3794.J3	Jayadeva, 12th cent. (Table P-PZ40)
	Jayadeva, 13th cent , see PK3794.J332
3794.J332	Jayadeva, son of Mahādeva (Table P-PZ40)
3794.J338	Jayadevakavi (Table P-PZ40)
3794.J344	Jayamangalasūri, 18th cent. (Table P-PZ40)
3794.J3472	Jayanta Bhaṭṭa, fl. 850-910 (Table P-PZ40)
3794.J35	Jayarāma Piṇḍye (Table P-PZ40)
3794.J356	Jayaratha, 12th/13th cent. (Table P-PZ40)
3794.J358	Jayaśekharasūri (Table P-PZ40)
3794.J36	Jayasena (Table P-PZ40)
3794.J365	Jayata, 14th cent. (Table P-PZ40)
3794.J372	Jayavallabha (Table P-PZ40)
3794.J4435	Jinabhadrasūri, 12th cent. (Table P-PZ40)
3794.J4442	Jinapāla, fl. 1205-1238 (Table P-PZ40)
3794.J45	Jinaratnasuri, 13th cent. (Table P-PZ40)
3794.J452	Jinasena (Table P-PZ40)
3794.J454	Jinasena, 8th cent. (Table P-PZ40)
3794.J47	Jīva Gosvāmī (Table P-PZ40)
3794.J48	Jīvadevācārya, 15th cent. (Table P-PZ40)
3794.J53	Jñānasāgarasūri, 15th cent. (Table P-PZ40)
3794.J55	Jñanaśrimitra (Table P-PZ40)
3794.K28	Kāḷe Dhuṇḍhirājā Rāmacandra (Table P-PZ40)
	Kālidāsa (Table P-PZ40)
3795.A1	Collected works. Selections. By date
3795.A6-Z	Translations. By language, A-Z
3796.A-Z	Separate works, A-Z
	Subdivide each work like PK3796.K6 PK3796.K8
	Abhijñanaśakuntalā, see PK3796.S3+
3796.K6-K8	Kumārasambhava
3796.K6	Texts
	Translations
3796.K69	Polyglot
3796.K7	English
3796.K73	French
3796.K75	German
3796.K76	Italian

PK

Sanskrit (Post-Vedic) literature
Individual authors or works, through 1800
Bid - Kal
Kālidāsa
Separate works, A-Z
Kumārasambhava
Translations -- Continued

3796.K77	Scandinavian
3796.K78	Spanish
3796.K79	Other, A-Z
3796.K8	Criticism
3796.M2-M4	Mālavikāgnimitra
3796.M5-M7	Meghadūta
3796.P7-P9	Puṣpabanavitāsam
3796.R2-R4	Raghuvaṃsa
3796.R6-R8	Ṛtusaṃhāra
3796.S3-S5	Ṣakuntalā
3796.S7-S9	Śṛngāratilaka
3796.S96-S963	Śrāmalādaṇḍaka
3796.S97-S973	Śyāmalānavaratnamālikā
3796.V6-V8	Vikramorvaṣi
3797	Biography and criticism
3798	Kal - Z (Table P-PZ40, or P-PZ43)
3798.K26	Kalya Lakṣmīnṛṣiṃha, 18th cent. (Table P-PZ40)
3798.K27	Karṇapūra, b. 1524? (Table P-PZ40)
3798.K45	Kauṭalya (Table P-PZ40)
3798.K55	Kavīndrācārya Sarasvatī, Sarvavidyānidhāna, 17th cent. (Table P-PZ40)
3798.K572	Kavirāja, 12th cent. (Table P-PZ40)
3798.K577	Kīrtiratnasūri, 1392-1468 (Table P-PZ40)
3798.K5852	Krishnadeva Raya, King of Vijayanagar, d. 1529 or 30 (Table P-PZ40)
3798.K5864	Kṛṣṇa, 16th cent. (Table P-PZ40)
3798.K5868	Kṛṣṇabhaṭṭa, 14th cent. (Table P-PZ40)
3798.K5869	Kṛṣṇadāsa (Table P-PZ40)
3798.K587	Kṛṣṇadāsa, b. 1531 (Table P-PZ40)
3798.K58712	Kṛṣṇadāsa Kavirāja Gosvāmi, b. 1518 (Table P-PZ40)
3798.K5872	Kṛṣṇadatta Maithila (Table P-PZ40)
3798.K59	Kṛṣṇalīlāśukamuni, 1193-1293 (Table P-PZ40)
3798.K65	Kṛṣṇamiśra (Table P-PZ40)
3798.K69	Kṛṣṇaśricandana, 18th cent. (Table P-PZ40)
3798.K73	Kṣemendra, fl. 1050 (Table P-PZ40)
3798.K74	Kṣemīśvara (Table P-PZ40)
3798.K78	Kulacēkarar, 9th cent. (Table P-PZ40)
3798.K79	Kulaśekharavarma (Table P-PZ40)
3798.K822	Kumāradāsa (Table P-PZ40)
3798.K84	Kūranārāyana, 11th cent. (Table P-PZ40)
3798.L3	Lakṣmaṇādhvari, 17th cent. (Table P-PZ40)
3798.L34	Lakṣmīdāsa, 14th cent. (Table P-PZ40)
3798.L36	Lakṣmīdhara, 11th cent. (Table P-PZ40)
3798.L58	Lokānandācārya (Table P-PZ40)

Sanskrit (Post-Vedic) literature
Individual authors or works, through 1800
Kal - Z -- Continued

3798.L6 Lokanātha Bhaṭṭa, 17th cent. (Table P-PZ40)
3798.L652 Lolimbarāja (Table P-PZ40)
3798.M16 Madana, fl. 1210-1218 (Table P-PZ40)
3798.M168 Mādhava, son of Māyana, called Vidyāraṇya, d. 1386 (Table P-PZ40)
3798.M182 Mādhavabhaṭṭa, fl. 1610 (Table P-PZ40)
3798.M186 Madhuravāṇi, 17th cent. (Table P-PZ40)
3798.M188 Madhusūdana Tarkapañcanana (Table P-PZ40)
3798.M215 Māgha (Table P-PZ40)
3798.M224 Mahādeva Tīrtha (Table P-PZ40)
3798.M226 Mahendra Vikrama Varma, King of Kanchi, fl. 600-630 (Table P-PZ40)
3798.M2274 Mahimabhaṭṭa, 11th cent. (Table P-PZ40)
3798.M228 Mallācārya, 14th cent. (Table P-PZ40)
3798.M229 Mallanārādhya (Table P-PZ40)
3798.M23 Mānavavāstulakṣaṇa (Table P-PZ40)
3798.M24 Mānaveda, d. 1658 (Table P-PZ40)
3798.M243 Maṇḍalakavi (Table P-PZ40)
3798.M25 Maṇika, 14th cent. (Table P-PZ40)
3798.M254 Māṇikyasundarasūri, 16th cent. (Table P-PZ40)
3798.M26 Mankha, fl. 1135-1150 (Table P-PZ40)
3798.M288 Mārkaṇḍeya, 16th cent. (Table P-PZ40)
3798.M289 Mathurādāsa, 15th cent. (Table P-PZ40)
3798.M296 Māyideva, fl. 1419-1446 (Table P-PZ40)
3798.M3 Mayūra (Table P-PZ40)
3798.M45 Meghavijaya, fl. 1652-1703 (Table P-PZ40)
Meghavijayopādhyāya, fl. 1652-1703, see PK3798.M45
3798.M55 Mitramiśra, 17th cent. (Table P-PZ40)
3798.M752 Mūkaśankara (Table P-PZ40)
3798.M762 Munibhadrasūri (Table P-PZ40)
3798.M82 Murāri (Table P-PZ40)
3798.N23 Nāga Bhaṭṭa (Table P-PZ40)
3798.N24 Nāgadeva (Table P-PZ40)
Nallakavi, see PK3791.B66
3798.N273 Narasiṃha, 14th cent. (Table P-PZ40)
3798.N276 Narayaṇa, 16th cent. (Table P-PZ40)
3798.N2765 Nārāyana, son of Brahmadatta (Table P-PZ40)
3798.N277 Nārāyaṇa Bhaṭṭa (Table P-PZ40)
3798.N313 Nārāyaṇa Paṇḍitācārya, 13th cent. (Table P-PZ40)
3798.N317 NārāyaṇabhaÞ jadeva, 16th cent. (Table P-PZ40)
3798.N32 Nārāyanabhaṭṭapāda (Table P-PZ40)
3798.N323 Nārāyaṇacarya, 1623-1676 (Table P-PZ40)
3798.N324 Nārāyaṇadīkṣita, 17th cent. (Table P-PZ40)
3798.N325 Nārāyaṇakavi (Table P-PZ40)
3798.N33 Nārāyaṇatīrtha, 17th cent. (Table P-PZ40)
3798.N372 Nayacandrasūri (Table P-PZ40)
Nīlakaṇṭha, 1610-1670, see PK3798.N554
3798.N53 Nīlakaṇṭha, of Rājamangalam (Table P-PZ40)
3798.N54 Nīlakaṇṭha Dīkṣita, 17th cent. (Table P-PZ40)

PK

Sanskrit (Post-Vedic) literature
Individual authors or works, through 1800
Kal - Z -- Continued

3798.N554 Nīlakaṇṭhaśukla, 17th cent. (Table P-PZ40)
3798.N556 Nityānanda, 17th/18th cent. (Table P-PZ40)
3798.P15 Padmagupta (Table P-PZ40)
3798.P17 Padmanābhamiśra, 17th cent. (Table P-PZ40)
3798.P172 Padmanābhaśastrin, Srīhari (Table P-PZ40)
3798.P177 Padmasāgara, 16th cent. (Table P-PZ40)
3798.P18 Padmasundara, pupil of Padmameru, fl. 1558-1569 (Table P-PZ40)
Padmasundarasūri, fl. 1556-1575, see PK3798.P18
3798.P3 Pancastavī (Table P-PZ40)
Panchatantra, see PK3741
3798.P35 Paṇḍitācārya, fl. 1400-1432 (Table P-PZ40)
3798.P37 Paramānanda, 16th cent. (Table P-PZ40)
3798.P372 Paramānanda, Kavindra (Table P-PZ40)
3798.P38 Patañjali (Table P-PZ40)
3798.P66 Prabodhānanda Sarasvatī (Table P-PZ40)
3798.P7 Prataparudra II, King of Warangal, fl. 1295-1323 (Table P-PZ40)
3798.P772 Pṛthvīdhara (Table P-PZ40)
3798.P8 Punaṃnampūtiri, 15th cent. (Table P-PZ40)
3798.P813 Puṇyakoṭi (Table P-PZ40)
3798.P816 Puṇyakusalagaṇi, 17th cent. (Table P-PZ40)
3798.P823 Pūrṇamalla, Kavi (Table P-PZ40)
3798.P825 Pūrṇasarasvatī (Table P-PZ40)
3798.P827 Purusottamadeva, King of Orissa, fl. 1466-1497 (Table P-PZ40)
3798.P83 Puṣpadanta, 10th cent. (Table P-PZ40)
3798.R23 Raghunātha Dāsa, Gosvāmī (Table P-PZ40)
3798.R238 Raghūttamatīrtha, 17th cent. (Table P-PZ40)
3798.R24 Raghuvaryatīrtha, 1630-1712 (Table P-PZ40)
3798.R26 Rājacūḍāmaṇi Dīkṣita (Table P-PZ40)
3798.R264 Rājanātha Diṇḍima (Table P-PZ40)
3798.R265 Rājaśekhara, ca. 880-ca. 920 (Table P-PZ40)
3798.R268 Rājavallabha, fl. 1429-1456 (Table P-PZ40)
3798.R2713 Rāmabhadra Dīkṣita, 17th cent. (Table P-PZ40)
3798.R2715 Rāmabhaṭṭa (Table P-PZ40)
3798.R2717 Rāmacandra, 12th cent. (Table P-PZ40)
3798.R27173 Rāmacandra, 16th cent. (Table P-PZ40)
3798.R2718 Rāmacandra Bhāratī (Table P-PZ40)
3798.R273 Rāmacandrakavi (Table P-PZ40)
3798.R2734 Ramacandramakhi, 17th cent. (Table P-PZ40)
3798.R274 Rāmagopāla, 18th cent. (Table P-PZ40)
3798.R2747 Rāmakavi, 18th cent. (Table P-PZ40)
3798.R275 Rāmakṛṣṇa (Son of Devaji) (Table P-PZ40)
3798.R2753 Rāmakṛṣṇa Kādamba, fl. 1803-1840 (Table P-PZ40)
3798.R276 Rāmānandarāya (Table P-PZ40)
3798.R277 Rāmānandathakkura (Table P-PZ40)
3798.R2862 Rāmāpaṇivāda, ca. 1707-ca. 1775 (Table P-PZ40)
3798.R2872 Raṇachoḍabhaṭṭa, fl. 1661-1681 (Table P-PZ40)

Sanskrit (Post-Vedic) literature
Individual authors or works, through 1800
Kal - Z -- Continued

3798.R2878 Ratnākara, Rājānaka, 8th/9th cent. (Table P-PZ40)
3798.R2879 Ratnakheta Śrīnivāsādhvarīndra (Table P-PZ40)
3798.R35 Raviṣeṇa, fl. 678 (Table P-PZ40)
3798.R77 Rudra, son of Ananta, fl. 1596 (Table P-PZ40)
3798.R8 Rudrabhaṭṭa, 11th cent.? (Table P-PZ40)
3798.R819 Rupacandragaṇi, 18th cent. (Table P-PZ40)
3798.R83 Rūpagosvāmī, 16th cent. (Table P-PZ40)
3798.R862 Rūparasika Devācārya, 16th cent. (Table P-PZ40)
3798.S17 Ṣaḍakṣarīśa, 17th cent. (Table P-PZ40)
3798.S25 Sāgara Rāmācārya, 17th cent. (Table P-PZ40)
3798.S317 Sahajakīrti, fl. 1605-1648 (Table P-PZ40)
3798.S32 Sāhajī, King of Tanjore, fl. 1684-1712 (Table P-PZ40)
3798.S3217 Śakalakīrti, 1380 or 81-1442 or 3 (Table P-PZ40)
3798.S33 Śaktibhadra, 9th cent. (Table P-PZ40)
3798.S332 Śaktivallabha Arjyāla, 18th cent. (Table P-PZ40)
3798.S334 Sāmarājadīkṣita, fl. 1655-1700 (Table P-PZ40)
3798.S335 Ṣāmba (Table P-PZ40)
3798.S3372 Śambhu, 11th cent. (Table P-PZ40)
3798.S3432 Sanātana Gosvāmī, 1484-1558 (Table P-PZ40)
3798.S345 Śandhyākaranandin (Table P-PZ40)
3798.S348 Ṣankarabhaṭṭa, 16th cent. (Table P-PZ40)
3798.S35 Ṣankarācārya (Table P-PZ40)
3798.S355 Śankarakavi (Table P-PZ40)
3798.S36 Ṣankaramiśra, 15th cent. (Table P-PZ40)
3798.S37 Śankhadhara, 12th cent. (Table P-PZ40)
3798.S383 Ṣaptarṣi, 18th cent. (Table P-PZ40)
3798.S386 Śatānandakavīndrasūnu (Table P-PZ40)
3798.S43 Śesayyangār, 17th cent. (Table P-PZ40)
3798.S46 Siddhacandragaṇi, 16th cent. (Table P-PZ40)
3798.S48 Ṣiddharṣigaṇi (Table P-PZ40)
3798.S51 Śilhaṇa Miśra (Table P-PZ40)
3798.S584 Ṣingabhūpāla (Table P-PZ40)
3798.S59 Śivakavi (Table P-PZ40)
3798.S61 Śivasvamīn, fl. 855 (Table P-PZ40)
3798.S73 Somadeva Sūri, 10th cent. (Table P-PZ40)
3798.S734 Somanāthamiśra (Table P-PZ40)
3798.S737 Somaprabhācārya, 12th cent. (Table P-PZ40)
3798.S75 Ṣomeśvaradeva, 13th cent. (Table P-PZ40)
3798.S76 Śrīharṣa (Table P-PZ40)
3798.S77 Śrīharṣa, 12th cent. (Table P-PZ40)
3798.S776 Ṣrīkṛṣṇabhaṭṭa, 18th cent. (Table P-PZ40)
3798.S786 Ṣrinivasa Kavi, 18th cent. (Table P-PZ40)
3798.S793 Ṣrīrāmakarṇāmrta (Table P-PZ40)
3798.S795 Śrīvallabhagaṇi, fl. 1597-1604 (Table P-PZ40)
3798.S8 Ṣubandhu, 6th cent. (Table P-PZ40)
3798.S83 Śubhacandra, fl. 1516-1556 (Table P-PZ40)
3798.S87 Ṣudarśana (Table P-PZ40)
3798.S91 Śūdraka (Table P-PZ40)

Sanskrit (Post-Vedic) literature
Individual authors or works, through 1800
Kal - Z -- Continued

3798.S9418 Sukṛtidattapantasūri, 1823-1875 (Table P-PZ40)
3798.S942 Sukumārakavi (Table P-PZ40)
3798.S947 Sūrya Paṇḍita (Table P-PZ40)
3798.S962 Śyāmilaka (Table P-PZ40)
3798.T5 Tirumalamba, consort of Achyuta Raya, King of Vijayanagar (Table P-PZ40)
3798.T7 Trivikrama Bhaṭṭa, fl. 915 (Table P-PZ40)
3798.T72 Trivikramapaṇḍita (Table P-PZ40)
3798.U27 Udaya, 16th cent. (Table P-PZ40)
3798.U28 Udayaprabhadevasūri, 13th cent. (Table P-PZ40)
3798.U3 Uddaṇḍa (Table P-PZ40)
3798.U42 Umāmaheśvaraśāstri, 18th cent. (Table P-PZ40)
3798.U44 Umānandanātha, 18th cent. (Table P-PZ40)
3798.U8 Utpala, fl. 900-950 (Table P-PZ40)
3798.U83 Utprekṣāvallabha, 16th cent. (Table P-PZ40)
3798.V13 Vādimīkara (Table P-PZ40)
3798.V14 Vādirāja, 16th cent. (Table P-PZ40)
3798.V15 Vādirāja Sūri, fl. 1025-1042 (Table P-PZ40)
3798.V1512 Vāgbhaṭa (Son of Dahāṭa) (Table P-PZ40)
3798.V1514 Vallabhācārya, 1479-1531? (Table P-PZ40)
3798.V15177 Vāmana Bhaṭṭa, Bāṇa (Table P-PZ40)
3798.V15182 Vaṃśīdharamiṣra (Table P-PZ40)
3798.V15184 Vañchanatha, 18th cent. (Table P-PZ40)
3798.V15192 Vararuci (Dramatist) (Table P-PZ40)
3798.V1524 Vāsudeva, 9th cent. (Table P-PZ40)
3798.V1526 Vāsudevaratha, 18th cent. (Table P-PZ40)
3798.V153 Vatsarāja (Table P-PZ40)
3798.V1682 Vātsya Varadācārya (Table P-PZ40)
3798.V1715 Vedakavi (Table P-PZ40)
3798.V175 Venkāmātya, 18th cent. (Table P-PZ40)
3798.V177 Venkatādhvarin, 17th cent. (Table P-PZ40)
3798.V185 Veṇkatanātha, 1268-1369 (Table P-PZ40)
3798.V188 Venkaṭasubrahmaṇyādhvari, 18th cent. (Table P-PZ40)
3798.V2 Vetālapañcaviṃśati (Table P-PZ40)
3798.V45 Vidyākara Purohita, son of Vaidyeśvara, 16th cent. (Table P-PZ40)
3798.V47 Vidyānandi, fl. 1442-1481 (Table P-PZ40)
3798.V474 Vidyānātha (Table P-PZ40)
3798.V48 Vidyāpati Thākura, 15th cent. (Table P-PZ40)
3798.V69 Vikramacarita (Table P-PZ40)
3798.V75 Viṇāvāsavadatta (Table P-PZ40)
3798.V76 Vīṇāvāsavadattakathā (Table P-PZ40)
3798.V78 Vinayacandrasūri, 13th cent. (Table P-PZ40)
3798.V792 Vīranandi, 10th cent. (Table P-PZ40)
3798.V8-V83 Viṣākhadatta (Table P-PZ40)
3798.V8372 Visvanath Singh, Maharaja of Rewa, 1789-1854 (Table P-PZ40)
3798.V842 Viśvanātha, fl. 1316 (Table P-PZ40)
3798.V845 Viśvanātha Cakravartin (Table P-PZ40)

Sanskrit (Post-Vedic) literature
Individual authors or works, through 1800
Kal - Z -- Continued

3798.V848 Viśvanātha Kavirāja (Table P-PZ40)
3798.V854 Viśvanāthabhaṭṭa, fl. 1650-1709 (Table P-PZ40)
3798.V86 Viśveśvara, 18th cent. (Table P-PZ40)
3798.V88 Viṭṭhalanātha, 1518-1588 (Table P-PZ40)
3798.Y3 Yaśovijaya, 1634-1688 (Table P-PZ40)
3799 Individual authors or works, since 1800 (Table P-PZ40, or P-PZ43)
e. g.
3799.A42 Alasingabhatta, fl. 1834-1836 (Table P-PZ40)
3799.A49 Anūpanārāyaṇa Bhattācāryya (Table P-PZ40)
3799.B4415 Bhagavati Subrahmaṇya Śastrikaḷ, 1870-1925 (Table P-PZ40)
3799.C35 Caṇḍīdāsa (Table P-PZ40)
3799.D55 Dānakelicintāmaṇi (Table P-PZ40)
3799.D82 Dvivedi, Durgaprasada (Table P-PZ40)
3799.G53 Godavarma, 1800-1851 (Table P-PZ40)
3799.G578 Gopāla Mairāla, 1814-1872 (Table P-PZ40)
3799.H33 Harisūri (Table P-PZ40)
3799.J475 Jha, Badarinatha (Table P-PZ40)
3799.J48 Jha, Dharmadatta, 1860-1918 (Table P-PZ40)
3799.K29 Kañcanācāryya (Table P-PZ40)
3799.K36 Kāntānātha Bhaṭṭa, 18th/19th cent. (Table P-PZ40)
3799.K6 Korāḍa Rāmacandṛa, 1816-1900 (Table P-PZ40)
3799.K686 Krsnācāryula, Kāśī, 1872- (Table P-PZ40)
3799.L25 Lakshmana Suri, M., 1859-1928 (Table P-PZ40)
3799.M34 Maheśacandratarkacūḍāmaṇi, 1841-1909 (Table P-PZ40)
3799.M83 Mukunda, fl. 1850-1860 (Table P-PZ40)
3799.N365 Nandakiśora, d. 1865 (Table P-PZ40)
3799.N373 Narayana Das, Azzada Adibhatla, 1864-1945 (Table P-PZ40)
3799.N376 Nārāyanakavi, 1868-1935 (Table P-PZ40)
3799.N53 Nīlakaṇthaśarman, Punnaśśerī, 1858-1935 (Table P-PZ40)
3799.P2744 Panta Viṭhṭhala, 19th cent. (Table P-PZ40)
3799.R27 Raghavācārya, 1770-1831 (Table P-PZ40)
3799.R28 Raghavan, V., 1908-1979 (Table P-PZ40)
Raghavan, V. (Venkatarama), see PK3799.R28
3799.R353 Rāmarāya, Bellankoṇḍa, 1875-1914 (Table P-PZ40)
3799.R37 Rāśivadekara, Appāśāstrī, 1873-1913 (Table P-PZ40)
3799.S14 Sacchidananda Siva Abhinava Narasimha Bharati, Swami, 1858-1912 (Table P-PZ40)
3799.S145 Ṣaccidananda, Brahmacari (Table P-PZ40)
3799.S2 Śankaralāla (Table P-PZ40)
Śāstrī, Paramānanda, 1926- , see PK3799.S3947
3799.S3947 Shastri, Parmanand, 1926- (Table P-PZ40)
3799.S843 Sundararāja (Table P-PZ40)
3799.T3 Tarkalankara, Candrakanta, 1836-1910 (Table P-PZ40)

Sanskrit (Post-Vedic) literature
Individual authors or works, since 1800 -- Continued
3799.T55 Thakkura, Kṛṣṇasiṃha, 1848-1921 (Table P-PZ40)
3799.T75 Trivikrama, 19th cent. (Table P-PZ40)
3799.V32 Vakulabhooshanam, Jaggu, 1902- (Table P-PZ40)
Vakulabhūsana, Jaggu, 1902- , see PK3799.V32
3799.V334 Varadācārya (Table P-PZ40)
3799.V42 Veṅkaṭācārya, Bāladhanvi Jaggu, 1874- (Table P-PZ40)
3799.V49 Visvanathasuri, 19th cent. (Table P-PZ40)
3799.V9 Vyas, Ambika Datt, 1850-1900 (Table P-PZ40)
Vyāsa, Ambikādatta, 1850-1900, see PK3799.V9
3800.A-Z Local. Special provinces, regions, etc., A-Z
Under each:
1 History
2 Collections
Special subjects
(3801) Philosophy
Cf. Catalogue of manuscripts of India office
(3811) Sankhya
(3821) Yoga
(3831) Nyāya
(3841) Vaiṣeshika
(3851) Mīmāṃsā
(3861) Vedānta (Uttara-mīmāṃsā)
(3881) Other schools
Religion
For original texts, commentaries and textual interpretations only
Cf. Monier-Williams, Brahmanism and Hinduism, 4th ed. 1891; R.G. Bhandakar, Vaiṇavism, Śaivism, and minor religious systems, 1913
For treatises on the various religions of India, see BL
(3901-3908) Brahmanism
(3901.A2-A39) Collections
(3901.A5-Z) Individual authors or works
Translations
(3903) Oriental
see PJ-PL
(3905) Western. By language, A-Z, and date
see BL1110+
Commentaries, interpretation, etc.
(3907) Oriental
see PK-PL
(3908) Western
(3911-3918) Hinduism
Class here general and miscellaneous collections representing various systems
Divide like PK(3901-3908)
(3921-3928) Vaiṣṇavism
Divide like PK(3901-3908)

Sanskrit (Post-Vedic) literature
Special subjects
Religion
Hinduism -- Continued
(3931-3938) Śaivism
Divide like PK(3901-3908)
(3941-3948) Vaikhānasa cult
Divide like PK(3901-3908)
Minor religious systems
(3951-3958) Śāktras (Śakti worshippers). Tantras.
Tantrik texts
Divide like PK 3901-3908
(3961) Gāṇapatyas
(3963) Skanda (Kārttikeya)
(3965) Sauras (Sun worshippers)
(3966-3667) Pāñarātra texts
(3966) General
(3967) Special texts, A-Z
e. g.
(3967.A4) Ahirbudnya-saṃhitā
(3971-3978) Buddhism
Sanskrit only, Cf. PK4501 +
Divide like PK(3901-3908)
(3981-3988) Jainism
Sanskrit only, cf. PK5001 +
For translations, see BL1310.3 +
(3991) Foreign systems
e.g. Zoroastrianism
(3996) Christian
History and geography
(4001) General
(4011) Biography. Genealogy
(4021) Ethnology. Caste
(4031) Law
(4051) Music and dancing
Art
(4061) General
(4065) Architecture
(4071) Sculpture
(4081) Painting
(4091) Other
Philology
(4111) General works
Grammar, see PK501
Lexicography, see PK920 +
(4121) Metrics
(4131) Poetics. Dramaturgy, etc.
(4141) Rhetoric
Science
(4161) General
(4171) Mathematics. Arithmetic. Geometry
(4191) Astronomy. Astrology

PK

Sanskrit (Post-Vedic) literature
Special subjects
Science -- Continued
(4211) Other (Natural history. Plants. Animals. Minerals)
(4221) Medicine
(4231) Technical arts and sciences
(4241) Gastronomy
(4251) Occult sciences. Magic. etc.
Translations into foreign languages (from Sanskrit and Indic literature, general)
4471 Greek
4472 Latin
4473 Dutch. Flemish
4474 English
4475 French
4476 German
4477 Italian
4478 Portuguese
4479 Spanish
4480 Scandinavian
4483 Slavic
4485.A-Z Other, A-Z
Pali literature
History and criticism
(4501.A1) Periodicals. Yearbooks. Societies. Congresses
Publications of the Pali Text Society PK4541
see PK1001
(4501.A2) Collections
Series. Monographs by different authors, see PK1002.A+
Collected works, studies, essays, of individual authors, see PK1002.A+
4501.A3 Encyclopedias. Dictionaries
(4501.A4) Study and teaching
see PK1011
History
General
4503 Treatises. Compends. Textbooks
4505 Outlines, syllabi, etc.
4507 Collected essays
4509 Lectures, addresses, pamphlets
General special
4511 Relations to history, civilization, culture, etc.
4512 Relations to other literatures. Translations
4513 Treatment of special subjects, classes, etc.
Biography
4515 Collective
Individual
see PK4591, PK4601
4516 Literary topography
4517 Women authors

Pali literature
History and criticism
History -- Continued
By period
(4519) To 200 A.D.
see PK4503
4521 200-1800
4523 1800-
Poetry
4525 General
4526 Special
Prose. Fiction
4529 General
4530 Special
e.g. Dialogs. Legends
4535 Other. Miscellaneous
Local, see PK4641+
Collections
4541 General and miscellaneous
e. g.
4541.P3-P6 Pali Text Society's publications
4541.S5 Pali texts in Siamese characters (Collection)
4543 Inedited works. By editor, A-Z
4545 Selections. Anthologies
Tripiṭaka, see BQ1100+
(4546.A1) Complete editions of the three parts
(4546.A2) Partial
4546.A3 Selections. Anthologies
(4546.A7-Z5) Criticism
(4546.Z9) Dictionaries. Indexes. Concordances
Editions of the separate parts
Vinayapiạka
(4548.A1) Comprehensive
(4548.A2) Partial
(4548.A3) Selections. Anthologies
(4548.A4A-Y) Editions of special parts. By title
(4548.A7-Z5) Criticism. Commentaries
(4548.Z9) Dictionaries. Indexes. Concordances
Suttapiṭaka
(4551.A1) Comprehensive
(4551.A2) Partial
(4551.A3) Selections. Anthologies
(4551.A4A-Y) Editions of special parts. By title
(4551.A7-Z5) Criticism. Commentaries
(4551.Z9) Dictionaries. Indexes. Concordances
Abhidammapiṭaka
(4555.A1) Comprehensive
(4555.A2) Partial
(4555.A3) Selections. Anthologies
(4555.A4A-Y) Editions of special parts. By title
(4555.A7-Z5) Criticism. Commentaries
(4555.Z9) Dictionaries. Indexes. Concordances
4563 Poetry (i.e. modern collections)

PK

Pali literature
Collections -- Continued
4565 Prose
4571 Inscriptions
4591.A-Z Individual authors and works, A-Z
Subarrange each author by Table P-PZ40 unless otherwise specified
(4591.A6) Anguttaranikāya (Table P-PZ40)
see BQ1340-BQ1349.5
4591.B87 Buddhappiya, fl. 1229-1246
(4591.D2) Dhammapada (Table P-PZ40)
see BQ1370-BQ1379.5
(4591.D55) Dīgha-nikāya (Table P-PZ40)
see BQ1290-BQ1299.5
4591.H38 Hatthavanagallavihāravamśa
(4591.I8) Itivuttaka (Table P-PZ40)
see BQ1400-BQ1409
(4591.J3) Jātakas (Table P-PZ40)
see BQ1460-BQ1470
(4591.K3) Kathāvatthu (Table P-PZ40)
see BQ2540-BQ2549
(4591.M3) Mahānāma, 5th cent. (Table P-PZ40)
see BQ2600-BQ2609
(4591.P8) Puggala-paññatti (Table P-PZ40)
see BQ2530-BQ2539
(4591.S8) Suttanipāta (Table P-PZ40)
see BQ1410-BQ1419.5
(4591.T5) Theragāthā (Table P-PZ40)
see BQ1440-BQ1449
4591.V55 Vinayaprabha, ca. 1367-1432 or 3
Translations
(4621) Eastern languages
see PJ-PL
(4631) Western languages
see BL
References for translations are to be made here according to the following scheme, subarranged by date
.E5 English
.E5A1 Collections. General and miscellaneous
.E5A2 Tripitaka (Complete or partial)
.E5A3 Vinayapitaka (Complete or partial)
.E5A4 Suttapitaka
.E5A5 Abhidhammapitaka
.E5A6 Noncanonical writings
.E5A7-.E5Y Separate works
Pali literature outside of India and Sri Lanka
Burma
History
4641 General
4642 Special
Texts

Pali literature
Pali literature outside of India and Sri Lanka
Burma
Texts -- Continued
4643 Collections and selections
4644 Separate authors and works
4651-4654 Tibet
Divide like PK4641-PK4644
4661-4664 China
Divide like PK4641-PK4644
4671-4674 Japan
Divide like PK4641-PK4644
4681.A-Z Other countries, A-Z
Prakrit literature
History and criticism
4990 Periodicals. Societies. Congresses
4992 Collections
4994 General works
Biography
4996 Collective
Individual, see PK5013.A +
Jaina literature
5001.A1 Periodicals. Societies. Congresses
5001.A2-A3 Collections of monographs
5001.A2 Various authors
5001.A3A-Z Particular authors
5001.A5-Z3 Treatises, compends
Including treatises confined to canonical literature
5001.Z5A-Z Lectures, addresses, etc.
5001.1 General special
e.g. relations to history, civilization, literature, etc.
5001.6 Poetry
5001.7 Drama
5001.8 Prose: Fiction, legends, tales, etc.
Collections
5003.A1-A29 General and miscellaneous
5003.A4 Selections. Anthologies
(5003.A5-A9) Siddhānta (Jaina canon)
see BL1310 +
5003.A92-Z Other collections, A-Z
5006 Poetry
5007 Drama
5008 Prose: Fiction, legends, tales, etc.
5009 Inscriptions
For Asoka inscriptions, see PK1480 +
5013.A-Z Individual authors or works, A-Z (Table P-PZ40, or P-PZ43)
5013.B7 Brahma Jinadāsa, 1393-1473 (Table P-PZ40)
5013.D48 Devendrasūri, 13th cent. (Table P-PZ40)
5013.D53 Dharmadāsagaṇi (Table P-PZ40)
5013.D54 Dharmaghoṣasūri (Table P-PZ40)

PK

Prakrit literature
Individual authors or works, A-Z -- Continued
5013.G79 Guṇāḍhya (Table P-PZ40)
5013.H3 Hāla (Table P-PZ40)
5013.H35 Haribhadra Sūri (Table P-PZ40)
Haribhadrasūri, 700-770, see PK5013.H35
5013.K7 Kṛṣṇalīlāśukamuni, 1193-1293 (Table P-PZ40)
5013.L35 Lakṣmaṇagaṇi, 12th cent. (Table P-PZ40)
5013.M24 Maheśvarasūri, 11th cent. (Table P-PZ40)
5013.N33 Nayacandrasūri, 15th cent. (Table P-PZ40)
5013.N42 Nemicandrasuri, fl. 1072-1083 (Table P-PZ40)
5013.P7 Pravarasena (Table P-PZ40)
5013.P8 Puṣpadanta, 10th cent. (Table P-PZ40)
5013.R3 Rājaśekhara, ca. 880-ca. 920 (Table P-PZ40)
5013.R34 Rāmapāṇivāda, ca. 1707-ca. 1775 (Table P-PZ40)
5013.R84 Rudradāsa, 17th cent. (Table P-PZ40)
5013.S29 Sanghadāsagani (Table P-PZ40)
5013.S292 Sanghatilakācārya, 14th cent. (Table P-PZ40)
5013.S3 Sāntisūri, Acārya (Table P-PZ40)
5013.S92 Svayambhū (Table P-PZ40)
5013.U3 Uddyotana Sūrī, fl. 779 (Table P-PZ40)
5013.V3 Vākpati, 8th cent. (Table P-PZ40)
5013.V57 Viśveśvara, 18th cent. (Table P-PZ40)
Translations
From Prakrit into other languages
For canonical works, see BL1310, with added entry here
5045-5046 Collections (Table P-PZ30)
Individual works, see PK5013.A+
Modern Indo-Aryan literature
Cf. PK1501+, Modern Indo-Aryan languages
Cf. PK1549.2+, Particular modern Indo-Aryan languages and dialects
5401-5446 History and collections (Table P-PZ22)
5447.A-Z Local, A-Z
Translations (Collected)
5461 English
5471.A-Z Other languages, A-Z
Iranian philology and literature
Philology
6001-6091 General
Divide like PJ3001-PJ3091
History of Persian literature
6097 Comprehensive treatises (Old, Middle, and New Persian)
New Persian, see PK6406
6099 General special
6102-6107 Avestan (Old Bactrian) (Table P-PZ8a, nos. 1-7)
Including works on both Avestan and Old Persian
6108 Metrics
6109 Other special
6111-6119 Avesta (Text)

Iranian philology and literature
Avestan (Old Bactrian)
Avesta (Text) -- Continued
6111 Editions. By date
The manuscripts of the three books Vendidād, Vīspered and Yasna appear in two different forms according as they are accompanied, or not, by a Pahlavī version. If the books are kept separate as three divisions, each part is usually accompanied by a Pahlavī version. If for liturgical purposes portions of one book are mingled with another, and arranged in the order in which thay are to be used in the service, the Pahlavī translation is omitted, and the collection is called the Vendidād Sādah or "Vendidād pure", i.e. text without commentary. The second group comprising the minor prayers and the Yashts is called the Khordah Avesta or "small Avesta." Cf. A.V.W. Jackson, Avesta grammar I
Including editions of the Vendidād
6112.A-Z Selections. By editor, A-Z
6113 Particular books
Books denoted by letters, A - G
1. Yasna = A, Chapters 28-34, 43-51, 53 are known as Gāthās; 2. Vīspered = B; 3. Vendidād = C; 4. Yashts = D; 5. Minor texts = E; , e g. Nyāishes, Gāhs,; 6. Gāthās = F; 7. Fragments, quoted in Pahlavī books = G
Translations and commentaries
Eastern
Translations
6114 Pahlavī
6114.2 Persian
Other languages
see PJ - PL
Cf. PK3991, Sanskrit
Commentaries
6115 Pahlavi
6115.2 Persian
Other languages
see PJ - PL
Western
6116.A-Z Translations. By language, A-Z
6117 Textual and philological criticism
6118 Special topics (not A-Z)
(6119) Indexes, glossaries, etc.
see PK6106+
6121-6127 Old Persian (Table P-PZ8a nos. 1-7)
Including language of the Achaemenian inscriptions
Inscriptions
6128.A1 Collections. By editor
6128.A3-A7 Translations. By language

PK

Iranian philology and literature
Old Persian
Inscriptions -- Continued
6128.A8-Z Special, A-Z
e. g.
6128.D3 Inscription of Darius I
6129 Other special
6131 Median language
6132 Inscriptions
Middle Iranian languages
6135 General works
Pahlavī (Middle Persian, 226-642 A.D.)
6141-6186 Language (Table P-PZ5)
Included in Pahlavī are Husvarish (containing both Iranian words and Aramaic logograms), Pazend (transcription in Avesta letters) and Parsee (transcription in Persian (Arabic) and Gujarātī script)
6150 Alphabet. Writing
6151 Grammar in Oriental languages
6177.A-Z Dictionaries with definitions in other languages, A-Z
Linguistic geography
Dialects, provincialisms, etc.
6185.A-Z Local. By region, place, etc., A-Z
e. g.
6185.P3 Parthia
Literature
6190 History
Texts
6191 Collections
6192 Selections
Special
6193 Sassanid inscriptions
Cf. CN
6194 Papyri
(6195) Avesta translations
see PK6114
6197 Other religious works
6198 Non-religious works
6199 Translations (Table P-PZ30)
6199.4-5 From Pahlavī into other languages
6199.7 Khorezmi (Table P-PZ15)
6199.8 Khotanese (Table P-PZ15)
6199.85 Sarmatian (Table P-PZ15)
6199.9 Sogdian (Table P-PZ15)
New Persian
6201-6399 Language (Table P-PZ3)
(6252) Transliteration
see P226
Literature
Inscriptions
6400 History and criticism

Iranian philology and literature
New Persian
Literature
Inscriptions -- Continued
Collections
6400.2 General
6400.4 Museums. Institutions
6400.5 Private collections
6400.6.A-Z By place where found, A-Z
6400.7 Individual inscriptions
History and criticism
6401 Periodicals. Societies. Serials
6402 Collected works of individual authors
6403 Encyclopedias. Dictionaries
6404 Study and teaching
6406 General works
6408 Lectures, addresses, etc.
General special
6409 Relations to history, civilization, etc.
6410 Relations to other literatures
6411 Translations (as subject)
6412.A-Z Treatment of special subjects, classes, etc., A-Z
Biography
6413 Collective
Individual, see PK6450.9+
6413.5.A-Z Special classes of authors, A-Z
6413.5.P7 Prisoners
6413.5.W65 Women
By period
(6414) Origins and classic period (to ca. 1500) see PK6406
Modern, 1500-
6415 General
6415.2 1500-1800
6415.4 19th century
6415.5 20th century
By form
Poetry
6416 General
(6417) Origins and classic period (to ca. 1500) see PK6416
6418 Modern, (1500-)
6419 Special
Including epic, romantic, lyric, didactic and mystic
6420.A-Z Other forms and subjects, A-Z
e. g.
6420.E83 Ethics. Islamic ethics
6420.G3 Gazel (Amatory ode, wine-song or religious hymn)
6420.H86 Hunting
6420.I7 Iran

Iranian philology and literature
New Persian
Literature
History and criticism
By form
Poetry
Special
Other forms
and subjects, A-Z -- Continued

6420.I84 Islam
Islamic ethics, see PK6420.E83
6420.K5 Kings and rulers as poets
6420.L39 Laylī and Majnūn
6420.Q3 Qasīdā (Encomiastic, elegiacor satirical poem)
6420.R8 Rubāi (Quatrain, epigram)
6420.S8 Sufism. Sufi poetry
6420.W65 Women poets
Drama
6421 General
6422 Special
Prose. Prose fiction
6423 General works
6424.A-Z Special topics, A-Z
6424.C58 Civilization, Western
6425 Wit and humor
(6426) Folk literature
see GR290-GR291.2
6426.5 Children's literature (General)
Local (within Iran)
6427.A-Z By region, province, etc., A-Z
6427.3.A-Z By city, etc., A-Z
Outside Iran
6427.5 General works
6427.6.A-Z By country, A-Z
Collections
6428 General
6429 Selections. Anthologies
By period
6430 Through 1500
6431 Since 1500
Poetry
6433 General
6434 Selections. Anthologies
By period
6435 Through 1500
Prefer PK6433
6436 Since 1500
Special
6438.A-Z By form, A-Z
Divide like PK6420.A-PK6402.Z
6439.A-Z By subject, A-Z
6439.A4 'Alī ibn Abī Ṭālib, caliph

Iranian philology and literature
New Persian
Literature
Collections
Poetry
Special
By subject, A-Z -- Continued
6439.I73 Iranian Revolution, 1979
6439.K47 Khomeini, Ruhollah
6439.L6 Love
6439.M3 al-Mahdī, Muḥammad ibn al-Ḥasan
6439.M85 Muḥammad, The prophet
6439.N48 New year. Nawrūz
6439.P36 Patriotic poetry
6439.R38 Revolutionary poetry
6439.R8 Russia
6439.S94 Sufism
6440 Drama
6443 Prose. Prose fiction
Local (within Iran)
6445.A-Z By region, province, etc., A-Z
6446.A-Z By city, etc., A-Z
Outside Iran
6447.A-Z By region or country, A-Z
Translations (Table P-PZ30)
6449 From Persian into foreign languages
English
6449.E1 General and miscellaneous
6449.E5 Poetry
6449.E6 Drama
6449.E7 Prose
(6449.E9) Individual authors'
see PK6451+
6449.F1-F9 French
Divide like PK6449.E1-PK6449.E9
6449.G1-G9 German
Divide like PK6449.E1-PK6449.E9
6449.I1-I9 Italian
Divide like PK6449.E1-PK6449.E9
6449.R1-R9 Russian
Divide like PK6449.E1-PK6449.E9
6449.S1-S9 Spanish
Divide like PK6449.E1-PK6449.E9
6450.A-Z Other languages, A-Z
Individual authors or works (Table P-PZ39, P-PZ40, or P-PZ43)
6450.9-6559 To 1870
6450.9 Anonymous works. By title, A-Z
6451 A - F
6451.A22 ʻAbdī Bayg Shīrāzī, Zayn al-ʻĀbidīn ʻAlī, 1515-1580 or 81 (Table P-PZ40)
6451.A29 Abū Ṭāhir Ṭarsūsī, Muḥammad ibn Ḥasan (Table P-PZ40)

PK

Iranian philology and literature
New Persian
Literature
Individual authors or works
To 1870
A - F -- Continued

6451.A295 Adīb al-Mamālik, Muḥammad Ṣādiq ibn Ḥusayn, 1860-1917 or 18
6451.A3 Adīb Ṣābir ibn Ismā'īl Tirmizī, d. 1147?
6451.A37 Āfarīn Lāhūrī, Faqīr Allāh, d. 1741 or 2
6451.A39 Afghāni, Jamāl al-Din, 1838-1897
6451.A43 Ahlī Khurāsānī, d. 1527 or 8
6451.A5 Ahmad, sultan of Bagdad (Table P-PZ40)
6451.A533 Aḥmad Shāh Durrānī, Amir of Afghanistan, ca. 1723-1772
6451.A566 'Alī Qulī Khān Vālih, 1712-1756
6451.A5723 Alisher Navoiĭ, 1441-1501
6451.A59 Amīr Khusraw Dihlavī, ca. 1253-1325
6451.A62 Anvarī, Awḥad al-Dīn, d. 1189 or 90
6451.A68 'Arif Ardabīlī, 14th cent.
6451.A69 'Ārifī, d. ca. 1449
6451.A77 'Ashiq, Kalyān Singh, 1751 or 2-1822
6451.A783 Ashrafī, Muḥammad Īljī ibn Muḥammad Muhsin

'Aṭṭar, Farīd al-Dīn, d. ca. 1230, see PK6451.F4

6451.A82 'Awfī, Muḥammad, fl. 1228
6451.A84 'Ayyūqī
6451.A85 'Aẓīm Tattavī, 'Aẓīm al-Dīn, 1749 or 50-1814
6451.B25 Bābā-Ṭāhir
6451.B32 Bandah Navāz, 1321-1422
6451.B35 Bardsīrī Kirmanī, Shams al-Dīn Muḥammad
6451.B49 Bīdil, 'Abd al-Qādir, 1644-1720 or 21
6451.B5 Bīdpaī. Persian version. Anvar i Suhaili
6451.B53 Bīghamī, Muḥammad ibn Aḥmad
6451.C32 Callisthenes, Pseudo-

Calleddin, Rmī, Mevln, see PK6478+

6451.D34 Dairi, Raja Koul Arzbegi, 1828-1900
6451.D348 Daqāyiqī, Shams al-Dīn Muḥammad, 13th cent.
6451.D5 Dilshād Pasrūrī
6451.F28 Fakhr al-Dīn Gurgānī, fl. 1048
6451.F3 Falakī Shirwānī (Table P-PZ40)
6451.F4 Farīd al-Dīn 'Aṭṭar, 13th cent.
6451.F46 Fawzī, Shaykh, d. ca. 1747
6451.F47 Fayzī, Abū al-Fayz ibn Mubārak, 1547 or 8-1595
6451.F65 Fighānī, Bābā, d. 1519
6455-6460 Firdawsī

Iranian philology and literature
New Persian
Literature
Individual authors or works
To 1870
A - F
Firdawsī -- Continued
6455.A1 Comprehensive editions
Including comprehensive editions of the Shāhnāma
6455.A2 Selections
6455.A3-Z Episodes
Translations
6456 Western
Under each:
1 Comprehensive works
2 Special parts, A-Z
3 Extracts. Selections
English
6456.A1 Comprehensive works
6456.A12 Special parts
6456.A13 Extracts. Selections
French
6456.A2 Comprehensive works
6456.A22 Special parts
6456.A23 Extracts. Selections
German
6456.A3 Comprehensive works
6456.A32 Special parts
6456.A33 Extracts. Selections
6456.A5-Z Other languages, A-Z
6456.5.A-Z Oriental languages, A-Z
Under each:
.x Comprehensive works
.x2 Special parts, A-Z
.x3 Extracts. Selections
6457 Adaptations. Paraphrases, etc. (English)
Juvenile works, see subclass PZ
Commentaries
6458 Oriental
6459 Western
6460 Yusuf and Zuleikha
6463 Firdawsī - Hāfiz
6463.G38 Ghālib, 1796?-1869
6463.G39 Ghanī, Muḥammad Ṭahir, d. 1668 or 9
6463.G4 Ghanīmat, Muḥammad Akram, fl. 1685-1696
6463.G43 Ghāzalī Mashhadī, 1526 or 7-1572 or 3
6463.G45 Ghāzīuddīn Khān, 1736-1800
6465 Hāfiz, 14th cent. (Table P-PZ39)
6465.A1 Editions. By date
6465.A2 Selections
6465.A3-Z2 Separate works, A-Z

PK

Iranian philology and literature
New Persian
Literature
Individual authors or works
To 1870
Hafiz, 14th cent.
Separate works -- Continued

6465.D5	Diwan (Collection of 537 short odes, or sonnets, called ghazals)
6465.K5	Kit'as (42 fragments)
6465.R8	Ruba'iyat, or tetrastics (69)
6465.Z3-Z79	Translations
6465.Z3-Z36	English
6465.Z3	Complete works. By translator and date
6465.Z31	Selections. By translator, A-Z
6465.Z32	Dīwān. By translator, A-Z
6465.Z34	Kit'as. By translator, A-Z
6465.Z36	Ruba'iyat. By translator, A-Z
6465.Z4-Z46	French
6465.Z4	Complete works. By translator and date
6465.Z41	Selections. By translator, A-Z
6465.Z42	Dīwān. By translator, A-Z
6465.Z44	Kit'as. By translator, A-Z
6465.Z46	Ruba'iyat. By translator, A-Z
6465.Z5-Z56	German
6465.Z5	Complete works. By translator and date
6465.Z51	Selections. By translator, A-Z
6465.Z52	Dīwān. By translator, A-Z
6465.Z54	Kit'as. By translator, A-Z
6465.Z56	Ruba'iyat. By translator, A-Z
6465.Z6-Z66	Italian
6465.Z6	Complete works. By translator and date
6465.Z61	Selections. By translator, A-Z
6465.Z62	Dīwān. By translator, A-Z
6465.Z64	Kit'as. By translator, A-Z
6465.Z66	Ruba'iyat. By translator, A-Z
6465.Z7-Z79	Other languages (alphabetically)
6465.Z8-Z99	Biography. Criticism
6470	Haf -Ibn (Table P-PZ40)
6470.H19	Ḥakīm Lāhaurī, Shāh 'Abdulhakīm, 1700-1758 (Table P-PZ40)
6470.H338	Ḥasan Dihlavī, 1253 or 4-ca. 1338 (Table P-PZ40)
6470.H38	Hātifī, d. 1520 or 1 (Table P-PZ40)
6470.H5	Hisābī, 16th cent. (Table P-PZ40)
6470.H75	Humā Shīrāzī, 1797 or 8-1873 or 4 (Table P-PZ40)
6470.H88	Ḥusayn Mīrzā ibn Manṣūr, Sultan of Khorasan, 1438-1506 (Table P-PZ40)
	Ibn Yamīn, Fakhr al-Dīn Maḥmūd (Table P-PZ40)
6475.A1	Editions. By date
6475.A3-Z3	Translations. By language, A-Z

Iranian philology and literature
New Persian
Literature
Individual authors or works
To 1870
Ibn Yamīn, Fakhr al-Dīn Maḥmūd -- Continued
6475.Z5 Criticism
6477 Ibn - Jal (Table P-PZ40)
6477.I385 'Imād ibn Muḥammad al-Na'rī, 14th cent. (Table P-PZ40)
6477.I82 Isfarangī, Sayf al-Dīn, 1185 or 6-1267 or 8 (Table P-PZ40)
Jalāl al-Dīn Rūmī, Maulana, 1207-1273
6478 Complete works. By date, or editor
6479 Selections. By date, or editor
6480.A-Z Translations. By language, A-Z
Subarrange by translator
6481 Separate works
Under each:
1 Complete editions and selections. By date and editor
2 Separate books. By number
3 Translations. By language
4 Criticism
6481.D4-D7 Dīwan-i-Shams-i-Tabriz
Apply table at PK6481
6481.M2-M5 Maktūbāt
Apply table at PK6481
6481.M6-M9 Masnavī
Apply table at PK6481
6481.R6-R9 Rubā'iyāt
Apply table at PK6481
6482 Biography and criticism
6485 Jalal to Jāmī (Table P-PZ40)
6485.A43 Jamālī, Ḥamid ibn Fazl Allāh, d. 1535 or 6 (Table P-PZ40)
6490 Jāmī, 1414-1492
6495 J - N (Table P-PZ40)
6495.K3 Kamāl al-Dīn Ismā'īl, d. 1237 (Table P-PZ40)
6495.K33 Kamāl Khujandī, d. ca. 1400 (Table P-PZ40)
6495.K34 al-Kātib al-Samarqandī, Muḥammad ibn 'Alī (Table P-PZ40)
6495.K35 Khāqānī, Afzal al-Dīn Shirvānī, ca. 1126-1198 or 9 (Table P-PZ40)
6495.K358 Khayālī Bukhārāyī, d. ca. 1446 (Table P-PZ40)
6495.M454 Manūchihrī Dāmghānī, Abū Najm Aḥmad ibn Qawṣ (Table P-PZ40)
6495.M47 Mas'ūd Sa'd Salmān, 1046 or 7-1121 or 2 (Table P-PZ40)

PK

Iranian philology and literature
New Persian
Literature
Individual authors or works
To 1870
J - N -- Continued

6495.M49 Mazhar Jān Janān, Habīb Ullah, 1699-1780 (Table P-PZ40)
6495.M56 Mīr Ḥusaynī Haravī, Ḥusayn ibn 'Ālim, 1272 or 3-ca. 1317 (Table P-PZ40)
6495.M565 Mīrzā Āqā Tabrīzī (Table P-PZ40)
6495.M57 Mīrzā Malkum Khān, 1833-1908 (Table P-PZ40)
6495.M58 Mirzā Sharaf Jahān Qazvīnī, 1496-1560 (Table P-PZ40)
6495.M84 Mu'īnuddīn Ḥasan Cishtī Sanjārī Ajmerī, 1143?-1234? (Table P-PZ40)
6495.M8415 Mu'izzī, Amīr 'Abd Allāh Muḥammad, d. 1048 or 9 (Table P-PZ40)
6495.M842 Mujīr al-Dīn Baylaqānī, d. 1197 or 8 (Table P-PZ40)
6495.M847 Mullā Ḥamīdullāh Shāhābādī, d. 1848 (Table P-PZ40)
6495.M86 Munavvar, Nūr al-Dīn Bukhārī, 1789-1852 (Table P-PZ40)
6495.N22 Nakhjavānī, Aḥmad ibn al-Hasan (Table P-PZ40)
6495.N24 Nakhshabī, d. 1350 (Table P-PZ40)
6495.N26 Nanda Lāla, 1633-1705 (Table P-PZ40)
6495.N27 Naqī, 'Alī, 1546 or 7-ca. 1622 (Table P-PZ40)
6495.N29 Nashāṭ, 'Abd al-Vahhāb, 1761 or 2-1849 or 50 (Table P-PZ40)
6495.N297 Nāsir Bukhārā'ī, Nāṣir, 1320?-1388? (Table P-PZ40)
6495.N3 Nāṣir-i Khusraw, 1004-ca. 1088 (Table P-PZ40)
6495.N5 Ni'mat Allāh Valī, 1330?-1431 (Table P-PZ40)
6495.N54 Nisārī Bukhārī, Bahā' al-Dīn, Ḥasan, fl. 1566 (Table P-PZ40)
6499 Niẓāmī 'Arūzī, fl. 1110-1153
6499.C6 Chahār maqāla
6501 Niẓāmī Ganjavī, 1140 or 41-1202 or 3 (Table P-PZ40)
Niẓāmī of Ganja, the more famous Niẓāmī
The five works named below are known as the Khamsah, the Quintet, or the Five Treasures
6501.A1 Editions
Translations
6501.A2-A29 English. By translator

Iranian philology and literature
New Persian
Literature
Individual authors or works
To 1870
Niẓāmī Ganjavī, 1140 or 41-1202 or 3
Translations -- Continued

6501.A3-A39 French. By translator
6501.A4-A49 German. By translator
6501.A5-A59 Other. By language
Separate works
Under each subdivide for translations
6501.H4 Haft paykar
6501.H43W5 Wilson's translation of Haft Paykar
6501.I8 Iskandarnāmah
6501.K4 Khusraw va Shīrīn
6501.L3 Laylī va Majnūn
6501.M3 Makhzan al-asrār
6501.Z8-Z99 Biography and criticism
Omar Khayyām
6510.A1 Editions. By date
Editions with translations
Subarrange by editor
6511.A1 Polyglot
6511.A2-Z By language
Translations
Cf. Dole's Multi-variorum edition, vol. II, app. 49
6512 In three or more languages, by editor
If in two languages, classify with the less known
English
Fitzgerald's translation
6513.A1 Editions
6513.A15 Editions with Vedder's illustrations
6513.A2 Selections
6513.A3A-Z Concordances
(6513.A5-Z) Criticism
see PK6525
Translations. By language
6514.A-Z European, A-Z
e. g.
6514.S2-S4 Scandinavian
6514.S2 Danish. Dano-Norwegian
6514.S3 Icelandic
6514.S4 Swedish
6514.S5-S79 Slavic
6514.S5 Bohemian
6514.S6 Polish
6514.S7 Russian
6514.S71-S79 Minor Slavic
6515.A-Z Oriental and other, A-Z
e. g.

Iranian philology and literature
New Persian
Literature
Individual authors or works
To 1870
Omar Khayyām
Translations
English
Fitzgerald's translation
Translations. By language
Oriental and other, A-Z -- Continued

6515.J3	Japanese
6516.A-Z	Other English translations. By translator, A-Z
6516.A1-A19	Anonymous
6517	Translations into languages other than English
	Excluding versions of Fitzgerald's translation for which, see PK6514
6517.D8	Dutch. Flemish. Frisian
6517.F5	French
6517.G3	German
6517.I5	Italian
6517.P6	Portuguese
	Scandinavian
6517.S3	Danish. Dano-Norwegian
6517.S4	Icelandic
6517.S6	Swedish
6517.S8	Spanish
6518.A-Z	Other languages, A-Z
	e. g.
	Subarrange by translator
6518.A5	Albanian
6518.I7	Irish
6524	Biography
6524.A2	Societies. Periodicals. Collections
6525	Criticism and interpretation
6526	Omar - Oz
6527	P (Table P-PZ40)
6527.U87	Pūriyā-yi Valī, Maḥmūd Khvārazmī, d. 1419 or 20 (Table P-PZ40)
6528	Q (Table P-PZ40)
6528.A4	Qādirī, Muḥammad, 17th cent. (Table P-PZ40)
6528.A55	Qāni'i, 16th cent. (Table P-PZ40)
6529	R - Rud (Table P-PZ40)
6529.A35	Rābi'ah-'i Balkhī, 10th cent. (Table P-PZ40)
6529.A93	Rawnaq 'Alī Shāh, Muḥammad Ḥusayn farzand-i Muḥammad Kāẓim, d. 1814 or 15 (Table P-PZ40)
6529.I93	Riyāẓī, d. 1479 or 80 (Table P-PZ40)

Iranian philology and literature
New Persian
Literature
Individual authors or works
To 1870 -- Continued
6530 Rūdakī, 10th cent. (Table P-PZ37)
6532 Ruf - Ruz (Table P-PZ40)
6532.K55 Rukn-i Ṣāyin Harvī, 14th cent. (Table P-PZ40)
Rumi, see PK6478+
6532.P32 Rup Narāyan, 18th cent. (Table P-PZ40)
Sa'dī, ca. 1184-1191
6540.A1 Editions. By date
6540.A2 Selections. By editor
Separate works
6540.B2 Būstān (Orchard). By date
6540.D2 Dīwān (Collection of lyrics)
6540.G2 Gulistan (Rose-garden)
6540.P3 Pand namah (Scroll of wisdom)
6540.T3 Tayyibāt (Odes)
Translations
6541 English
Subdivide by individual work and translator
6542.A-Z Other European languages, A-Z
e.g. Gulistan in French, translated by Defrmery, PK6542.F5G23; Gulistan in French, translated by Semelet, PK6542.F5G27
Subdivide by language, individual work and translator
6543.A-Z Oriental and other languages, A-Z
Subdivide like PK6542
6546 Biography and criticism
6549 S - T
6549.S214 Saccal Sarmast, 1739-1829 (Table P-PZ40)
6549.S218 Ṣādiq Munshī (Table P-PZ40)
6549.S225 Safā'ī, Aḥmad ibn Mahdī, 1771-1829 (Table P-PZ40)
6549.S234 Ṣāfī, 'Alī Shāh, Ḥasan, 1835-1899 (Table P-PZ40)
6549.S24 Sa'ib Tabrīzī Muḥammad 'Alī, d. ca. 1670 (Table P-PZ40)
6549.S27 Salīm Tihrānī Muḥammad Qulī, d. 1647? (Table P-PZ40)
6549.S3 Sanā'ī, of Ghazni, d. ca. 1150 (Table P-PZ40)
6549.S33 Sarfarāz Khānu 'Abbāsī, Miyān, d. 1776 (Table P-PZ40)
6549.S35 Sarmad Shahīd, 1618-1660 or 61 (Table P-PZ40)
6549.S44 Shabistarī, Maḥmūd ibn 'Abd al-Karīm, d. ca. 1320 (Table P-PZ40)

Iranian philology and literature
New Persian
Literature
Individual authors or works
To 1870
S - T -- Continued
6549.S5 Shams al-Dīn Fakīr, 18th cent (Table P-PZ40)
6549.S557 Shibli Numani Muḥammad, 1857-1914 (Table P-PZ40)
6549.S57 Simnānī, Aḥmad ibn Muḥammad, 1261-1336 (Table P-PZ40)
6549.S77 Sūfī Māzandarānī, Muḥammad, d. 1623? (Table P-PZ40)
6549.S84 Sulṭān, Valad, 1226-1312 (Table P-PZ40)
6550 T - Z
6550.T29 Taftah, Munshī Hargopāl, 1799-1879
Ṭāhir of Hamadān, see PK6451.B25
6550.T33 Tair-zade, Mirza-Alekber, 1862-1911
6550.T34 Tālib Āmulī, d. 1626?
6550.T35 Tarzī Afshār, fl. 1616-1650
6550.T8 Ṭūṭīnāmah
6550.U2 ʻUbayd Zakani, Niẓam al-Dīn, d. ca. 1370
6550.U5 'Unsurī, Abū al-Qāsim Ḥasan, fl. 1009-1041
6550.U7 'Urfī Shīrāzī, Muḥammad, 1555 or 6-1590
6550.V3 Vaḥhī, Yazdī, d. 1583
6550.V325 Vālah Iṣfahānī, Muḥammad Kāẓim, d. 1813 or 14
6550.V39 Vaysī, Fatḥ 'Alī, 1825-1886
6550.Y34 Yaqhmā Jandaqī, Abū al-Ḥasan, ca. 1782-1859
6559 Z
6559.Z28 Ẓafar Khān, Aḥsan Allāh, 1605 or 6-1662 or 3
6559.Z3 Ẓahīr Fāryābī, Abū al-Fazl Ṭāhir ibn Muḥammad, d. 1201 or 2
6559.Z5 Zīb ; un-Nisā, begam, 17th cent.
6559.Z75 Zuh;urī, Nūr al-Dīn Muḥammad, 1537 or 8-1616 or 17
6561 Individual authors, 1870-
e. g.
6561.A99 'Azīz Janq, Nawab
6561.T284 Ṭarzī, Maḥmūd
(6599) Folk literature
see GR290-GR291.2
(6599.7) Proverbs
see PN6519.P5
Afghan (Pashtō, Pushto, Pushtu, etc.)

Iranian philology and literature
Afghan (Pashtō, Pushto, Pushtu, etc.) -- Continued
6701-6799 Language (Table P-PZ4)
Substitute for PK6717: Grammar in Oriental languages
Under each author subdivide by successive cutter numbers:
0 Texts
1 Translations
2-3 Commentaries
2 Eastern
3 Western
4 Indexes, glossaries, etc.
6800-6818 Literature (Table P-PZ23)
Individual authors or works, A-Z
Subarrange each author by Table P-PZ40 unless otherwise specified
6818 To 1800
6818.K53 Khwushḥāl Khān, 17th cent (Table P-PZ40)
6818.R3 Rahmān, ʻAbd al-Raḥmān, fl. 1641-1708 (Table P-PZ40)
6819 19th century
6820 20th century
6851-6859 Baluchi (Table P-PZ8a)
6871-6879 Dari (Table P-PZ8a)
6901-6909 Kurdish (Table P-PZ8a)
6908.9.A-Z Individual authors or works, A-Z (Table P-PZ40, or P-PZ43)
6951-6959 Ossetic (Table P-PZ8a)
6958.9.A-Z Individual authors or works, A-Z (Table P-PZ40 or P-PZ43)
e. g.
6958.9.K45 Khetagurov, Konstantin Levanovich, 1859-1906
6971-6979 Tajik (Table P-PZ8a)
6978.9.A-Z Individual authors or works, A-Z
e. g.
6978.9.A75 Ạsiṛi, toshkhoja, 1864-1916
6978.9.D65 Donish, Ahmadi, 1826-1897
6978.9.D9 Dzhalil, Rakhim Jalil
6978.9.H69 Hoziq, Junaĭdullo, d. 1843
Jalil, Rahim, 1909- , see PK6978.9.D9
6978.9.M57 Mirzo Barkhudori Farohī
6978.9.N69 Nozili Khujandī
6978.9.S53 Shohin, Shamsiddin-makhdum, 1859-1894
6978.9.V67 Vosifī, Zaĭnuddin Mahmud ibn Abdujalil, 1485-ca. 1551
Minor Iranian dialects
e. g.
6991.A-Z Groups, A-Z
6991.C3 Caspian
Ghalchah, see PK6991.P3
6991.P3 Pamir. Ghalchah
6996.A-Z Particular dialects, A-Z

PK

Iranian philology and literature
Minor Iranian dialects
Particular dialects, A-Z -- Continued
6996.B3 Bartang
6996.G3 Gabri
6996.G54 Gilaki
6996.H3 Hazara language
6996.I7 Ishkashmi
6996.K4 Kashani
6996.K8 Kumzari
6996.M8 Munji
6996.O75 Ormuri
6996.R6 Roshan
6996.S3 Sarikoli
6996.S5 Shughni
6996.S6 Sivendi
6996.T3 Talysh
6996.T35 Tat
Cf. PJ5089.297, Judeo-Tat
6996.W3 Wakhi
6996.Y2 Yaghnōbī
6996.Y3 Yazghulami
6996.Z4 Zebaki
7001-7075 Dardic (Pisacha) languages
7001 General
Dard group
Class here languages spoken in Dardistan
7005 General
7010 Shiṇā
7015.A-Z Dialects, A-Z
7015.B75 Brokpa
7021-7037 Kāshmīrī
7021-7028 Language (Table P-PZ8a)
7029 Dialects
7029.A2 Kashṭwāṛī (Kishtwārī)
7029.A5-Z Other
7029.P6 Pōgulī
7029.R3 Rāmbanī
Literature
7031 History
7033 Collections
Individual authors or works, A-Z (Table P-PZ40, or P-PZ43)
e. g.
7035.H32 Ḥabbah Khātūn, d. 1605 (Table P-PZ40)
7035.L3 Laldyadā, 14th cent. (Table P-PZ40)
7035.M35 Maḥmūd Gāmī, 1765-1855 (Table P-PZ40)
7035.N84 Nund-Rishi (Table P-PZ40)
7035.R38 Rāzdān, Kṛṣṇa, 1850-1926 (Table P-PZ40)
7037 Translations
Kōhistānī
Group of languages spoken in the Panjkora, Sivat, and Indus Kohistans

Dardic (Pisacha) languages
Dard group
Kōhistānī -- Continued
7040 General
7045.A-Z Particular dialects, A-Z
7045.G3 Gārwī
7045.M3 Maiyā (Indus-Kōhistānī)
7045.T6 Tōrwālī
7045.W6 Wotapuri-Katargalai
7050 Nuristani (Kāfir) group
Languages spoken in Nuristan
General, see PK7050
7055.A-Z Special, A-Z
7055.A8 Ashkund (Ashku)
7055.B3 Bashgali (Table P-PZ16)
7055.W3 Waigali (Table P-PZ16)
7055.W4 Wasi-veri (Vernon, Prēsun, or Prasu) (Table P-PZ16)
Languages spoken outside of Kafiristan.
Kalāshā-Pashai subgroup
(7060) General
see PK7050
7065.A-Z Special, A-Z
7065.D5 Dīrī
7065.G3 Gawar-bati (Narsātī)
7065.K3 Kalāshā
7065.P3 Pashai (Laghmānī; Dēhgānī
7065.T5 Tirahī
7070 Khōwār (Table P-PZ15a)
7075 Phalura
(7501) Lost ancient or medieval Indo-European languages of Asia
see P901+
Armenian language and literature
Language
8001-8099 General and Old (Classical) Armenian (Table P-PZ4)
Under each author subdivide by successive cutter numbers:
0 Texts
1 Translations
2-4 Commentaries
2 Eastern
3 Western
4 Indexes, glossaries
8017 Popular
Grammars formerly classed in this number are to be reclassed in PK8018+ as appropriate according to Table P-PZ4 without distinction between those in Oriental and non-Oriental languages
8017.5 Script
Inscriptions
8196 Collections. By editor
8196.7 By place where found, A-Z

Armenian language and literature
Language
Inscriptions -- Continued
8197 Translations. By language
8198.A-Z Special, A-Z
8301-8349 Middle Armenian (10th-15th centuries) (Table P-PZ5)
8310 Grammar in Oriental languages
Grammars formerly classed in this number are to be reclassed in PK8311+ as appropriate according to Table P-PZ5 without distinction between those in Oriental and non-Oriental languages
8351-8449 Modern Armenian (Table P-PZ4)
8367 Grammar in Oriental languages
Grammars formerly classed in this number are to be reclassed in PK8368+ as appropriate according to Table P-PZ4 without distinction between those in Oriental and non-Oriental languages
8450 Modern West Armenian
8450.1 Grammar
8450.2 Exercises. Readers. Phrase books, etc.
8450.3 Etymology
8450.4 Dictionaries
8451-8499 Modern East Armenian (Table P-PZ5)
8451.F5 F.N. Finck, Lehrbuch der neuostarmenischen literatursprache
Literature
8501-8546 History and collections (Table P-PZ22)
Individual authors or works, A-Z
Subarrange individual authors by Table P-PZ40 unless otherwise specified
8547 Through 1800
8547.A57 Arak'el Siwnets'i, 1350-1422 (Table P-PZ40)
8547.A6 Aray Geghets'ik ew Shamiram (Table P-PZ40)
8547.F7 Frik, b. ca. 1236 (Table P-PZ40)
8547.G56 Ghowl Hovhannēs, ashowgh, 1740?-1834 (Table P-PZ40)
8547.G7 Gregory, Narekatzi, Saint, 951-1003 (Table P-PZ40)
8547.G715 Grigor IV Tghay, Catholicos of Armenia, d. 1193 (Table P-PZ40)
8547.G73 Grigoris, Aght'amarts'i, d. 1545 (Table P-PZ40)
8547.H57 Hovhan Mamikonian, Bp. of Mamikoniank' (Table P-PZ40)
8547.H58 Hovhannēs, T'lkurants'i, 14th-15th cent. (Table P-PZ40)
8547.M37 Martiros, Ghrimets'i, d. 1683 (Table P-PZ40)
8547.M5 Mkhit'ar Sebastats'i, 1676-1749 (Table P-PZ40)
8547.N29 Naghash Hovnat'an (Table P-PZ40)
8547.N3 Nahapet K'owch'ak, 16th cent. (Table P-PZ40)
8547.N38 Nerses Mokats'i, ca. 1575-1625 (Table P-PZ40)

Armenian language and literature
Literature
Individual authors or works, A-Z
Through 1800 -- Continued

8547.N4	Nersēs Shnor'hali, Saint, ca. 1100-1173 (Table P-PZ40)
8547.P32	Patmowt'iwn Tarōnoy For the text itself, see BX122
8547.S26	Sargis apuch'ekhts'i (Table P-PZ40)
8547.S27	Sasownts'i Dawit' (Table P-PZ40)
8547.S3	Sayat'-Nova, 1712-1795 (Table P-PZ40)
8547.S56	Simeon Aparanets'i, 16th cent. (Table P-PZ40)
8547.U73	Urbat'agrik' (Table P-PZ40)
8547.V35	Vardan Aygekts'i, 12th cent. (Table P-PZ40)
8548	1801- e. g.
8548.A25	Abovian, Khach'atowr, 1805-1848 (Table P-PZ40)
8548.A292	Agapyan, Arshak, 1860-1905 (Table P-PZ40)
8548.A296	Aghayan, Ghazaros, 1840-1911 (Table P-PZ40)
8548.A33	Aharonian, Awetis, 1866-1948 (Table P-PZ40)
8548.A815	Arp'iarian, Arp'iar, 1852-1908 (Table P-PZ40)
8548.A838	Asatowr, Zapēl H., 1863-1934 (Table P-PZ40)
8548.A8385	Asatur, Hrant, 1862-1928 (Table P-PZ40)
8548.A8456	Atrpet, 1860-1937 (Table P-PZ40)
8548.B37	Bashalean, Lewon, 1868-1943 (Table P-PZ40)
8548.B48	Biwrat, Smbat, 1862-1915 (Table P-PZ40)
8548.D395	Demirchian, Derenik, 1877-1956 (Table P-PZ40)
8548.D6	Dowrian, Petros, 1852-1872 (Table P-PZ40) Duryan, Petros, see PK8548.D6
8548.G314	Galēntēr, Melkón, b. 1855 (Table P-PZ40)
8548.G57	Gisak, 1860-1902 (Table P-PZ40)
8548.H27	Hakobian, Hakob, 1866-1937 (Table P-PZ40)
8548.H48	Hisarian, M.H. (Table P-PZ40)
8548.H6724	Hovhannisyan, Hovhannes, 1864-1929 (Table P-PZ40)
8548.I8	Isahakyan, Avetik', 1875-1957 (Table P-PZ40)
8548.L35	Leo, 1860-1932 (Table P-PZ40)
8548.L38	Leyli, 1892-1951 (Table P-PZ40)
8548.M215	Malēzian, Vahan, 1871-1967 (Table P-PZ40)
8548.M65	Mowrats'an, 1854-1908 (Table P-PZ40)
8548.N22	Nalbandiants', Mik'ayuēl, 1829-1866 (Table P-PZ40)
8548.N25	Nar-Dos, 1867-1933 (Table P-PZ40)
8548.N26	Nar-pēy, Khorēn, 1832-1892 (Table P-PZ40)
8548.O764	Oskean, Karapet A. (Karapet Aristakēs), 1869-1901 (Table P-PZ40)
8548.O77	Otian, Erowand, 1869-1926 (Table P-PZ40)
8548.P24	Panosian, Aghek'sandr, 1859-1919 (Table P-PZ40)
8548.P28	P'ap'azian, Vrt'anēs, 1866-1920 (Table P-PZ40)
8548.P29	Paronian, Hakob, 1943-1891 (Table P-PZ40)
8548.P3	Patkanyan, Rhap'ayel, 1830-1892 (Table P-PZ40)
8548.P33	Perch, b. 1863 (Table P-PZ40)
8548.P36	Pēshikt'ashlian, Mkrtich', 1828-1868 (Table P-PZ40)

Armenian language and literature
Literature
Individual authors or works, A-Z
1801- -- Continued
8548.P38 Peshtimalchian, Grigor (Table P-PZ40)
8548.P49 Pilēzikchian, Barhnabas (Table P-PZ40)
8548.R3 Raffi, 1835-1888 (Table P-PZ40)
Sahakyan, Leĭli, 1892-1951, see PK8548.L38
8548.S35 Sēfērean, Z.A. (Table P-PZ40)
8548.S44 Set'ian Hovhannēs, 1853-1930 (Table P-PZ40)
8548.S5 Shant', Lewon, 1869-1951 (Table P-PZ40)
8548.S515 Shirvanzade, 1858-1935 (Table P-PZ40)
8548.S54 Sipilian, Kghemēs, 1824-1878 (Table P-PZ40)
8548.S6 Sowndowkiants', Gabriēl, 1825-1912 (Table P-PZ40)
Sundukian, Gabriel, 1825-1912, see PK8548.S6
8548.T22 T'aghiadian, Mesroup Dawt'ian, 1803-1858 (Table P-PZ40)
8548.T375 Tēmirchipashian, Eghia, 1851-1908 (Table P-PZ40)
8548.T5 T'lkantints'i, 1860-1915 (Table P-PZ40)
8548.T67 T'owmanian, Hovhannēs, 1869-1923 (Table P-PZ40)
8548.T69 Tsatowryan, Alek'sandr, 1865-1917
8548.T7 Tserents', 1822-1888 (Table P-PZ40)
T'umanyan, Hovhannes, 1869-1923, see PK8548.T67
8548.V276 Vanandets'i, Hovhannēs Mirzayean, 1772-1841 (Table P-PZ40)
8548.Z55 Zōhrap, Grigor, 1861-1915 (Table P-PZ40)
Local
Cf. PK8096+, 8341+, 8441+
By region, province, or place
Armenia and Turkey
History
8561 General
8562 Special forms, poetry, etc.
Collections
8563 General
8564 Special forms, poetry, etc.
8565.A-Z By place, A-Z
8566-8699 Outside of Armenia
Under each 5-numbered place:
1-2 History and criticism
1 General
2 Special forms, poetry, etc.
3 Collections
4 By state, region, etc.
5 By place, A-Z
(8566-8570) Turkey
For reference only; see PK8500+, PK8561+
Other parts of Asia
8571-8575 Palestine
Apply table at PK8566-8699
8576-8580 Iran
Apply table at PK8566-8699

Armenian language and literature
Literature
Local
By region, province, or place
Outside of Armenia
Other parts of Asia -- Continued
8581-8585 India
Apply table at PK8566-8699
8591.A-Z Other, A-Z
Europe
8601 General
8611-8615 Austria
Apply table at PK8566-8699
8621-8625 Great Britain
Apply table at PK8566-8699
8631-8635 Greece
Apply table at PK8566-8699
8641-8645 Italy
Apply table at PK8566-8699
8651-8655 Soviet Union
Apply table at PK8566-8699
8661.A-Z Other, A-Z
Africa
8671 General
8675.A-Z Special, A-Z
America
8681-8689 United States and Canada (Table P-PZ24)
8689.A-Z Individual authors, A-Z
8689.D49 Devrish, K., 1883-1963
Keljik, Krikor Arabel, see PK8689.D49
8691 Spanish America
8695 Brazil
8697 Australia and New Zealand
8699.A-Z Pacific Islands, A-Z
Translations into Armenian
8701 Translations from several languages
Ancient literature
8711.A1 General
Greek
Collections
8711.G1 General and miscellaneous
8711.G3 Poetry
8711.G5 Drama
8711.G8 Prose
8711.G9 Individual authors or works
Latin
Collections
8711.L1 General and miscellaneous
8711.L3 Poetry
8711.L5 Drama
8711.L8 Prose
8711.L9 Individual authors or works
Syriac

Armenian language and literature
Literature
Translations into Armenian
Ancient literature
Syriac -- Continued
Collections
8711.S1 General and miscellaneous
8711.S3 Poetry
8711.S5 Drama
8711.S8 Prose
8711.S9 Individual authors or works
Modern literature
Divide like PK8711.G1-PK8711.G9
8761.E1-E9 English
8761.F1-F9 French
8761.G1-G9 German
8761.I1-I9 Italian
8761.R1-R9 Russian
8761.S1-S9 Spanish
8769.A-Z Other languages, A-Z
Translations from Armenian into other languages
English
8831.E1 General and miscellaneous
8831.E3 Poetry
8831.E5 Drama
8831.E7 Prose. Prose fiction
(8831.E9) Individual authors
see PK8547+
8831.F1-F9 French
Divide like PK8831.E1-(.E9)
8831.G1-G9 German
Divide like PK8831.E1-(.E9)
8831.I1-I9 Italian
Divide like PK8831.E1-(.E9)
8831.R1-R9 Russian
Divide like PK8831.E1-(.E9)
8831.S1-S9 Spanish
Divide like PK8831.E1-(.E9)
8835.A-Z Other languages, A-Z
Caucasian languages
9001 Periodicals. Societies. Collections
9003 General works. History of philology. Biography
(9003.9) Bibliography. Bio-bibliography
see class Z
9004 Languages (History. Relations, etc.)
9005 Study and teaching
Grammar
9007 Treatises
9009 Phonology. Phonetics
9013 Morphology. Inflection. Accidence
9014 Parts of speech (Morphology and syntax)
9015 Syntax
9020 Lexicology

Caucasian languages -- Continued
9021 Etymology
Lexicography
9025 Dictionaries
9027 Linguistic geography. Dialects, etc.
Literature
9030 History and criticism
9040 Collections
Particular groups
9048 Abhazo-Adyghian
Nakho-Daghestan
9049 General works
9050 Nakh
9051 Daghestan (Table P-PZ15a)
9052 Kartvelian
Particular languages
Georgian (Grusinian)
9101 Periodicals. Societies. Collections
9103 General works. History of philology
Biography
9103.2 Collective
9103.3.A-Z Individual, A-Z
(9103.9) Bibliography. Bio-bibliography
see class Z
9104 Language (History. Relations, etc.)
9105 Study and teaching
9105.5 Old Georgian (Table P-PZ15)
Grammar
9106 Treatises (Advanced)
9107 Textbooks
9108 Readers. Chrestomathies
9109 Phonology. Phonetics
9111 Alphabet. Transliteration
Cf. P211, P226
9113 Morphology. Inflection. Accidence
9114 Parts of speech (Morphology and syntax)
9115 Syntax
9117 Style. Composition. Rhetoric
9119 Prosody. Metrics. Rhythmics
Etymology
9122 Lexicology
Lexicography
9125 Dictionaries
9127 Linguistic geography. Dialects
9130 Adzhar
9132 Gurian (Table P-PZ15)
9135 Imeretian
9136 Ingilo
9138 Kakhetia
9140 Kartlia
9141 Mingrelian
9151 Laz
9160-9169 Literature (Table P-PZ24)

Caucasian languages
Particular languages
Georgian (Grusinian)
Literature -- Continued

9169.A-Z Individual authors or works, A-Z (Table P-PZ40, or P-PZ43)
e. g.
9169.A7 Aragvispireli, Šio, 1867-1926 (Table P-PZ40)
9169.A72 Arč'ili, 1647-1713 (Table P-PZ40)
9169.B28 Bagrationi, Ioana, t'avadi, 1768-1830 (Table P-PZ40)
9169.B328 Barat'ašvili, Mamuka, 18th cent. (Table P-PZ40)
9169.B33 Barat'ašvili, Nikoloz, t'avadi, 1817-1845 (Table P-PZ40)
9169.C38 Cavcavaze, Ilia, t'avadi, 1837-1907 (Table P-PZ40)
9169.C47 Ceret'eli, Akaki, 1840-1915 (Table P-PZ40)
9169.D3 Dadiani, Shalva Nikolaevich, 1874- (Table P-PZ40)
9169.D39 Davit' IV, King of Georgia, ca. 1073-1125 (Table P-PZ40)
9169.E67 Erist'avi, Rap'iel, t'avadi, 1824-1901 (Table P-PZ40)
9169.E86 Evdošvili, Irodion, 1873-1916 (Table P-PZ40)
9169.G52 Gogebašvili, Iakob, 1840-1912 (Table P-PZ40)
9169.G8 Guramišvili, Davit', 1705-1792 (Table P-PZ40)
9169.K5 Kldiashvili, David, 1862-1898 (Table P-PZ40)
9169.M2 Mač'abeli, Ivane, 1854-1898 (Table P-PZ40)
9169.M62 Mose, Xoneh, 11th/12th cent. (Table P-PZ40)
9169.O718 Orbeliani, Grigol, 1804-1883 (Table P-PZ40)
9169.O72 Orbeliani, Sulxan-Saba, 1658-1725 (Table P-PZ40)
9169.P87 P'urc'elaze, Anton (Table P-PZ40)
9169.R8 Rustaveli, Shota, 12th-13th cent. (Table P-PZ40)
(9169.S3) Savva, monk, 1659-1725
see PK9169.O72
9169.T85 T͡Sit͡sishvili, Nodar, d. 1658 (Table P-PZ40)
9169.V38 Važa-P'šavela, 1861-1915 (Table P-PZ40)
9201.A-Z Other, A-Z
9201.A2 Abazin (Table P-PZ16)
9201.A3 Abkhaz (Table P-PZ16)
9201.A4 Adygei (Table P-PZ16)
Adzhar, see PK9130
9201.A6 Agul (Table P-PZ16)
9201.A7 Akhwakh (Table P-PZ16)
9201.A73 Akkinski (Table P-PZ16)
9201.A77 Archi (Table P-PZ16)
9201.A9 Avaric (Table P-PZ16)
9201.B34 Bagulal (Table P-PZ16)
9201.B36 Bats (Table P-PZ16)
9201.B49 Bezhta (Table P-PZ16)

Caucasian languages
Particular languages
Other, A-Z -- Continued

9201.B67 Botlikh (Table P-PZ16)
9201.B83 Budukh (Table P-PZ16)
9201.C2 Chamalal (Table P-PZ16)
9201.C3 Chechen (Table P-PZ16)
9201.C5 Circassian (Table P-PZ16)
9201.D3 Dargwa (Darghi, Dargin) (Table P-PZ16)
9201.G5 Ginukh (Table P-PZ16)
9201.G63 Godoberi (Table P-PZ16)
9201.H5 Hinalugh (Table P-PZ16)
9201.I6 Ingush (Table P-PZ16)
9201.K3 Kabardian (Table P-PZ16)
9201.K45 Karata (Table P-PZ16)
9201.L3 Lak (Table P-PZ16)
Laz, see PK9151
9201.L5 Lezghian (Table P-PZ16)
Mingrelian, see PK9141
Oubykh, see PK9201.U3
Päkhy, see PK9201.U3
9201.R87 Rutul (Table P-PZ16)
9201.S3 Samur (Table P-PZ16)
9201.S8 Svan (Table P-PZ16)
9201.T3 Tabasaran (Table P-PZ16)
9201.T4 Tapanta (Table P-PZ16)
9201.T7 Tsakhur (Table P-PZ16)
Tsova-Tush, see PK9201.B36
9201.U3 Ubykh (Oubykh, Päkhy) (Table P-PZ16)
9201.U4 Udi (Ude, Udic) (Table P-PZ16)
(9601) Romany (Gipsy, Gypsy)
see PK2896+

A

Epigraphical Hybrid Sanskrit: PK1470
Erotic literature
  Arabic
    Literary history: PJ7519.E76
  Indo-Aryan
    Literary history: PK2907.E7
Essays
  Hebrew
    Collections: PJ5047
    Literary history: PJ5032
  Hindī
    Collections: PK2078.E8
  Hindustānī
    Collections: PK2078.E8
  Sanskrit (Post-Vedic): PK3760
Ethico-didactic literature
  Indo-Aryan
    Literary history: PK2935+
Ethico-didactic poetry
  Sanskrit (Post-Vedic): PK3741
Ethics in literature
  Arabic
    Collections
      Poetry: PJ7632.E65
    Literary history
      Poetry: PJ7542.E65
  New Persian
    Literary history
      Poetry: PK6420.E83
Ethiopian languages: PJ8991+
Ethiopic (Geez) language: PJ9001+
Ethiopic literature: PJ9090+
Ethmology
  Talmudic (Mishnaic) Hebrew: PJ4931+
Etymology
  Arabic (Oriental languages): PJ6172+
  Arabic (Western languages): PJ6571+
  Assamese: PK1555
  Assyriology: PJ3450+
  Bengali: PK1681
  Berber: PJ2347
  Caucasian: PK9021
  Coptic: PJ2161
  Cushitic: PJ2409
  Egyptology: PJ1350+
  Ethiopic (Geez): PJ9083
  Georgian: PK9121
Etymology
  Hebrew: PJ4801+
  Indo-Iranian: PK65
  Lahnda: PK2268
  Marāṭhī
    Western languages: PK2371
  Modern Arabic dialects: PJ6731
  Modern Indo-Aryan languages: PK1531
  Oriental languages (General): PJ183
  Pali: PK1083
  Phenician-Punic: PJ4181
  Prakrit: PK1221
  Sanskrit: PK901+
  Semitic: PJ3065
  Sinhalese: PK2831
  Sumerian: PJ4031
  Syriac: PJ5483
  Vedic: PK361
Eulogies
  Arabic
    Collections: PJ7632.E8
    Literary history
      Poetry: PJ7542.E8
Europe in literature
  Arabic
    Collections: PJ7604.E87
    Literary history: PJ7519.E87
Europeans in literature
  Arabic
    Collections: PJ7604.E87
    Literary history: PJ7519.E87
Exiles in literature
  Arabic
    Collections
      Poetry: PJ7632.E85
    Literary history
      Poetry: PJ7542.E85
Exiles in literture
  Arabic
    Literary history
      Fiction: PJ7572.E95
Expatriation in literature
  Hebrew
    Literary history
      Fiction: PJ5030.E94
Eye in literature
  Arabic
    Collections
      Poetry: PJ7632.E9
    Literary history: PJ7519.E94
      Poetry: PJ7542.E9

F

Fables
Indo-Aryan
Literary history: PK2935+
Faisal, King of Saudi Arabia, 1906-1975, in literature
Arabic
Collections
Poetry: PJ7632.F35
Literary history
Poetry: PJ7542.F35
Falasha
Agau dialect: PJ2443
Fate and fatalism in literature
Arabic
Literary history: PJ7519.F37
Fātiḥah
Language of the Koran: PJ6696.Z6F36
Feminism in literature
Arabic
Collections: PJ7604.F45
Literary history: PJ7519.F45
Fiction
Arabic
Collections: PJ7671+
Literary history: PJ7571+
Hebrew
Collections: PJ5044+
Literary history: PJ5028+
Hindī
Collections: PK2077
Hindustānī
Collections: PK2077
Jaina
Literary history: PK5001.8
Literary history
Mohammedan: PJ836
Pali
Literary history: PK4529+
Prakrit
Collections: PK5008
Sanskrit (Post-Vedic): PK3750+
Yiddish
Collections: PJ5128
Literary history: PJ5124
Figures of speech
Language of the Hadīth: PJ6697.Z5F5
Language of the Koran: PJ6696.Z5F5
Figures of speech in literature
Indo-Aryan
Literary history: PK2907.F55
Fini Hindi (Hindustānī dialect): PK2000.F54
Fishes in literature
Indo-Aryan
Literary history: PK2907.F57
Folk songs
Hindī: PK2085
Hindustānī: PK2085
Food in literature
Arabic
Collections: PJ7604.F6
Poetry: PJ7632.F66
Literary history: PJ7519.F6
Poetry: PJ7542.F66
Forests in literature
Indo-Aryan
Literary history: PK2907.F6
Funeral offerings, Liturgy of
Egyptology: PJ1559.L6+

G

Gabri (Iranian dialect): PK6996.G3
Gadi (Western Pahāṛī dialect): PK2610.G3
Gafat (Ethiopian dialect): PJ9285
Galilee in literature
Hebrew
Literary history: PJ5012.G3
Galla
Eastern Cushitic language: PJ2471+
Gaṛhwālī (Central Pahāṛī dialect): PK2605.G3
Gārwī (Kōhistānī dialect): PK7045.G3
Gawar-bati (Nuristani language): PK7065.G3
Gazel
New Persian
Literary history
Poetry: PK6420.G3
Gedeo dialect
Sidamo group: PJ2501
Geez
Ethiopic language: PJ9001+

Generosity in literature
  Arabic
    Literary history
      Poetry: PJ7542.G35
Geography
  Assyrian clay tablets:
    PJ3921.G4
Geography in literature
  Indo-Aryan
    Literary history: PK2907.G4
Geogrian (Grusinian) language:
    PK9101+
Ghadames
  Modern Libyan dialect: PJ2359
Ghalchah (Iranian dialect):
    PK6991.P3
Ghat
  Tuareg dialect: PJ2382.G4
Ghazal in literature
  Arabic
    Collections
      Poetry: PJ7632.G4
    Literary history
      Poetry: PJ7542.G4
Gilaki (Iranian dialect):
    PK6996.G54
Gilgamesh
  Assyriology: PJ3771.G5+
Gimirra language
  West Cushitic: PJ2570
Ginukh (Caucasian language):
    PK9201.G5
Gipsy (Modern Indo-Aryan
  languages): PK2896+
Gnomic-erotic literature
  Sanskrit (Post-Vedic): PK3771
Godoberi (Caucasian language):
    PK9201.G63
Gods in literature
  Indo-Aryan
    Literary history: PK2907.G63
Gonga language
  West Cushitic: PJ2572
Grammar
  Arabic (Oriental languages):
    PJ6101+
  Armenian
    Oriental languages: PK8367
  Assamese: PK1551+
  Assyriology: PJ3231+
  Bengali: PK1661+
  Berber: PJ2345
  Caucasian: PK9007+
Grammar
  Coptic: PJ2029+
  Cushitic: PJ2405
  Egyptology: PJ1121+
  Ethiopic (Geez): PJ9019+
  Georgian: PK9106+
  Hebrew: PJ4553+
  Indo-Iranian: PK21
  Marāṭhī: PK2356+
  Middle Indo-Aryan dialects:
    PK1472
  Modern Arabic dialects: PJ6713
  Modern Indo-Aryan languages:
    PK1511+
  Oriental languages (General):
    PJ120+
  Oromo: PJ2471.12
  Pali: PK1017+
  Phenician-Punic: PJ4175+
  Prakrit: PK1206+
  Sanskrit: PK475+
  Semitic: PJ3021+
  Sinhalese: PK2811+
  Sumerian: PJ4010.9+
  Syriac: PJ5419+
  Talmudic (Mishnaic) Hebrew:
    PJ4911+
  Vedic: PK231+
  Yiddish: PJ5115+
Grief in literature
  Hebrew
    Literary history
      Fiction: PJ5030.G74
Guanche (Extinct language)
  Berber: PJ2371
Gudella dialect
  Sidamo group: PJ2503
Gujarati (Modern Indo-Aryan
  languages): PK1841+
Gujuri (Modern Indo-Aryan
  languages): PK1911
Gulf States
  Modern Arabic dialects: PJ6851+
Gurage (Ethiopian dialect):
    PJ9288
Gurian (Georgian dialect):
    PK9132
Gypsy (Modern Indo-Aryan
  languages): PK2896+

H

Hadendoa
Beja dialect: PJ2457
Hadith, Language of the: PJ6697.A6+
Hadramaut
South Arabian languages: PJ6971
Hadya dialect
Sidamo group: PJ2503
Halbī (Modern Indo-Aryan languages): PK1914
Hallāj, al-Ḥusayn ibn Manṣūr, 858 or 9-922, in literature
Arabic
Collections: PJ7604.H33
Literary history: PJ7519.H33
Hallenga
Beja dialect: PJ2459
Hamir
Agau dialect: PJ2435
Hamitic languages: PJ991+
Hamito-Semitic languages: PJ991+
Hammurabi, Age of
Literature: PJ3621
Hamta
Agau dialect: PJ2437
Hanumān (Hindu deity) in literature
Indo-Aryan
Literary history: PK2907.H36
Harari (Ethiopian dialect): PJ9293
Hāṛauṭī (Modern Indo-Aryan languages): PK1921+
Harer
Oromo dialect: PJ2476
Harranian authors
Arabic literature
Literary history: PJ7525.4.H35
Harsūsī
Modern South Arabian dialect: PJ7141+
Hawiyya dialect
Somali: PJ2537
Hazara language (Iranian): PK6996.H3
Hebrew
Oriental philology and literature: PJ4501+
Heroes in literature
Arabic
Collections: PJ7604.H4
Poetry: PJ7632.H4
Literary history: PJ7519.H4
Poetry: PJ7542.H4
Heroism in literature
Arabic
Collections
Poetry: PJ7632.H4
Literary history
Poetry: PJ7542.H4
Hieratic literature: PJ1650+
Hieroglyphic writing: PJ1091+
Hijā' in literature
Arabic
Collections
Poetry: PJ7632.S3
Literary history
Poetry: PJ7542.S3
Himachali (Modern Indo-Aryan languages): PK2606+
Himyaritic
South Arabian languages: PJ6965
Hinalugh (Caucasian language): PK9201.H5
Hindī (Modern Indo-Aryan languages): PK1931+
Hindko (Lahnda dialect): PK2269.H5
Hinduism in literature
Indo-Aryan
Literary history: PK2907.H55
Hindustānī (Modern Indo-Aryan languages): PK1981+
History
Demotic literature: PJ1895
Hebrew literature: PJ5008+
History (of Assyriology): PJ3151+
History (of Egyptology)
Oriental philology and literature: PJ1051+
History (of language)
Hebrew: PJ4545
History (of the decipherment)
Cunieform: PJ3197
History in literature
Syriac
Collections: PJ5643
History of Arabic philology: PJ6051+

I

K

Mothers in literature
Arabic
Collections: PJ7604.M6
Literary history: PJ7519.M6
Mu'āraḍāt in literature
Arabic
Collections
Poetry: PJ7632.M74
Literary history
Poetry: PJ7542.M74
Muḥammad, d. 632 and Mohammedan literature: PJ814.M83
Muḥammad, Prophet, d. 632, in literature
Arabic
Collections: PJ7604.M76
Literary history: PJ7519.M76
Muḥammad, the prophet, in literature
New Persian
Collections
Poetry: PK6439.M85
Muḥummad, the prophet, in literature
Arabic
Collections
Poetry: PJ7632.M75
Literary history
Poetry: PJ7542.M75
Munji (Iranian dialect): PK6996.M8
Muwashshah in literature
Arabic
Collections
Poetry: PJ7632.M8
Literary history
Poetry: PJ7542.M8
Mystic poetry
New Persian
Literary history: PK6419
Mythology
Demotic literature: PJ1881
Mythology in literature
Arabic
Collections: PJ7604.M9
Poetry: PJ7632.M9
Literary history: PJ7519.M9
Poetry: PJ7542.M9
Mythology in literture
Arabic
Literary history
Fiction: PJ7572.M94
Mythology, Indic, in literature
Indo-Aryan
Literary history: PK2907.M94
Mzab
Berber language: PJ2395.M97

N

Nabataean inscriptions: PJ5239.A1+
Nakh (Nakho-Daghestan language): PK9050
Nakho-Daghestan (Caucasian languages): PK9049+
Names
Pali: PK1084
Names, Personal, in literature
Indo-Aryan
Literary history: PK2907.N35
Nāpuri (Marāṭhī dialect): PK2378.N34
Narration in literture
Arabic
Literary history
Fiction: PJ7572.N37
Narrative poetry
Arabic
Collections: PJ7632.N27
Literary history: PJ7542.N27
Sanskrit (Post-Vedic): PK3600+
Narratives
Indo-Aryan
Literary history: PK2941+
Narsātī (Nuristani language): PK7065.G3
Nasser, Gamal Abdul, pres., United Arab Republic, 1918-1970, in literature
Arabic
Collections
Poetry: PJ7632.N3
Literary history
Poetry: PJ7542.N3
Nasser, Gambal Abdel, 1918-1970, in literature
Arabic
Literary history: PJ7519.N27

Physicians as authors
  Arabic literature
    Literary history: PJ7525.4.P45
Pigeons in literature
  Arabic
    Literary history
      Poetry: PJ7542.P49
Pilgrims and pilgrimages in literature
  Indo-Aryan
    Literary history: PK2907.P56
Pkhy (Caucasian language): PK9201.U3
Plagiarism in literature
  Arabic
    Collections
      Poetry: PJ7632.P53
    Literary history
      Poetry: PJ7542.P53
Plants in literature
  Indo-Aryan
    Literary history: PK2907.P59
Pleiades in literature
  Arabic
    Collections
      Poetry: PJ7632.P54
    Literary history
      Poetry: PJ7542.P54
Poems
  Egyptology: PJ1569
Poetry
  Arabic
    Collections: PJ7631+
    Literary history: PJ7541+
  Assyriology: PJ3751+
  Bengali: PK1710
  Collections
    Mohammedan: PJ856
  Hebrew
    Collections: PJ5039+
    Literary history: PJ5022+
  Hindī
    Collections: PK2057+
    Literary history: PK2040+
  Hindustānī
    Collections: PK2057+
    Literary history: PK2040+
  Indo-Aryan
    Literary history: PK2916
  Jaina
    Literary history: PK5001.6
  Literary history
    Mohammedan: PJ827
  New Persian
    Collections: PK6433+
    Literary history: PK6416+
  Pali
    Collections: PK4563
    Literary history: PK4525+
  Papyri: PJ1725
  Prakrit: PK5006
  Sanskrit (Post-Vedic): PK3600+
  Sumerian: PJ4061+
  Syriac
    Collections: PJ5617
    Literary history: PJ5604
  Yiddish
    Collections: PJ5126
    Literary history: PJ5122
Poets in literature
  Arabic
    Collections: PJ7604.P58
    Literary history: PJ7519.P58
Pŏgulī (Kashṭwāṛī dialect): PK7029.P6
Politics
  Demotic literature: PJ1895
Politics in literature
  Arabic
    Collections: PJ7604.P6
      Poetry: PJ7632.P64
    Literary history: PJ7519.P6
      Poetry: PJ7542.P64
  Hebrew
    Literary history: PJ5012.P64
      Fiction: PJ5030.P64
  Indo-Aryan
    Literary history: PK2907.P65
Politics in literture
  Arabic
    Literary history
      Fiction: PJ7572.P64
Polysemy
  Language of the Koran: PJ6696.Z5P64
Poor in literature
  Arabic
    Collections: PJ7604.P64
    Literary history: PJ7519.P64
Post-Biblical Hebrew: PJ4865

S

T

Tabasaran (Caucasian language): PK9201.T3
Tahaggart
  Tuareg dialect: PJ2382.T3
Tajik (Iranian philology and literature): PK6971+
Talmudic (Mishnaic) Hebrew: PJ4901+
Talysh (Iranian dialect): PK6996.T3
Tamashek
  Berber language: PJ2381+
Tamazight
  Berber language: PJ2395.T3
Tapanta (Caucasian language): PK9201.T4
Targums of Onkelos (Pentateuch), Language of the: PJ5251+
Taste in literature
  Arabic
    Collections
      Poetry: PJ7632.T3
    Literary history
      Poetry: PJ7542.T3
Tat (Iranian dialect): PK6996.T35
Tawarek
  Berber language: PJ2381+
Technical Arabic: PJ6119.5
Temissa
  Modern Libyan dialect: PJ2367
Terminology
  Hebrew: PJ4554
  Modern Indo-Aryan langauges: PK1514
Thaḷī (Mārwāṛī (Ḍ;ingaḷ) dialect): PK2469.T3
Tharu (Bihārī dialect): PK1820
Theological and ascetic literature
  Ethiopic (Geez): PJ9098
Theology in literature
  Syriac
    Collections: PJ5621+
Tifinag
  Berber languages: PJ2344
Tigré (Ethiopian dialect): PJ9131
Tigrinya (Ethiopian dialect): PJ9111
Time in literature
  Arabic
    Collections
      Poetry: PJ7632.T5
    Literary history
      Poetry: PJ7542.T5
  Indo-Aryan
    Literary history: PK2907.T55
Time in literterure
  Arabic
    Literary history
      Fiction: PJ7572.T54
Tirahī (Nuristani language): PK7065.T5
Tirhutia (Bihārī dialect): PK1811+
Topography
  Assyrian clay tablets: PJ3921.G4
Tōrwālī (Kōhistānī dialect): PK7045.T6
Touch in literature
  Arabic
    Collections
      Poetry: PJ7632.T6
    Literary history
      Poetry: PJ7542.T6
Towns in literature
  Arabic
    Collections
      Poetry: PJ7632.C56
    Literary history
      Poetry: PJ7542.C56
Translating
  Arabic (Oriental languages): PJ6170
  Arabic (Western languages): PJ6403
  Indo-Aryan languages: PK1528
  Sanskrit: PK868
  Sinhalese: PK2828
Translations
  Armenian inscriptions: PK8197
  Asoka inscriptions: PK1485
  Assyriology: PJ3951+
  Egyptian: PJ1941+
  Ethiopic literature: PJ9101.A+
  Indo-Aryan: PK2977+
  Indo-Iranian: PK85
  Kāshmīrī: PK7037
  Modern Indo-Aryan: PK5461+

U

V

Y

Z